PRENTICE-HALL
FOUNDATIONS OF MODERN SOCIOLOGY SERIES

Alex Inkeles, Editor

second edition
THE SOCIOLOGY OF SMALL GROUPS

THEODORE M. MILLS
Center for the Study of Human Groups
State University of New York at Buffalo

Prentice-Hall, Inc., Englewood Cliffs, New Jersey 07632

Library of Congress Cataloging in Publication Data

Mills, Theodore M.
    The sociology of small groups.
    (Foundations of modern sociology)
    Bibliography.
    Includes index.
    1. Small groups. I. Title. II. Series: Prentice-Hall foundations of modern
sociology series.
HM133.M5 1984   302.3'4   83-13902
ISBN 0-13-820910-3
ISBN 0-13-820902-2 (pbk.)

To Mary Jane

Editorial/production supervision: Colleen Brosnan
Manufacturing buyer: John B. Hall

©1984, 1967 by Prentice-Hall, Inc., Englewood Cliffs, New Jersey 07632

Printed in the United States of America

10 9 8 7 6 5 4 3 2 1

ISBN 0-13-820902-2 {pbk}
ISBN 0-13-820910-3

Prentice-Hall International, Inc., *London*
Prentice-Hall of Australia Pty. Limited, *Sydney*
Editora Prentice-Hall do Brasil, Ltda., *Rio de Janeiro*
Prentice-Hall Canada Inc., *Toronto*
Prentice-Hall of India Private Limited, *New Delhi*
Prentice-Hall of Japan, Inc., *Tokyo*
Prentice-Hall of Southeast Asia Pte. Ltd., *Singapore*
Whitehall Books Limited, *Wellington, New Zealand*

The second attraction of the series was the opportunity to share with teachers and students some of our troubles in small group research, perhaps eliciting their talent and imagination in overcoming them. Among these are (1) the resistance of modern cultures to learning about groups—the more we learn about groups, the more we seem to threaten those we seek to enlighten; (2) the observer and experimenter effects—groups "clam up" when observed, and subjects play-act for experimenters; (3) the enlightenment effect—groups learn what researchers have discovered and modify their actions accordingly; (4) the historical effects—ideas and values change from one decade to another.

I raise these issues in this book not only because they are about as fundamental as you can get in social science research but also because the small group setting offers special advantages to those attempting to work them out.

Acknowledgements to First Edition. I wish to thank Robert N. Bellah, François Bourricaud, Donald R. Matthews, Luciano Gallino, and William P. Yohe, my colleagues at the Center for Advanced Study in the Behavioral Sciences, for fruitful discussions on modern sociological theory from which this book benefits; graduate students in the Department of Sociology, Yale University, too numerous to list but including Peter J. Burke and Michael Farrell, whose dual concern for relevance and clarity helped define the book's emphasis; Philip E. Slater, J. Zvi Namenwirth, and George Huaco, for critical reviews of selected chapters; and Anna Tower (of the Center), Mary Elizabeth Hintze, and Nora C. Quiocho, for their assistance in typing and for suggested improvements in exposition. I am especially grateful to Alex Inkeles, General Editor of Prentice-Hall's Foundations of Modern Sociology Series, for his criticism and suggestions during the book's early stages and for his patience and support throughout a later period of formulation and reformulation.

Acknowledgements to Second Edition. I wish to thank Alex Inkeles, General Editor of the Foundations of Modern Sociology Series, for his continued guidance; Michael P. Farrell of the State University of New York at Buffalo and Madeline Schmitt of the University of Rochester for their generosity in sharing their experiences in using the first edition and for their thoughtful suggestions for the second; the reviewers, invited by Prentice-Hall, for the care with which they undertook their task and the clarity of their reports; and Edward H. Stanford and Susan J. Taylor of Prentice-Hall and their staffs for enacting standards of excellence in their craft. I am especially grateful both to my own students and to the teachers and students from colleges and universities in many sectors of the world who, in response to their use of the first edition, have written and influenced my thought. Their contributions have made this edition more of a joint effort, which pleases me.

CONTENTS

PREFACE

This book is an invitation for you to take a new look at the human groups about you, to consider a sociological way of thinking about them, and possibly to join those who are attempting to create a science of group dynamics advanced enough to explain their mysteries and concrete enough to guide members in their group experiences.

When Professor Alex Inkeles asked me to contribute to the Foundations of Modern Sociology Series, I found the idea of the series most appealing. The plan was to produce a "shelf" of quality monographs that reflected the advanced thought in various sectors of sociology. Teachers could select and compose their own "text," students could invest according to their individual interests, and authors could bring up-to-date thinking and research directly to the classroom, hopefully avoiding a predigested style and the tendency to write down to students. The plan promised something of value to each in the triangle of teacher, student, and author.

The series notion was especially attractive to me, in small groups, for two reasons. First, our field is without a conceptual center. At present we have no single perspective, nor a single theory that adequately accounts for what has been observed. Instead, we have an array of different approaches, each tending to be more committed to the interests of a profession (such as psychiatry, social psychology, and so on) than to a comprehension of human groups in their own right. Using simple language I have tried to present the essentials of selected theoretical models (so that each may be compared) and then later on to bring together certain of their ideas into a single analytical scheme. This scheme assumes that groups are purposeful systems responding not only to practical day-to-day demands but also, in varying degrees, to the fulfillment of deep needs and the realization of ultimate values. My hope is that the scheme will help you attain the type of overall view of groups that is useful for gaining insight into their dynamics, for guiding group action, and for designing scientific research.

INTRODUCTION

We are quite possibly in the midst of a revolutionary trend on the part of human beings to learn about themselves, individually and collectively, through the mode of scientific inquiry. Over the past 50 years in particular, new interest, new talent, new skills, new resources, and a new confidence, along with a new receptivity to what is being learned, have combined to produce energetic expansion in social science research. Even within this general trend, the increase since World War II in research on the small human group has been remarkable. Once the group was singled out as an object of study, enthusiasm spread to many branches of the social sciences, including psychology, social psychology, psychiatry, sociology, political science, and anthropology, as well as to the related fields of applied mathematics, cybernetics, and general systems theory. Seeking a new understanding of group dynamics, investigators in these fields directed their attention to what happens when people meet, live and work together.[1]

Then, in the late 1960s, the field underwent a traumatic crisis. From outside the field came political demands to produce "truths" that were "relevant"; from inside came discoveries (such as the effect of the experimenter on subjects and the influence of personal values on the experimenter's selection of research problems) for which investigators themselves were unprepared. The field experienced a crisis not just of confidence but of perspective. Because of its importance in the history of social science we consider this crisis in the brief history that follows. Although some saw the crisis itself as a sign of weakness and possible failure, others saw change as a challenge worthy of response in developing valid empirical research, part of the often difficult task of making a science that can indeed help us learn about ourselves as humans.[2]

What are these groups that have attracted so much interest? One answer is that they are the immediate, interpersonal contexts in which we live, work, make decisions, and play. Another more personal answer might come to mind if the reader considers these questions: Looking back on your life so far, what group of individuals has been most important to you? What group has been most significant in your life? Which has had the most impact? If the images that come to mind include your family, playmates, an athletic team, a gang, roommates, or a counseling group, then they illustrate what we call *small groups*. Other examples range from construction gangs, hunting parties, ceremonial dance teams, jazz combos, astronaut crews, surgical teams, and army buddies, to research seminars and office staffs. To say that there are many more is to understate the case. With some 4.25 billion individuals in the world, each belonging to five or six groups, on an average, and even allowing for overlap in memberships, any reasonable estimate of the total number of small groups that currently exist would run to eight or ten billion.

Many of these billions are *primary* groups which Dunphy defines as "a group which persists long enough to develop strong emotional attachments between members, at least a set of rudimentary, functionally differentiated roles, and a subculture of its own which includes an image of the group as an entity and an informal normative system which controls group-relevant action as members."[3] Whether life in such groups is easygoing and pleasant or turbulent and disturbing, members tend to be attached to one another, to be "significant" to one another, as would be indicated by a sense of personal loss when a member is separated from the group.

Such primary groups are at one end of a scale. At the other, impersonal end of the scale are *secondary* groups whose value is largely extrinsic. They are organized chiefly to get a job done, to produce objects or services that have exchange value, usually for outsiders. Performance according to standards of effectiveness or excellence takes precedence over personal feelings and attachments. Often members are considered replaceable in the service of high-quality group performance, as in a surgical team, an astronaut crew, or a string quartet. Beyond their variation in "primaryness," the billions of groups that exist vary in other respects including size, duration of existence, reward to members, usefulness to the community, and the degree to which their structure and activities are governed by custom or law (the Supreme Court is highly structured and governed by law; children at play are not).

WHY STUDY GROUPS?

Groups may be numerous and various, but why study them? One reason is curiosity about the human condition. The billions of groups referred to before are settings in which the men, women, and children of the world pursue their daily activities of work and play. Whatever form they take, we can assume that their structures and internal dynamics make a difference not only to the lives of their members but also to the character and history of the communities of which they are a part. As we all know, the newborn infant cannot become human without "a mothering group," and reciprocally, groups can neither maintain themselves nor accomplish collective goals without having gained commitment from individuals. This interdependence between person and group is elemental, both in the origin and development of group life among humans and in individual lives—elemental enough to raise further questions, such as, How do these groupings tend to shape personalities? What part do they play throughout the life cycle of individuals? What do groups give to and require from individuals? What is actually required for individuals to live, work, and play together? What are the dynamics of these small centers of human existence?

On another level, how do networks of such groups contribute to the life of communities? What groups influence the course of history of a community in what ways? How do these relations—among persons and the group, among groups and the community—differ from one region to another, or from one culture to another? Are there general laws that tend to govern such relations? One can see that interest in the human condition is likely to lead quite naturally to questions about human groups whether one is a historian, psychologist, anthropologist, sociologist or a scholar in related fields.

For some, curiosity leads back through time to the origin and early development of social life among *homo sapiens*, as best it can be reconstructed. Whether the role of the male (as some are currently arguing[4]) or the role of the female (as others are arguing[5]) was critical in its formation, scholars generally agree that the sustained human group was a social invention of critical evolutionary importance. The human group originated presumably through mutual interaction among factors such as parental care, the growth of a larger brain, development of language, extended childhood, exchange behavior, and play. Once the sustainable group emerged, it became a valuable social form. First, it became a means to accomplish tasks and reach goals that were simply impossible for the individual alone, including care of the young after the death of the mother, the hunting of large animals, the spanning of wide chasms, fishing in gangs, building complex structures, performing certain music and dance forms, playing certain games, conducting communal ceremonies, and defending effectively against attack. Second, the group became a source not only of physical sustenance but also of warmth and affection, of tenderness and support, and of a sense of identity and collective security. Third, the group became both a creator and a transmitter of culture: language and technical know-how, beliefs and art forms, games and ceremonies, and in general, a set of meanings for interpreting existence, including life in the group itself. Fourth, human groups, each bound together by mutual trust, became building blocks to be joined together to form larger social units, ranging from the small outfit or band, to the clan, the tribe, the city, the society, and eventually to the highly complex political and economic organizations which now span the globe. Quite naturally, in the face of the new possibilities of, and demands on, these supra-structures, the form and substance of the original groups gave way to radically new forms that have led to today's wide variety of primary and secondary groups.

The second reason to study groups is to better understand the psychology of the individual. "Human nature, " wrote Cooley, "is developed and expressed in those simple, face-to-face groups that somehow are alike in all societies: groups of the family, the playground, and the neighborhood . . . . In these, everywhere human nature comes into existence."[6] The humanizing processes that occur between the newborn child and the family are often so intricately interwoven that the boundaries between person and group are not clear. Consequently, those who wish to advance our knowledge about personality development are finding it enormously helpful, if not essential, to comprehend the interpersonal dynamics in the formative group. As research has brought more of those dynamics to light, it has become apparent that although some families are effective in socializing their young, others are not, and in the extreme some are dehumanizing—presenting confusion, inflicting pain, and tending to become, in Jules Henry's words, "pathways to madness."[7] It was partly a growing realization of the critical importance of the group in inducing madness that inspired practitioners to turn the matter around by using the family group as an instrument of therapy to help clear away confusion, reduce pain, and develop competence in dealing with the world.[8] Thus, both as a source of difficulties and as a therapeutic instrument, the group has become increasingly relevant to personality psychologists, psychiatrists, therapists, and counselors in various professions. With interest currently directed at the different stages in the life cycle, we can expect more research on the effects of shifts in group relations between each stage of life.

The third reason to study groups is to better understand larger social units, such as organizations, institutions, communities, and societies.[9] Ordinarily, these larger units are composed of overlapping smaller groups connected through various types of obligations and responsibilities. Because of interdependencies in a given network, groups small in themselves may nonetheless have important or even critical effects upon the rest of the system. We are familiar with the general tendency for decision making to migrate to the top of a power network where often a small group of executives and advisors makes the final decision. Insofar as the internal relations (loyalties, jealousies, coalitions) of that small group affect its decisions, then its dynamics have an impact on the larger system. Examples from recent history include (1) The way the brother relation between John and Robert Kennedy (among other factors) lent resolve to their position in the Cuban Missile Crisis, and (2) how the friendship between President Nixon and John Mitchell combined with animosity toward John Dean weakened Nixon's defense, contributing to his resignation and a change in the presidency. At the grassroots level, widely distributed decisions made separately but similarly by a multitude of groups can also have an emphatic overall impact—for example, when many individual families decide to emigrate, or when many would-be parents decide to practice birth control. Both at the top and at the grassroots level the dynamics of small units can be a major source of variance in determining changes in the larger system. The more important they are as a source of variance, the more essential it becomes for those who want to understand change in the larger system to study the dynamics of the smaller groups. For these reasons, students of organizations, communities, and larger societies find the study of small groups relevant.

A fourth reason to study groups is to contribute to the development of sociology as a science.[10] Since sociology's special task is to advance our understanding of social systems in whatever form they appear, "why not," as Homans has asked, "begin by studying a system small enough so that we [can], so to speak, see all the way around it?"[11] This strategy becomes even more significant when we remember that small human groups are not just microsystems. They are in certain ways microcosms of larger societies, for when closely observed they can be seen to exhibit, in miniature, "societal" features, such as division of labor, a code of ethics, a government, media of exchange, prestige ranking, ideologies, myths, and even religious practices. One can imagine the small group becoming to sociology what the fruitfly has been to genetics. Through the study of small groups, theoretical models can be constructed and compared to models of other forms of social systems, as one step of the many steps in the scientific task of constructing theoretical models that can be applied successfully across all systems. Although the study of groups has the advantage of dealing with relatively rapidly changing and accessible systems, it bears the burden of determining when the dynamics of the smaller correspond to the dynamics of the larger and when they do not. When study successfully bears that burden, then it contributes to more useful ways of thinking about social systems in general.

The fifth reason to study groups is to aid sociologists themselves in becoming better scientists through understanding how groups influence them personally and consequently how the content of their sociology is affected. Sociologists are human, of course, and are subject to the same group influences as those they observe. Group residues (including influences from sociologists' families, neighborhood friends, teachers, fellow students, and professional colleagues) are part of the mental apparatus employed in interpreting the social world. As Cooley recognized earlier and Shils has emphasized more recently,[12] although it is true that similarities between the observers and the observed are a potential source of affinity, possibly leading to deeper empathy and sharper insight, the task remains for those who wish to develop a science of social phenomena outside themselves to distinguish and somehow take into account the effects inner residues have upon their observations and interpretations. In the study of the interchange between the individual and the group the sociology of groups can help investigators sort the subjective from the objective. As an additional aid researchers may gather together in work groups to compare their observations and interpretations. Members can review each others' work and note subjective distortions; together they can consider the latent assumptions that might be governing the thinking of the team as a whole. This work complements, but does not replace, systematic empirical observation with tests for reliability and validity. It is the study of group influences upon the investigators themselves that can better enable them to correct for such influences within themselves and to more accurately interpret the other, whether the other is person, group, or society.

In summary, small groups are studied (1) out of curiosity about the human condition, (2) to help understand the psychology of the individual, (3) to help understand the structure and dynamics of larger social units, (4) to advance social system theory in general, and (5) to help social scientists understand how groups affect their actions and thoughts as scientists.

THE STORY OF THE STUDY
OF SMALL GROUPS

Scientific study of groups is largely a twentieth-century phenomenon; nineteenth-century sociologists were understandably preoccupied with major historical trends.[13] Given the newly emerging capitalist societies and bureaucratic states, the formation of new class structures and the dissolution of the intimate groupings in the traditional community, attention was drawn more to what was forming than to what was breaking up—and a dichotomy existed between the dislodged individual and the large system. It is true that Durkheim appreciated the importance of primary group ties in the operation of both social[14] and personal control[15] and that Simmel conceived of the mutuality in social relations,[16] yet these were exceptions: small groupings were overlooked and the dichotomy remained. The new psychology dealt with the individual, the new sociology with the total society.

Partly in response to this gap, Cooley, in the United States, emphasized the affinity between the person and the group: the infant savage becomes socialized through intimate and prolonged interaction in the primary family group;[17] throughout life, close ties with other persons sustain individuals, stabilize their thought, and give them a sense of direction. Cooley noted the ease with which the boundaries between the individual and group are magnified, and the difficulty in recognizing the connections between them. Such connections were demonstrated in the work of Thomas, who showed that when groups disintegrate, the psyche of persons attached to them tends to disintegrate,[18] and in the work of Thrasher, who found that delinquent gangs train their recruits to crime, gain their loyalty, and protect them against society.[19] (This type of criminal behavior is as much a group phenomenon as an individual one.)

The therapeutic effect of groups was discovered in Boston, quite by accident, by Pratt, who noted that his deeply discouraged tuberculosis patients gave each other a kind of aid in discussions about their problems that he could not provide professionally.[20]

Before long, important advances were made to well beyond the point of merely recognizing that "groups made a difference." Industrial output, Mayo found, was materially affected by the network of group relations among workers:[21] not only did the workers fit their output to the standards of the informal team, but their identification with the company, their sense of being part of the larger unit, depended upon close primary relations of respect and affiliation between agents of the company and the informal team. Primary ties linked the individual, the team, and the company. Later field work affirmed the fruitfulness of Mayo's formulation. For example, research showed that the combatants in World War II found their strength and security through loyalty to their immediate comrades. Their motivation to fight was local: they could not let their buddies down. Also, the coordination required to carry out the missions of a mammoth military organization was seen to depend in essence upon an overlapping network of primary personal ties.[22]

Early Visions[23]

Kurt Lewin gave impetus to the study of groups. His program and approach were twofold: Research should lead to social action; action should serve research.[24] Human behavior, no matter how idiosyncratic, was lawful. The laws were to be discovered through knowledge of the field of psychological and sociological forces serving at any moment as causes of action. The science of groups depended upon locating and measuring these forces. One technique Lewin and associates used was to create different groups with known characteristics, then observe their operation. For instance, they set up groups under different styles of leaders, observed how the leaders acted and how the members responded, compared the results, and then drew empirically based conclusions about the dynamic effects of leadership. Through these and other simple, yet scientifically sound, procedures, they demonstrated that theoretically relevant hypotheses could be tested in the experimental laboratory. Coupled with this approach to science were values of an

> emphasis on participatory democracy and the psychotherapeutic stress on openness, spontaneity, closeness, warmth, expression of feelings and authenticity. The framework presupposes that man is preeminently a group animal and that he fulfills himself through active, responsible, cooperative participation in the affairs of his group as an equal with other members . . . . It further posits that groups (organizations, communities, etc.) which are controlled democratically . . . are more likely to be more productive and more gratifying to their members than groups which are not so controlled.[25]

The advancement of science and the liberation of the individual in society were complementary, not contradictory.

Meanwhile, a more distinctly sociological approach was being taken at Harvard where there was interest in establishing the reality of the social system as a complex of mutually dependent elements. Whyte went to the North End of Boston where he encountered Doc and members of Doc's gang whose life together Whyte detailed at firsthand. His association with these young men led not only to the classic *Street Corner Society* but also to lifelong relationships (generously described in the third edition of Whyte's book).[26] Homans, once a commander of small warships, having written on his experience as a leader of groups at sea and having studied workers in business and industry, brought his scheme together in *The Human Group*, where he then applied it to a number of field studies.[27] From there he singled out a series of testable propositions about dynamic relations in social systems that held up empirically in case studies. These propositions implied wider applications and intimated a vision of the *universal social system*—an image that was almost simultaneously being brought into focus by Parson's work on action theory, which conceived of personalities, groups, and societies as different forms of the more general class of action systems.[28] Were there variables by which all such systems could be analyzed? Were there principles that could be applied both within and across all types of human systems?

In close contact with Parsons and Shils and influenced by their conceptual scheme in *Toward a General Theory of Action*, Bales presented a sociological theory of group interaction and an empirical scoring technique to go with it.[29] Groups confront standard problems, such as how to adapt to the realities of the immediate situation, how to accomplish the group's goal, how to hold the group together, and how to satisfy members' needs. Groups must address themselves to these problems if they are to continue to operate. Since most interaction among members represents attempts to resolve these problems, one may classify each act according to the problem to which it is addressed. Although groups vary in their cultures, they all confront a similar set of problems, and consequently problem-oriented categories may be used universally. By applying a standard method of classifying interaction over a wide range of groups, one can discover universal responses to system problems, including trends from the beginning to the end of a meeting, tendencies for members to divide their labor, and how attempts to resolve one problem complicate others.

The importance of Bales's approach was that it shifted attention from the group's effect on people and the situation to the effects of people and the situation upon the group: *group processes themselves were the phenomena to be accounted for and explained*. How do variables such as group size, personalities of members, emotional attachments, and so on, affect the interaction process? What laws explain the process we observe? What laws explain the observable interaction throughout all small groups? The elegant simplicity of Bales's technique has led to its wide use as a standard research method. It has also led to the development of supplementary methods to tap additional dimensions of group process, such as the content of what is said and the emotional orientation of members toward others (mentioned later).

Conceiving of the group as a type of social system, as did Parsons, Bales, Shils and Homans, helped investigators think in more abstract and in more general terms than previously; experience in studying the act-by-act process among members in groups also encouraged investigators to think in dynamic terms. These factors combined with others to stimulate new interest in formulating dynamic mathematical models of group processes. Although the idea of expressing complex system processes in mathematical terms is, of course, borrowed from physical scientists, it seemed that it might be adapted to social processes and, in fact, has become one of the exciting current trends in the field of small groups.[30]

The vision of the group as a *therapeutic setting* gained clarity during World War II. Historically, its roots were in the work of Burrow, who in the 1920s presented a rationale for group therapy:[31] Emotional disorders are due to unresolved problems occurring in a network of interpersonal relations—knowledge about them can be better gained when the patient is interacting with a variety of persons rather than in the traditional, one-to-one doctor and patient relationship; one's distorted view of oneself is reflected through many eyes—one's confused ways of dealing with others can be brought to light and clarified. But Burrow's argument was not well received, and group therapy lay dormant until World War II. The demands of wartime, coupled with shortages of psychiatrists, forced group treatment; finally physicians began to realize some of the possibilities of this new type of therapy.

Bion and others in England, and Semrad in the United States, visualized the transformation of groups from being emotionally dependent to becoming autonomous as those participating in the process gained in confidence and strength.[32] In this way, the practices of psychoanalysis which seemed to work in the one-to-one setting might be applied (with suitable modifications) to the group setting, with the added therapeutic power of patients helping fellow patients. In practice, however, it soon became apparent that when patients meet together, they do more than simply present their "interpersonal past." Under the protection of the therapist, they draw together, create a new primary group with its own code and structure, and tend to value their group, feel loyal to it, and identify with it. Consequently, in order to know how to make appropriate modifications and to understand both individual and collective responses to modifications, the therapist needs to learn about group phenomena in their own right.

One means of studying group dynamics was to set up a special type of group which examined itself. At Harvard Semrad conducted seminars where medical students and young social scientists met together, observed their own interaction, and interpreted to each other what the group was doing.[33] The group was to be seen, and understood with depth, as a system. Similar study groups became part of training programs both at the Tavistock Institute in London and at the A. K. Rice Institute in the United States.

Although the therapeutic vision was oriented toward reducing pain, the *training vision* foresaw the face-to-face group as a setting for developing a high level of interpersonal competence on the part of professionals and executives, with the goal of altering existing organizations and institutions to be more "human," as well as more efficient.[34] Training was to come through interaction among the members "as they struggle to create a productive and viable organization, a miniature society; and as they work to stimulate and support one another's learning within that society. Involving experiences [would be] a necessary, but not the only, condition for learning .... Members [would establish] a process of inquiry in which data about their own behaviors are collected and analyzed simultaneously with the experience which generates the experience."[35]

In experiencing, observing, learning, managing, and reorganizing the T-group, members could become more skillful and competent as executives. The goals were to increase sensitivity toward group processes, and increase awareness of one's own group participation and ability to deal with a variety of group situations. T-groups and their variations continue to be an integral part of the training programs of the National Training Laboratories at Bethel, Maine.

Out of the legacy of progressive education and research on classroom behavior came the *pedagogical* vision of the "class as a primary group working through group processes rather than ignoring them."[36] At Chicago, Thelen organized his students into subgroups in which students collaborated in joint tasks.[37] Shortly thereafter Trow, Zander, Morse, and Jenkins, at Michigan, raised the question, "What are the implications of viewing the class not merely as a number of individuals in the same room but as a group?"[38] At Harvard case analysis courses were reoriented toward the creation of a group that could understand its own process and structure. The collective purpose of their members was to learn about their collective experience. Goals preoccupying other groups were set aside so the group was free to develop self-awareness, to discover what its "self" was where "self" meant the group. Through sometimes difficult periods of confusion and of group management the students had an opportunity to learn firsthand about human processes frequently discussed in the literature only as "principles and problems."[39]

Even with the variety of visions—the group as a setting for action and research, as microcosm, as therapist, as trainer, as teacher—certain common experiences became apparent. One experience was that many latent currents in the interpersonal situation (such as suppressed feelings and unconscious assumptions) were brought to attention, causing the participants to open their eyes to a wider field of vision. As they did so, they were often provided with an immediate and empirical base against which to judge the many myths and folk beliefs embedded in our culture. Such comparisons often resulted in a release from habits of seeing and thinking and allowed greater confidence in the participant's own observations and decisions. In short, the visions led into new territory, a territory that rewarded a sharp eye and realistic assessments.

Explosive Growth

Pursuing one or more of these visions and being guided by the experience of others, post-World War II investigators encountered a number of go-ahead signals that helped to accelerate activity in the field. Three in particular affirmed the directions early pioneers had taken and attracted literally thousands of others to the field, culminating in an extraordinary expansion of research on groups—in the first few years of the 1950s the number of publications tripled, and over the decade they increased almost tenfold! The expansion extended to many academic fields and professions: psychology, sociology, social psychology, psychiatry, psychoanalysis, anthropology, management, social work, education, and more.

The first green light came when experimenters found that, yes, one could conduct controlled experiments in the laboratory to test hypotheses; dependent variables could be adequately and reliably measured. Following closely behind Lewin, Lippitt, and White, Deutsch tested the differential effects of cooperation and competition upon groups;[40] Bavelas artificially controlled who in the group could send information to whom and tested the effects of such communication networks on group efficiency and group satisfaction;[41] Festinger, Schachter, and Back tested the effects of group cohesion upon pressures to conform to group norms.[42] These and other studies in the early 1950s inspired an expanding array of experiments. For instance, through selection, matching, and the use of control groups, the effects of individual characteristics upon group process were tested, including attitudes, values, age, gender, intelligence, and emotional needs; so also were the effects of group configurations tested (homogeneity or heterogeneity, status differences), the effects of group size, time working together, type of task, as well as emergent features such as power differences, coalitions, and emotional relations. Accumulating experience left little doubt that convincing experimental tests of a variety of hypotheses could be performed, although as indicated later there was growing concern about the relevance and importance of the hypotheses themselves.

The second go-ahead signal came when those studying the ongoing group process discovered that not only could the process be broken down and analyzed, but the resulting spectrum was far richer than imagined in the messages it conveyed about the individual actors and about the group as a whole. The process carried literally hundreds of messages, like a coaxial cable; it carried messages about the explicit, the implicit; the conscious, the unconscious; the personal, the transpersonal; the individual and the collective. It was expressive as well as instrumental; as much configurational as it was linear; not only unconscious but among members strangely collusive, often following unannounced directions; and often beyond measurement. As the details of group process opened into a fuller spectrum, new techniques were devised for systematically abstracting given elements for analysis. There soon were an enormous number—as shown by Simon and Boyer's anthology of some seventy scoring methods, presented in fourteen volumes, selected for their relevance to education alone![43]

The third green light was the almost unrecognized discovery that it was relatively easy to create a group. It took only a little ingenuity to set one up and get it underway, whether in the laboratory, the clinic, or at a training conference. It was especially easy in American society, particularly during the 1950s and 1960s. Readiness to participate came from students who wanted to pass a course, patients who needed help, people who were lonely, professionals who wanted to advance science, people curious about group process, and so on. Whether quick encounters or long-term groups, they were relatively easy to originate: all one needed was a purpose, a leader, and a readiness. Add to this ease the discovery that self-created groups were often rewarding—it can be deeply gratifying to have one's experimental procedures work well, to see the healing process at work in one's therapy group, or to experience insight and to see learning occur in one's study group.

Together these three factors encouraged the pioneers: it was possible to experiment with small groups; the group process was rich and informative; and they could be created fairly easily for many different purposes. Such encouragement combined with other factors to culminate in what Hare has called the "heyday" of small group research. Publications increased tenfold in the 1950s, as noted before; new laboratories were built; new observation schemes were devised; recording techniques like sound taping spread from the laboratory to the field; articles were collected in readers, such as the excellent Cartwright and Zander's *Group Dynamics*,[44] Hare, Borgatta, and Bales's *Small Groups*,[45] and somewhat later, Hare's *Handbook of Small Group Research*;[46] groups began to be videotaped for easy playback and review; training conferences both in England and America attracted more and more clients; an increasing number of psychiatrists were trying group therapy; many families as integral units entered self-study and therapy; and various forms of experiential groups, such as sensitivity training groups, began to appear.

Crisis in Experimentation

Only a few years later the picture changed dramatically from one of vision and pride ("Amongst all the social sciences, ours is the only which has managed to apply the techniques of laboratory experimentation to the development and testing of its propositions")[47] to one of disillusionment, even of despair, particularly in laboratories. Commenting on his annual review, Berkowitz in 1970 wrote:

> ... it seems to me ... that social psychology is now in a "crisis stage," in the sense that Kuhn used this term in his book *The Structure of Scientific Revolutions*. We seem to be somewhat at a loss for important problems to investigate and models to employ in our research and theory. It is certainly time to take stock, to see where we are and where we should go ....[48]

Smith, to whom Berkowitz was writing, agreed in stating that "our best scientists are floundering in search of a viable paradigm. It is hard to tell the blind alleys from the salients of advance .... The so-called scientist-professional model ... has been shattered, but all that is clear is that we have not found new directions."[49]

Although some interpreted the trauma as a melodramatic response to demands from outside the field to either become politically relevant or to close up shop, others pointed to growth within the field. New realizations and discoveries within social science accumulated and combined to present, if not red stop lights, then yellow lights of caution. The first caution arose from the growing gap between behavior in the laboratory and action in the outside world. According to Tajfel this gap was accentuated by theories which emphasized individual motivation to the neglect of the interaction between individual conduct and the social context. Tajfel stated that, ". . . owing to the 'individual' nature of the theories and the absence of cultural and social analysis in the design of the experiments and in the interpretation of the data, extrapolations to 'natural' social conduct are often either not possible, or they are irrelevant or trivial."[50]

The second caution arose when studies found that the experimenter was such an inextricable part of the system being studied that the meanings of many findings were altered fundamentally when his or her influence on the situation and the interplay between the experimenter and the subjects were fully taken into account.[51] Orne explored the set of "demand characteristics" generated by the experimenter and the laboratory setting, asking what impact they had upon results.[52] Rosenthal tested "the experimenter effect" in a series of imaginative and careful studies.[53] Subjects, he found, tended to give experimenters what they wanted; and experimenters, on their part, tended to find what they sought, in spite of safeguards. And there appeared no way to neutralize these tendencies.[54]

Tajfel suggested that this unintended effect of the experimenter on the subject inside the laboratory was compounded by unrecognized influences on the experimenters from outside the laboratory—influences due to social position, the institutional and social structure in which experimenters work and by the cultural values they internalize. Problems are selected and means are used; but values and assumptions governing selection remain implicit. Scientists may be unaware of the dynamics of their own choices while they are perhaps studying the dynamics of choice behavior in subjects. Thus the experimenter introduces noise into the process— the noise of the experimenter's own personal dilemmas.[55]

A third discovery was that small groups research was reflexive. It was suggested that the field needed not only "to know how studying and experimenting on groups alters them; [but] most of all ... how to create new theories to apply to group phenomena even after the groups themselves have become aware of the theories."[56] Seeley, to whom the problem seemed more serious than that of the crisis-provoking Heisenberg indeterminancy principle in the field of physics, stated that it

> is of the very essence in determining the status of a putative "human science": it lies in the fact that almost any "fact" stated about human beings is almost certain to be "heard" by them, to alter them in the hearing, and so to falsify, in the long run or the short, the statement made.[57]

Gergen referred to what he called "the enlightenment effect";[58] which as summarized by Elms produces

> change in behavior as the result of subjects' increasing awareness (and, indeed, increasing awareness by most members of our society) of social-scientific hypotheses and findings. According to Gergen, individuals who are knowledgeable about social psychology will intentionally alter their behavior in unpredictable ways; and as psychologists seek to offset such reactions, subjects will devise other means of asserting their individuality or their freedom from psychological laws, in an infinite regress of ploys and counterploys.[59]

Reactions to Crisis

Although the initial reaction to those developments was shock and dismay, later responses varied from being either defensive or diversionary, to adapting theories and methods to take into account what was being learned from the experience.

One of the defensive responses was denial: for instance, evidence of the "experimenter effect" was met with what Arthur Koestler called "a deep and profound silence" (comment made in introducing Rosenthal at the Center for the Study of Behavioral Science, Stanford, 1965). Many university departments and laboratories continued business as usual: Higbee and Wells have presented evidence "that the 1949–1959 trend toward experimentation on college students using analysis of variance designs was perpetuated during the 1960s."[60] Another defensive response was to reduce complexity, narrow the range of phenomena, and continue the pursuit of rigor in investigations, as exemplified by psychologists' work on cognitive consistency and among sociologists by a renewed attraction to B. F. Skinner's approach. A third defensive response was for investigators to discard both sophisticated hypotheses and statistical principles in experimental designs and return to open observation of subjects in elemental situations, such as when person meets person, or rat meets rat. A fourth and related response was to become an unobtrusive observer of action in naturalistic settings, as did Silverman, who argued that "if you agree ... that the only way to prevent a psychological subject from behaving like one is not to let him know that he is one, then [nonreactive, naturalistic research] methods are the only methods capable of generating valid data."[61] Closely associated was a move to loosen the demands placed both upon the observer and observed, to tolerate greater uncertainties and, in procedure, to de-differentiate toward simple description and interpretation of naturally occurring episodes, as did Harré, who suggested that, in any case, social psychology had not yet reached the stage at which it could pass from critical natural history to analytic science.[62]

In contrast some investigators reacted by reflecting on what was happening, first, to the working paradigms, second, to the investigators, and third, to the public's evaluation of the field. On the basis of those reflections, some began to state new working assumptions and to construct new paradigms. Israel and Tajfel edited their critical assessment; [63] Smith wrote his book on *Humanizing Social Psychology*;[64] Morton Deutsch wrote his article "On Making Social Psychology More Useful."[65] These were a few of a number of efforts at reconstruction. "Social psychologists," wrote Silverman, "have ... been the most self-reflective and critical group of scientists, inside or outside of psychology, and from this we may take hope."[66]

Reflection led investigators to reconsider the scope of forces operating in the research setting as they impinged upon both subjects and experimenters. Clearly the domain was more extensive and the influences more subtle than previously thought. Realizing this, a number of researchers turned to the research setting itself and quite deliberately applied their empirical techniques to the study of the laboratory culture,[67] the demand characteristics of the experimental setting,[68] variations in experimenter effect due to factors such as status and gender,[69] the effect of expectations,[70] unintended behavior,[71] the use of deception,[72] the role of suspicion,[73] the myth of the compliant subject,[74] the reciprocal influences between experimenter and subject,[75] as well as the contrast between the perceptual framework used by group participants and observers.[76] In making the research setting itself an object of study, investigators were, in a sense, seeking to know more thoroughly what had shocked them. Psychologists, in particular, were realizing that no matter how carefully they might try to isolate individual subjects, subjects responded in a group setting which needed to be understood sociologically.

Sensitivity to the lively influence on the subject of the many factors in the laboratory setting was one part of a more general expansion of the study of personal and social perception.[77] Building on previous research on interpersonal perception—the study of first impressions, stereotypes, differences between high- and low-status group members, differences in the accuracy of perception between strangers and friends, how accuracy of perception affects group effectiveness—additional work was done on the influence of the group's culture on members' perceptions, influence which varied according to emotional relations, readiness to disclose one's private life, reciprocity in disclosure and effects of disclosure on self-perception, and contrast between the viewpoints of actors in the group and observers outside. This and related research led to the development of *attribution theory*, a model of how and why we attribute certain qualities to objects, events, and actors; for example, assumptions about intentions of others, responsibility for events, or causality of events.[78] Social perception and attribution theory is, of course, relevant both to group members and to those studying groups.

Some investigators who were challenged by the crisis in their field explored feelings and emotions with new interest, with keener eyes, and with observation techniques finely tuned for detecting the expression of feeling and emotion and their impact on group life. Substantial progress in this regard had already been made by applying psychoanalysis to anthropology and sociology, specifically by the work of Moreno on emotional expression,[79] of Bion on dependence and affective collusion,[80] of Redl on "group emotion,"[81] of Jaques on defenses against anxiety,[82] of Schutz on affective orientations,[83] of Backman on affective relations,[84] and of Hall on "hidden" means of expressing ideas and feelings.[85] Mann and associates had devised and applied a method for tracing act-by-act both members' feelings about an authority figure and their levels of anxiety or sense of helplessness.[86] In the seventies, research included studies on love and attraction, hostility and resentment, the influence of feelings on perception, the role of emotions in group development, and how emotions are expressed (encoded) and how they are recognized (decoded) both by group members and by observers. Previously hidden dimensions were uncovered: the new field of proxemics (people's use of space) and the study of non-verbal processes evolved and flourished. These studies, together with experience in experiential groups where the power of emotional processes was apparent, reinforced a move on the part of psychologists to open the "black box" of personality to examination. This move helped American behaviorism to admit the existence and relevance of feelings and emotions (on the individual and collective levels) and the legitimacy of their scientific study.[87]

As cognitive and affective frontiers were being pushed back and as new elements entered the field for study, there were intimations of new dynamic relations among experimental variables. For instance, discovery of the experimenter effect stimulated a closer look at the relation between experimenter and subject, their contract, their perceptions of each other, and the consequences of those reactions. Perhaps because of this closer look, or perhaps because society itself was changing, subjects were found to be less naive than assumed, less compliant, more suspicious, and more demanding. Some experimenters and subjects were caught in the spiraling relation where deception leads to suspicion, requiring more subtle deception, which in turn arouses deeper suspicion, calling for new defensive maneuvers by both parties. Another example is the spiraling relations between self-perception, self-disclosure,[88] feedback from others,[89] self-awareness,[90] self-esteem, openness in presenting the self, and intimacy in relationships.[91] In this latter spiral one may see an opening up of the system, while in the former, a closing down. In either case such spiraling relations affect the investigator in the sense that opening up requires more subtle methods and closing down calls for a new working relationship with subjects.

In short, one set of responses to the new discoveries brought by the crisis in the field was to reexamine the working relations in the research laboratory, to expand the domain of cognitive and affective processes to be studied, to devise more highly discriminating techniques to detect and record the new features, and finally, to consider more subtle, dynamic relations among group processes.

Other Trends

Since from its beginning the study of groups had been varied and diverse, it was no surprise to find, in the 1960s and 1970s along with the expansion mentioned before, contrasting efforts to consolidate; that is, to bring together empirical findings, group conceptions, and fresh observations to form a new synthesis that either illuminated the group more fully or lent order and coherence to research findings.

One example of consolidation is Janis's conception of *Groupthink*—a syndrome that involves a group's loss of its capacity for critical thinking (as exemplified by the decision of President Kennedy and his "best and brightest" advisors to invade Cuba at the Bay of Pigs).[92] Citing a number of such critical decisions, Janis argued that a cause of the lapse of critical thinking was the high degree of cohesiveness among members of the group: most of all they wanted to be together and to advance together. As a concept, Groupthink connected several areas of concern: first it linked laboratory findings with the dynamics of actual groups; then it linked these observations with historical events well known to the public. Such illustrations not only clarified group phenomena, but showed that such study was relevant to our understanding of current history.

Bales's conception of a three-dimensional space within which group process occurs provides a second example of consolidation.[93] Grounded in extensive factor analyses of empirical observations, the dimensions of (a) *dominance-submission*, (b) *positive-negative*, and (c) *instrumental-expressive* defined a space in which to locate the orientations of actors, their actions and their symbolic references. Once each participant was located in the conceptual space, the resulting "shape" of the group itself (as it had become differentiated) could be shown simply and graphically. As a culmination of much work devoted to the discovery of universal tendencies in groups and to the creation of simple-yet-useful conceptions for their empirical study the concept of three-dimensional space helped order an enormous amount of data on various levels of group process and gave coherence to highly complex phenomena.

In addition to expansion and consolidation, there was a third trend: an effort to create abstract theories about highly selected processes. Emerson expressed the spirit of this approach when he wrote:

> Whenever people encounter one another in social interaction, most of the things social psychologists talk and write about are happening *all at once* . . . . No theory can possibly encompass it all. No mind can apprehend or comprehend it all at once. Thus, the aim of any theoretical perspective is to separate out a few attributes to be examined in purely analytic isolation . . . . We hope to gain intellectual orderliness within the narrow slice of reality we have chosen to study . . . .[94]

Social exchange theory is one of two examples. This theory stems from Homan's work in the sixties and is based on two assumptions: First, that when as social actors we find certain events beneficial we tend to act to induce their reoccurrence; and, second, that making them happen again depends often upon give-and-take relations with others. According to Emerson's recent progress report the theory has been sharpened, more clearly distinguished from economic theory, and generalized from the two-actor to the multiple-actor situation.

A second example of this trend is the *expectations state theory* being developed by Berger and associates at Stanford.[95] For their slice of reality they have selected those actions and social structures that seem to result from built-in expectations in the minds of actors, such as expectations on the part of both parties that one is superior to the other, whether the difference is based on competence, rank, age, race, gender, or other status characteristics. They suggest that such expectations are not only carried by culture, but in any given social or work setting their salience is relative to the collectively defined goals being pursued by members. The investigators' strategy has been to begin with the small group setting where they have been able to test their propositions experimentally and then (since expectations of differences exist throughout society) to move into the field to study organizations, communities, and the larger social system.

The crisis in small group research has appeared to have minimal effect on research activities in a number of previously popular areas, including the following: *deviance and group control* studies focused on pressures to conform,[96] normative structures of experiential groups,[97] and the effects of age and race on tendencies to conform;[98] on *triads* were studies looking at three-person games,[99] balance theory,[100] and expansion of the dyad to the triad;[101] *leadership* studies, continuing along previous lines.[102] In response to the growing awareness of the limitations of research with "instant" laboratory groups, increased attention has been given to the structural changes in the development of long-term groups.[103]

Meanwhile outside the laboratory an astonishing proliferation of groups—sensitivity training groups, encounter groups, transactional analysis groups, and so on—was taking place. These attracted the attention of social scientists who studied their internal dynamics, their effects on members, and the experiential group itself as a new form.[104]

Field studies have been extended to include children in Africa,[105] coalitions in Congress,[106] groups in sports,[107] isolated groups in Antarctica,[108] motorcycle clubs,[109] and groups on the battlefield;[110] comparisons have been made across cultures, including between American groups and Chinese,[111] Mexican,[112] African, and Filipino.[113]

Although the production of research articles slackened in the 1960s and 1970s the number of books on small groups has increased, reflecting the need to organize and order findings. The earlier collections of important papers by Cartwright and Zander; Hare, Borgatta, and Bales; and Lindzey and others, mentioned before, have been supplemented in particular by new anthologies by Bennis and others[114] and Ofshe;[115] and by new editions of Lindzey's handbook, and Hare's.[116] Survey and summary were the themes of a number of special issues of journals as the 1970s ended and the 1980s began.[117]

Conclusion

What seemed at first to have been a local crisis of confidence in social psychology is likely to be seen, in perspective, as part of what Boulding called a revolutionary change in man's awareness of himself and his societies.[118] Seeley wrote that "we [in America] are confronted with the possibility—perhaps now the inescapable necessity—of a highly self-conscious society of highly self-conscious individuals, a society that must sustain, cope with, or use all the new possibilities of 'vertical' complexity [awareness of the latent and the preconscious] in addition to the pre-existing ones of 'horizontal' complexity [inter-dependencies]. We have added a new dimension [the vertical]; and there is no more radical act."[119] Seeley warned that without courageous reconstruction of our working schemas and without imaginative inquiry, changes in societies, groups, and individuals would simply outdistance scientists and scholars.

In the study of groups it has become clear that Lewin's field of forces acting on group processes is more extensive, its network more intricate, and its synapses more subtle than earlier imagined. There is, as it were, a space around the earlier life-space. Horizontally in that space the observer and the observed, the experimenter and the subject, are within the same "field" and should be considered together in our theories. Over time they are linked by reflexivity for, as Seeley said, "Almost any 'fact' stated about human beings is almost certain to be 'heard' by them, to alter them in the hearing, and so to falsify, in the long run or in the short, the statement made."[120] Vertically in that space group processes are multileveled, multifaceted, multicaused, and multifunctional. Through them, using various grammars, the system speaks, sometimes clearly, sometimes obscurely. Often it seems that the factors accounting for much of the variance in the system are unknowable and beyond measure.

In short, one result of this expansion, both in our range of awareness and in our depth of experiences in groups (dramatized by the crisis in small group research), is the need to reexamine and reconstruct our theoretical paradigms.

AIMS OF THIS BOOK

This book, now in its second edition, is part of a larger task of constructing more effective ways of thinking about human groups. It anticipates not a single theory that will explain group phenomena but a set of theories from various fields of science, hopefully theories that will complement one another. Our approach is sociological; we try to gain a bird's eye view of the group, seeing "all the way around it," treating it as a dynamic and changing whole, yet still trying to remain in touch with both the inner lives of its members and the external realities the group must face. Thus, the first of four specific aims of the book is to introduce to you a sociological way of viewing groups. Six working models are presented and evaluated in Chapter 1, ranging from the psychoanalytic model to the more recent cybernetic model.

Secondly, this book attempts to show how a science of groups is possible. In Chapters 2 and 3 you are asked to put yourself in the place of the observer in the field and the experimenter in the laboratory. From that viewpoint you may be able to appreciate not only the difficulties the scientist, as an outsider, has in obtaining inside group information, but also come to understand how these difficulties are overcome and scientific inquiry is advanced. Selected observational methods are described in Chapter 2, and the exigencies of experimentation are discussed in Chapter 3.

The third aim is to enable you to more easily apprehend the ongoing process in groups; that is, to distinguish among the variety of signals, actions, and events, to sense the rhythm and order, and to find the underlying structures. Chapters 4 and 5 introduce five levels on which group processes occur (behavior, feelings, norms, goals, and values) and relate those levels to the subjective experience of group members. As the levels are presented you are invited to put yourself in the place of a pair of newcomers to the group and to follow their experience as they progress from one level to another—or more specifically, as they advance from novices who have yet to learn what the group is to members who eventually assume executive responsibility for the group as a whole and consequently require a way of conceiving of the whole.

Our final aim is to invite new theories about groups, not only as groups are found to be but also as they are in the process of becoming. Our view is that the group, as a whole, is a dynamic system with potential for change and growth. Although sociologists may agree on this general point, there is lack of agreement on its implications. Without attempting to take all points of view into account, Chapter 6 presents a paradigm which is based both on the cybernetic model (described in Chapter 1) and on the idea that group growth is not gradual but occurs instead through relatively sudden transformations from one type of system to another. Such transformations depend upon whether group members have adequately resolved certain critical organizational and emotional issues. Chapter 8 presents a continuum along which group formations vary from low to high potential for developing group capabilities.

In short, the book's emphasis is upon useful and effective ways of thinking about groups. It is hoped that with the present scheme and paradigm as an introduction, past and future accounts of research will gain fuller meaning and that you will have an added sense of excitement as you follow the venture of making a science of the sociology of small groups. A comprehensive review of current research findings can be found in those references given previously and in the context of selected issues that follow. Readings listed in Selected References include leads that you may follow to find additional reviews.

NOTES

1. For a balanced view of research and thought from the sociological perspective see Howard L. Nixon II, *The Small Group* (Englewood Cliffs, N.J.: Prentice-Hall, 1979). For earlier reviews of the development of the field, see Fred L. Strodtbeck and A. Paul Hare, "Bibliography of Small Group Research: 1900 through 1953," *Sociometry*, 17 (1954), 107–78; Edgar F. Borgatta, "Small Group Research," *Current Sociology*, 9 (1960), 173–200; and Robert E. L. Faris, "Development of the Small Group Research Movement," in Muzafer Sherif and M. O. Wilson (eds.), *Group Relations at the Crossroads* (New York: Harper & Row, Pub. 1953), pp. 155–84. For a recent review and a comprehensive bibliography see A. Paul Hare, *Handbook of Small Group Research*, 2nd ed. (New York: Free Press, 1976).

2. See the special issue, "What's Happened to Small Group Research," *The Journal of Applied Behavioral Science*, vol. 15, no. 3 (1979); and the special issue, "Small Groups: An Agenda for Research and Theory," *American Behavorial Scientist*, vol. 24 (May, June 1981).

3. Dexter C. Dunphy, *The Primary Group: A Handbook for Analysis and Field Research* (New York: Appleton-Century-Crofts, 1972), p. 5.

4. Donald C. Johanson and Maitland A. Edey, *Lucy: The Beginnings of Humankind* (New York: Simon & Schuster, 1981).

5. Nancy Makepeace Tanner, *On Becoming Human* (New York: Cambridge University Press, 1981).

6. Charles H. Cooley, *Social Organization: A Study of the Larger Mind* (New York: Scribner's, 1909), p. 30.

7. Jules Henry, *Pathways to Madness* (New York: Random House, 1965).

8. Clifford J. Sager and Helen Singer Kaplan, *Progress in Group and Family Therapy* (New York: Brunner/Mazel, 1972).

9. J. Sherwood Williams, B. Krishna Singh, Louis H. Gray, and Maxmillian H. Von Broembsen, "Small Groups as Simulates of Formal Organizations," *International Journal of Contemporary Sociology*, vol. 11 (January 1974), and Y. L. Kolomin-

skiy, "Sociopsychological Problems in Small Groups and Collectives," *Soviet Psychology*, 11, no. 1 (1972), 44–64.

10. Robert F. Bales, "The Equilibrium Problem in Small Groups," in Talcott Parsons, Robert F. Bales, and Edward A. Shils, *Working Papers in the Theory of Action* (New York: Free Press, 1953), pp. 111–61. For comments on the strategy and function of small group research see Lewis A. Coser, "The Functions of Small Group Research," *Social Problems*, 3 (Winter 1955–56), 1-6; Edgar F. Borgatta and Leonard S. Cottrell, "Directions for Research in Group Behavior," *American Journal of Sociology*, 63 (1957), 42–48; and Alan P. Bates and N. Babchuck, "The Primary Group: A Reappraisal," *Sociological Quarterly*, 3 (July 1961), 181–91. For a more recent appraisal see the special issue of *The Journal of Applied Behavioral Science*, vol. 15, no. 3 (July–Sept. 1979).

11. George C. Homans, *Sentiments and Activities* (New York: Free Press, 1962), p. 39.

12. Edward Shils, "The Calling of Sociology, "*Theories of Society*, Vol. II (New York: Free Press, 1961), pp. 440–41; Cooley, *Social Organization, A Study of the Larger Mind*.

13. For perceptive interpretations of origins and trends see Edward A. Shils, *"The Study of the Primary Group,"* in Daniel Lerner and Harold Lasswell, eds., *The Policy Sciences* (Stanford, Calif.: Stanford University Press, 1951), pp. 41–69, and Dunphy, *The Primary Group*, pp. 11–39. Also see Hare, *Handbook of Small Group Research*, 2nd ed., pp. 384–95.

14. Emile Durkheim, *The Division of Labor*, trans. George Simpson (New York: Free Press, 1933), especially pp. 1–31.

15. Emile Durkheim, *Suicide*, trans. John A. Spaulding and George Simpson (New York: Free Press, 1951), pp. 241–326.

16. Kurt H. Wolff, *The Sociology of Georg Simmel* (New York: Free Press, 1950), pp. 379–408; see also Georg Simmel, *Conflict and The Web of Group Affiliations*, trans. Kurt H. Wolff and Reinhard Bendix, respectively (New York: Free Press, 1955), pp. 125–95.

17. Cooley, *Social Organization: A Study of the Larger Mind*.

18. W. I. Thomas and Florian Znaniecki, *The Polish Peasant in Europe and America*, Vols. I–IV (Chicago: University of Chicago Press, 1918).

19. Frederic Thrasher, *The Gang* (Chicago: University of Chicago Press, 1927).

20. For a brief review of the origins of treatment in groups see Max Rosenbaum and Milton Berger, eds., *Group Psychotherapy and Group Function* (New York: Harper & Row, Pub. 1963).

21. Elton Mayo, *The Human Problems of an Industrial Civilization* (New York: Macmillan, 1933); see also the work of his associates in F. J. Rothlisberger and W. J. Dickson, *Management and the Worker: Technical vs. Social Organization in an Industrial Plant* (Cambridge, Mass.: Harvard University Press, 1939).

22. Edward A. Shils, "Primary Groups in the American Army," in Robert K. Merton and Paul F. Lazarsfeld, eds., *Continuities in Social Research: Studies in the Scope and Method of "The American Soldier"* (New York: Free Press, 1950), pp. 16–39.

23. In the sections that follow I adapt material from Theodore M. Mills, "Changing Paradigms for Studying Human Groups," *Journal of Applied Behavioral Science*, 15, no. 3 (July–Sept. 1979), 407–23. Copyright 1979 NTL Institute. Reproduced by special permission from the *Journal of Applied Behavioral Science*.

24. Kurt Lewin, "Frontiers in Group Dynamics," *Human Relations*, 1 (1947), 5–41; Kurt Lewin, "Frontiers in Group Dynamics: II," *Human Relations*, 1 (1947), 143–53; and Kurt Lewin and R. Lippitt, "An Experimental Approach to the Study of Autocracy and Democracy: A Preliminary Note," *Sociometry*, 1 (1938), 292–300.

25. Morton Deutsch, "On Making Social Psychology More Useful," *Items*, 30 (1976), 1-6. (New York: Social Science Research Council)

26. William F. Whyte, *Street Corner Society: The Social Structure of an Italian Slum* (Chicago: University of Chicago Press, 1943; 2nd ed., 1955; 3rd ed., 1981).

27. George C. Homans, *The Human Group* (New York: Harcourt Brace Jovanovich, Inc., 1950).

28. Talcott Parsons and Edward A. Shils, eds., *Toward a General Theory of Action* (Cambridge, Mass.: Harvard University Press, 1951).

29. Robert F. Bales, *Interaction Process Analysis: A Method for the Study of Small Groups* (Reading, Mass.: Addison-Wesley, 1950).

30. For a mathematical formulation of the theoretical system of Homans in *The Human Group*, see Herbert A. Simon, "A Formal Theory of Interaction in Social Groups," *American Sociological Review*, 17 (April 1952), 202–11; also see Joan Criswell, Herbert Solomon, and Patric Suppes, eds., *Mathematical Methods in Small Group Processes* (Stanford, Calif.: Stanford University Press, 1962); and Joseph Berger, Bernard Cohen, J. Laurie Snell, and Morris Zelditch, Jr., *Types of Formalization in Small Group Research* (Boston: Houghton Mifflin, 1962). For more recent examples of mathematical treatment see Thomas Mayer, *Mathematical Models of Group Structure* (Indianapolis: Bobbs-Merrill, 1975); Anatol Rappaport, "A Probabilistic Approach to Networks," *Social Networks*, 2 (1979), 1–18; and Kazuo Youraguchi, "A Mathematical Model of Friendship Choice Distribution," *Journal of Mathematical Sociology*, 7 (1980), 261–87.

31. Trigant L. Burrow, "The Group Method of Analysis," *Psychoanalytic Review*, 14 (1924), 268–80.

32. See W. R. Bion, *Experience in Groups and Other Papers* (New York: Basic Books, 1959); S. H. Foulkes, *Introduction to Group Analytic Psychotherapy* (London: Heineman Medical Books, 1948); Alexander Wolf, "The Psychoanalysis of Groups," *American Journal of Psychotherapy* (1949), pp. 15–50 and (1950), pp. 525–38; and J. Mann and Elvin V. Semrad, "Notes on the Use of Group Therapy in Psychosis," *Journal of Social Casework* (1948), pp. 176–81.

33. Elvin V. Semrad and John Arsenian, "The Use of Group Processes in Teaching Group Dynamics," *American Journal of Psychiatry*, C (1951), 358–63.

34. On training groups, see Leland P. Bradford, J. R. Gibb, and Kenneth D. Benne, eds., *T-Group Theory and Laboratory Methods* (New York: John Wiley, 1964); Edgar H. Schein and Warren G. Bennis, *Personal and Organizational Change through Group Methods: The Laboratory Approach* (New York: John Wiley, 1965).

35. Bradford, Gibb, and Benne, eds., *T-Group Theory and Laboratory Methods* pp. 1–2.

36. Dunphy, *The Primary Group*, p. 29.

37. Herbert A. Thelen, "Group Dynamics in Instruction," *School Review*, 57 (March, 1949), 139–48.

38. William C. Trow, Alvin F. Zander, William C. Morse, and David H. Jenkins, "Psychology of Group Behavior: The Class as a Group," *Journal of Educational Research*, 45 (Nov., 1951), 322–38.

39. Hugh Cabot and Joseph A. Kahl, *Human Relations: Concepts and Cases in Concrete Social Science* (Cambridge, Mass: Harvard University Press, 1953) and Philip E. Slater, *Microcosm: Structural, Psychological and Religious Evolution in Groups*, (New York: John Wiley, 1966).

40. Morton Deutsch, "An Experimental Study of the Effects of Cooperation and Competition Upon Group Process," *Human Relations*, 2 (1949), 129–52, 199–231.

41. Alex Bavelas, "Communication Patterns in Task Oriented Groups," *Journal of the Acoustical Society of America*, 20 (1950), 725–30, reprinted in Dorwin Cartwright and Alvin Zander, eds., *Group Dynamics*, 2nd ed. (Evanston, Ill.: Row, Peterson, 1960), pp. 669–82; for a follow-through study see Harold J. Leavitt, "Some Effects of Certain Communication Patterns on Group Performance," *Journal of Abnormal and Social Psychology*, 46 (1951), 38–50, reprinted in Guy E. Swanson, Theodore M. Newcomb, and Eugene L. Hartley, eds., *Readings in Social Psychology*, rev. ed. (New York: Holt, 1952).

42. Leon Festinger, Stanley Schachter, and Kurt W. Back, *Social Pressures in Informal Groups: A Study of Human Factors in Housing* (New York: Harper & Row, Pub., 1950); see also Stanley Schachter, "Deviation Rejection and Communication," *Journal of Abnormal and Social Psychology*, 46 (1951), 190–207, reprinted in Cartwright and Zander, eds., *Group Dynamics*, 2nd ed., pp. 260–85.

43. Anita Simon and E. Gil Boyer, eds., *Mirrors for Behavior: An Anthology of Observation Instruments*, Vols. I–XIV (Philadelphia: Research for Better Schools, 1970).

44. Cartwright and Zander, eds., *Group Dynamics*, 1st ed., 1953. Also see 2nd ed., 1960, and 3rd ed., 1965.

45. A Paul Hare, Edward F. Borgatta, and Robert F. Bales, *Small Groups: Studies in Interaction* (New York: Knopf, 1966).

46. Hare, *Handbook of Small Group Research*, 1st ed., 1962. Also see 2nd ed., 1976.

47. Henri Tajfel, "Experiments in a Vacuum," in Joachim Israel and Henri Tajfel, eds., *The Context of Social Psychology: A Critical Assessment* (New York: Academic Press, 1972), p. 106.

48. Quoted in M. Brewster Smith, "Is Psychology Relevant to New Priorities?" *American Psychologist* (June 1973), p. 464.

49. Ibid.

50. Tajfel, "Experiments in a Vacuum," in Israel and Tajfel, eds., *The Context of Social Psychology: A Critical Assessment*, p. 106.

51. Theodore M. Mills, 'A Sleeper Variable in Small Group Research: The Experimenter," *Pacific Sociological Review*, 5 (1962), 21–28.

52. Martin T. Orne, "On the Social Psychology of the Psychological Experiment: With Particular Reference to Demand Characteristics and Their Implications," *American Psychologist*, 17 (1962), 776–83.

53. Robert Rosenthal, *Experimenter Effects in Behavioral Research* (New York: Appleton-Century-Crofts, 1966).

54. Morris Rosenberg and Ralph H. Turner, *Social Psychology: Sociological Perspectives* (New York: Basic Books, 1981), p. xvii–xix.

55. Tajfel, "Experiments in a Vacuum."

56. Mills, "A Sleeper Variable in Small Group Research: The Experimenter," pp. 21–28.

57. John R. Seeley, *The Americanization of the Unconscious* (New York: International Science Press, 1967), p. 103.

58. Kenneth J. Gergen, "Social Psychology as History," *Journal of Personality and Social Psychology*, 26 (1973), 309–20.

59. A. C. Elms, "The Crisis of Confidence in Social Psychology," *American Psychologist* (October 1975), p. 969.

60. K. Higbee and M. G. Wells, "Some Research Trends in Social Psychology in the 1960s," *American Psychologist* (October 1972), p. 966.

61. Irwin Silverman, "Why Social Psychology Fails," *Canadian Psychological Review*, 17, no. 4 (1974), 355.   1977

62. Rom Harré, "Blueprint for a New Science," in N. Armistead, ed., *Reconstructing Social Psychology* (Middlesex, England: Penguin, 1974), pp. 240–58.

63. Israel and Tajfel, eds., *The Context of Social Psychology*.

64. M. Brewster Smith, *Humanizing Social Psychology* (San Francisco: Jossey-Bass, 1974).

65. Morton Deutsch, "On Making Social Psychology More Useful," *Items*, 30 (1976), 1–6. (New York: Social Science Research Council)

66. Irwin Silverman, "Why Social Psychology Fails," p. 358.

67. Karl E. Weich and David P. Gilfillian, "Fate of Arbitrary Traditions in a Laboratory Micro-culture," *Journal of Personality and Social Psychology* (February 1971), pp. 179–91.

68. Monte M. Page, 'Demand Characteristics and the Verbal Operant Conditioning Experiment," *Journal of Personality and Social Psychology* (September 1972), pp. 377–78; Sheldon H. Geller and Norman S. Endler, "The Effects of Subject Roles, Demand Characteristics, and Suspicion on Conformity," *Canadian Journal of Behavioral Science* (January 1973), pp. 46–54; and Keith F. Critchlow, Robert Herrup, and James M. Bobbs, Jr., "Experimenter Influence in a Conformity Situation," *Psychological Reports*, 23 (1968), 408–10.

69. Morton Deutsch, Donnah Canavan, and Jeffry Rubin, "The Effects of Size of Conflict and Sex of Experimenter upon Interpersonal Bargaining," *Journal of Experimental Psychology* (March 1971), pp. 258–67.

70. Ernest Timaeus, *Experiment and Psychology: On the Social Psychology of Psychological Experiments* (Göttingen: Hogrefe, 1974).

71. Yoshiyasu Uno, Judith H. Korvumaki, and Robert Rosenthal, "Unintended Experimenter Behavior as Evaluated by Japanese and American Observers," *Journal of Social Psychology*, 88 (October 1972), 91–106.

72. Davis S. Holmes and David H. Bennett, "Experiments to Answer Questions Raised by the Use of Deception in Psychological Research," *Journal of Personality and Social Psychology*, 29, no. 3 (1974), 358–67.

73. Lawrence J. Stricker, Samuel Messick, and Douglas N. Jackson, "Suspicion of Deception: Implications for Conformity Research, *Journal of Personality and Social Psychology*, 5, no. 4 (1967), 379–89; and David J. Martin, "Suspicion and the Experimental Confederate: A Study of Role and Credibility," *Sociometry*, 33 (June 1970), 178–92.

74. Leonard Berkowitz, "The 'Weapons Effect,' Demand Characteristics and the Myth of the Compliant Subject," *Journal of Personality and Social Psychology*, 20, no. 3 (1971), 332–38.

75. Peggy C. Marquis, "Experimenter-Subject Interaction as a Function of Authoritarianism and Response Set," *Journal of Personality and Social Psychology*, 25 (February 1973), 289–96.

76. Thomas L. Ruble, "Effects of Actor and Observer Roles on Attribution of Causality in Situations of Success and Failure," *Journal of Social Psychology*, 90 (June 1973), 41–44.

77. See A. Paul Hare, "Social Perception," Chap. 5 in Hare, *Handbook of Small Group Research*, 2nd ed., pp. 113–30.

78. Edward E. Jones and others, *Attribution: Perceiving the Causes of Behavior* (Morristown, N.J.: General Learning Press, 1972).

79. Moreno, *Who Shall Survive?*

80. Bion, *Experiences in Groups and Other Papers.*

81. Fritz Redl, "Group Emotion and Leadership," in Hare, Borgatta, and Bales, eds., *Small Groups*, pp. 86–87.

82. Elliott Jaques, "Social Systems as a Defense against Persecutory and Depressive Anxiety," reprinted in Theodore M. Mills and Stan Rosenberg, *Readings on the Sociology of Small Groups* (Englewood Cliffs, N.J.: Prentice-Hall, 1970), pp. 203–18.

83. William S. Schutz, *FIRO: A Three-Dimensional Theory of Interpersonal Behavior* (New York: Holt, Rinehart & Winston, 1958).

84. Carl W. Backman, "Attraction in Interpersonal Relations," in Rosenberg and Turner, eds., *Social Psychology: Sociological Perspectives*, pp. 235–68.

85. Edward T. Hall, *The Silent Language* (New York: Doubleday, 1959).

86. Richard D. Mann, Graham S. Gibbard, and John J. Hartman, *Interpersonal Styles and Group Development* (New York: John Wiley, 1967).

87. Magda Arnold, *Feelings and Emotions, The Loyola Symposium* (New York: Academic Press, 1970), pp. vii–x.

88. Sidney M. Jourard, *Self-Disclosure: An Experimental Analysis of the Transparent Self* (New York: John Wiley, 1971).

89. Kenneth J. Gergen, "The Effects of Interaction Goals and Personality Feedback on the Presentation of the Self," *Journal of Personality and Social Psychology*, 1, no. 5 (1965), 413–24.

90. James V. Clark, Samuel Culbert, and H. K. Babele, "Mutually Therapeutic Perception and Self-Awareness under Variable Conditions," *Journal of Applied Behavioral Science*, 5, no. 1 (1969), 65–72.

91. Carl W. Backman, "Attraction in Interpersonal Relations," in Rosenberg and Turner, eds., *Social Psychology: Sociological Perspectives*, pp. 235–68.

92. Irving L. Janis, *Victims of Groupthink: A Psychological Study of Foreign-Policy Decisions and Fiascoes* (Boston: Houghton Mifflin, 1972).

93. Robert F. Bales, *Personality and Interpersonal Behavior* (New York: Holt, Rinehart & Winston, 1970); and Robert F. Bales and Stephen P. Cohen with Stephen A. Williamson, *SYMLOG: A System for the Multiple Level Observation of Groups* (New York: Free Press, 1979).

94. Richard M. Emerson, "Social Exchange Theory," in Rosenberg and Turner, eds., *Social Psychology: Sociological Perspectives*, p. 31.

95. Joseph Berger and others, *Status Characteristics and Social Interaction: An Expectation State Approach* (New York: Elsevier North-Holland, 1977).

96. For example, Charles A. Kiesler, "Group Pressure and Conformity," in Judson Mills, ed., *Experimental Social Psychology* (New York: Macmillan, 1969), pp. 235–306.

97. Robert A. Luke, Jr., "The Internal Normative Structure of Sensitivity Training Groups," *Journal of Applied Behavioral Science*, 8 (July 1972), 421–37.

98. Fred Janney and others, "Conformity as a Function of Race and Age," *Psychological Reports*, 25 (1969), 591–97.

99. R. E. Overstreet, "Social Exchange in a Three-Person Game," *Journal of Conflict Resolution*, 16 (March 1972), 109–23.

100. Philip Brickman and Charles Horn, "Balance Theory and Interpersonal Coping in Triads," *Journal of Personality and Social Psychology*, 26 (June 1973), 247–355.

101. Richard H. Willis, "Coalitions in the Triad: Additive Case," *Psychonomic Science*, 92, no. 6 (1969), 347–48.

102. See Hare, *Handbook on Small Group Research*, 2nd ed., Chap. 15, pp. 278–303.

103. Bruce W. Tuckman, "Developmental Sequence in Small Groups," *Psychological Bulletin*, 62 (1965), 384–99; Michael P. Farrell, "Patterns in the Development of Self-Analytic Groups," *Journal of Applied Behavioral Science*, 12 (1976), 523–42; and Bruce W. Tuckman and Mary A. Jenson, "Stages in Small Group Development, Revisited," *Group Organizational Studies*, 2, no. 4 (December 1977), 419–27.

104. Morton A. Lieberman and others, *Encounter Groups: First Facts* (New York: Basic Books, 1973); Kurt W. Back, *Beyond Words* (New York: Russell Sage Foundation, 1972) and Kurt W. Back, "The Experiential Group and Society," *Journal of Applied Behavioral Science*, 9, no. 1 (1973) 7–20. Also see John J. Hartman, "Small Group Methods of Personal Change," *Annual Review of Psychology*, 30 (1979) 453–76 and Martin Lakin, "Experiential Groups: The Uses of Interpersonal Encounter, Psychotherapy Groups, and Sensitivity Training," in John Thibaut, Janet Spence, and Robert Carson, eds., *Contemporary Topics in Social Psychology* (Morristown, N.J.: General Learning Press, 1976), pp. 423–54.

105. Robert L. Munroe and Ruth H. Munroe, "Obedience among Children in an East African Society," *Journal of Cross-Cultural Psychology*, 3 (December 1972), 395–99.

106. Barbara Hinkley, "Coalitions in Congress: Size and Ideological Distance," *Midwest Journal of Political Science*, 16 (May 1972), 197–207.

107. N. G. Valentinova and V. V. Myedvyedyev, "Selected Problems of Small Groups in Sports Teams," *International Review of Sport Sociology*, 7, no. 1 (1973), 69–77.

108. L. P. Vermeulen, "Small-Group Behavior in Long-Term Isolation," *The South African Journal of Sociology*, 15 (April 1977), 35–40.

109. Randal Montgomery, "The Outlaw Motorcycle Subculture," *Canadian Journal of Criminology and Corrections*, 93 (October 1976), 332–42.

110. Charles W. Greenbaum, "The Small Group under the Gun: Uses of Small Groups in Battle Conditions," *Journal of Applied Behavioral Science*, 15 (July-September 1979), 392–405.

111. Robert D. Meade and William A. Barnard, "Conformity and Anticonformity among Americans and Chinese," *Journal of Social Psychology*, 89, no. 1 (1973), 15–24.

112. Charles G. McClintock, "Development of Social Motives in Anglo-American and Mexican-American Children," *Journal of Personality and Social Psychology*, 29, no. 3 (1974), 348–54.

113. A. Paul Hare and Dean Peabody, "Attitude Content and Agreement Set in Autonomy—Authoritarianism Items for United States, Africa and Philippine University Students," *Journal of Social Psychology*, 83 (1971), 23–31. For a recent review of cross-cultural studies see Harry C. Triandis and R. Brislin, eds., *Handbook of Cross-cultural Psychology: Social Psychology*, Vol. 5 (Boston: Allyn & Bacon, 1980).

114. Warren G. Bennis and others, eds., *Interpersonal Dynamics: Essays and Readings on Human Interaction*, 3rd ed. (Homewood, Ill.: Dorsey, 1973).

115. Richard J. Ofshe, ed., *Interpersonal Behavior in Small Groups* (Englewood Cliffs, N.J.: Prentice-Hall, 1973).

116. Gardner Lindzey and Elliott Aronson, eds., *The Handbook of Social Psychology*, 2nd ed., in 4 vols. (Reading, Mass.: Addison-Wesley, 1968); Hare, ed., *Handbook of Small Group Research*, 2nd ed.

117. Martin Lakin, ed., special issue: "What's Happened to Small Group Research?", *Journal of Applied Behavioral Science*, 15 (July-August-September 1979); and Edgar F. Borgatta and Paul M. Baker, eds., special issue: "Small Groups: An Agenda for Research and Theory," *American Behavioral Scientist*, 24 (May-June 1981).

118. Kenneth Boulding, *The Impact of the Social Sciences* (New Brunswick, N.J.: Rutgers University Press, 1966).

119. John R. Seeley, *The Americanization of the Unconscious* (New York: International Science Press, 1967), p. 16.

120. Ibid., p. 103.

CHAPTER 1
MODELS
OF
GROUPS

"My family was like a flower, quotes R. D. Laing. "Mother was the center and we were all petals. When I broke away, mother felt that she had lost an arm. They (sibs) still meet round her like that. Father never really comes into the family in that sense."[1]

Group members and sociologists alike have their own mental models of groups; through past experience we all accumulate impressions and compose images of what groups are like and how they operate. We "know" how boys play, what girls talk about, what families are like, how committees work. We "know" what is likely to happen in a lifeboat at sea, for we carry primitive notions or working models of "group nature" just as we carry concepts of "human nature." As Laing says, we map the outer scene as an image into our inner world so that the group out there becomes the group inside. And even if vague such inner images affect individual orientation to a group, and among all members influence the history of the group, particularly if the images are shared. Not only do such images tend to capture essentials of complex situations (as does the flower image in Laing's quote) but they also become the framework within which members think and act. When events fall within this framework they seem natural and normal, but when they fall outside, they are strange, even incomprehensible. Our subjective images set limits both on what we think will happen and on what we imagine to be possible. In this sense groups tend in their actions to fulfill the prophecy contained in their members' models.

These images in the immediate group are only part of the picture, for the culture of our communities and society contains images and models of groups just as it contains models of the earth and heavens, animals and plants. Some cultures, such as traditional Chinese, contain relatively sophisticated conceptions of human groups while others contain only rudimentary ones. In this regard American culture teaches us less about the inner dynamics of groups than it does about how to guard against the dynamics, rise above them, and use them. Most cultures exclude from their explicit models taboo topics such as incestuous or murderous and other socially disturbing feelings.

In its broadest sense the task of the sociology of small groups is to create, quite self-consciously, better and more workable models of groups. Better models in the sense that they cut through and correct the folk images in our cultures; more workable when they help organize disparate experience into a more coherent whole, when the models are stated clearly enough to be understood by others, when they seem to be consonant with our intersubjective experience of reality, and when their implications can be examined and tested and modified in terms of alternative models. Like group members, sociologists build their models out of experience and knowledge; and like group members, their models affect their own orientation to groups: The model provides a frame for defining what is relevant or irrelevant, what is observable and what is not, what is comprehensible and what is not, what is testable and what is not. To a large extent the model governs the sociologists' strategy of study and research. Often scientists are subject to pressures that cause them to ignore realities (which, though important, are seemingly irrelevant to their models) and to search for groups which because of their peculiar properties fulfill the prophecy contained in the model. Yet because a sociologist's attempt is both self-conscious and is performed in collaboration with fellow sociologists, he or she is subject to other pressures: pressures to formulate ideas clearly so they may be evaluated by others and to subject hypotheses continually to reexamination and test. Certainly a sociologist's model is useful when it contributes to sociology; it is no less useful when it helps group members understand their milieu.

Unfortunately for the student there is no single model accepted at present by most sociologists as the preeminent working model. The state of small-group theory is, as we have said, neither neat nor settled; rather, it is in flux.[2] This is partly because if small group researchers have discovered anything over the past forty or so years, it is that human groups are more complex, more varied, and perhaps more interesting than they first appear to be. One reaction has been to build more refined models of more highly selected features, as in some of the mathematical formulations of group interaction;[3] another has been to shift from closed to open models, from simplistic to more complex, from static to more dynamic, and from those models that assume a few types of groups to those that acknowledge a wide variety.[4] Our discussion in this chapter emphasizes the second trend; it provides a broader and less technical introduction to the field.

We should note, before presenting a selection of models, that since few working models are presented fully and explicitly in the literature and must therefore be reconstructed from the implicit notions underlying approaches to the study of groups, our sketches of models are interpretive. That is, they are our interpretations of the implicit ideas employed in various approaches.

PSYCHOANALYTIC MODELS

Freud argued that the transformation of a collection of individuals into a group with "we-feeling" occurs around a central authority who to others essentially controls and deprives. The "prototype of the primary group is a father and his sons. The father forces sexual abstinence on his sons, and the libido, denied discharge, is used to produce identifications between the sons and the father and among the sons."[5] In this sense the grouping of the sons together is a political alternative to the destruction of the depriving father. Freud dramatized this formative process when he depicted a primal horde where the chief claims all the females for himself and threatens other males with death if they interfere (see page 137). Rather than destroy the father, the sons each put him in the place of their ego-ideal, and in doing so identify with each other in their egos. To Freud, what holds groups together is a network of libidinal ties which are the outcome of inhibited sexual impulses and mutual identifications.

We interpret Freud's model as suggesting that when people come together (especially when they are working toward a goal or facing a common fate) the instinctual impulses of sex and aggression are aroused: the impulses to seek out someone to love and to identify would-be rivals. Sensitivity to others' bodies and style is heightened; qualities such as strength, size, beauty, sexiness, poise, vivacity, warmth, or "coolness" tend to guide the impulses of sex and aggression in their search for objects. Sometimes little or no fit occurs and individuals simply disperse with no group forming. Other times there are encounters where impulses are reciprocal or overlapping, resulting in the crystallization of a network of attractions and repulsions, perhaps close dyads, conflictful triangles, or possibly splits between the desirable and the undesirable; in any case a structure forms of interpersonal affect along the primary lines of sex and power. Individuals experience a pull toward immediate gratification, instead of waiting, and toward discharge rather than inhibition. As Freud said, they feel a pull toward the pleasure principle without regard to what that might mean to the group as a whole. However, the "father," or whoever symbolizes the depriving principle within the collectivity, prohibits such gratification and activates guilt within the collective as an inner control. Desires are protected as they are taken underground, made secret, and kept from the awareness not only of the "father" but also from the individuals themselves. Sexual and aggressive impulses and the network they generate are collusively suppressed, taking existence on the unconscious level as an affective understructure.[6] Even though the impulses to copulate and to kill surface only in dreams, jokes, and fairy-tale fantasies, they remain powerful enough that changes in their character (as from love to jealous hatred) may govern overt group action, like a magnet hidden below a compass needle.

Suppressed desire is overtly shielded by personal masks and protected by an implicit agreement to follow customary procedures. Group members (for they can now be called such) have entered into a compact against instinctual gratification—a compact not only to prevent sex and aggression from splitting the group but also for members to protect each other. What we as outside observers usually see is a more or less civilized enactment of the group's compact and its derivative culture, one function of which is to keep the affective processes under control and unknown.

In the two generations since Freud published his first sketch of this model others in psychoanalysis have presented extensions, modifications, and alternatives leaving at present more of a montage of partial models than either acceptance of the original or of a successor that fully supplants it. Redl extended Freud's original model to make it both more consistent with Freud's later theoretical distinctions and more applicable to the many groups that develop without the influence of a formal authority.[7] Redl suggested that groups may form around a variety of persons who turn out to be "central" to others, such as a boy whom others call a "bad influence," or a girl who becomes a group's "darling," or a young athlete who is a "hero" to others. Regardless of status or formal position, certain individuals become "central persons" around whom group feeling is evoked. They may become central as an object of identification not only as the ego-ideal Freud described (for example, a fine but strict coach) but also as one's conscience (a parish priest) or an object of fear (a cruel teacher); they may be objects of love (a favorite uncle) or objects of hostility (a smart but conceited student); or they may be sources of ego support, as when someone takes a dare that others would have liked to have taken. In all, Redl presented nine formulas for group formation supplementing Freud's original.

More clearly an alternative to Freud is a model that derives from the work of Melanie Klein,[8] the Washington School of Psychiatry, The Tavistock Institute in England, and the British object-relations group. Still in the process of development, some of its highlights are as follows:

It is not the father but the mother who is the first compelling power in human experience, argues Durkin.[9] It is not the father as Freud said, but the mother who is the "paramount and dangerous personality towards whom only a passive-masochistic attitude is possible, to whom one's will has to be surrendered."[10] "Surely the [baby's] mother must evoke such an image for it is she who unwittingly destroys his narcissistic bliss and who must bring to his awareness the deprivations and limitations of reality, as well as her love and sustenance. . . . [The baby's] experience with the mother must. . .be a terrifying and infuriating experience."[11] Later in life, the pressure of a group activates in its members not the image of the autocratic father but "traces of the pre-Oedipal mother image and the fears connected with it, causing [them] to become relatively submissive to the group and unusually suggestible."[12] At first glance this view might seem to parallel Freud's formulation, the simple difference being replacement of father by mother as the depriving one around whom mutual identification occurs and we-feeling develops. However, the difference may prove fundamental. Clinical research traces the associative processes involving the mother to a period earlier in the child's life than it is thought possible to identify with others in the sense of Freud's formula. This implies that still more elemental mechanisms are involved in group formation.

We interpret this model to suggest that whenever individuals encounter each other in anticipation of forming a group, or whenever an existing group is in crisis, or whenever a newcomer enters a group, the tension level goes up, the more so as the situation is unstructured and ambiguous. The internal mappings of "the world out there" and of the self's relation to it no longer apply and individuals experience what Durkheim called *anomie*—the absence of normative guidelines. In such circumstances tension is generated by a deep fear of being sucked into the group, of being engulfed by it, of fusing with others, and of losing one's sense of self. Yet as one imagines barricading oneself off, there is a fear of being excluded, rejected, and of being alone. On the one hand there is a fear of being swallowed up and, on the other, a fear of being starved—in either case by the mother.[13] Since one's usual adult mappings fail to serve in such situations, they tend to be replaced by fantasied relations from earlier periods in life, ultimately with images of self-with-mother when the self was neither engulfed nor starved. In short, in response to uncertainty and feelings of anxiety, adults tend, unconsciously, to return to their fantasied roots in infancy.

Group formation occurs through a cooperative search through earlier fantasied relations for those configurations that are sufficiently common among the individuals to serve as a foundation for working relations.[14] If and when such configurations are found, or compiled, and agreed upon, individual anxiety is relieved and the tension between persons decreases, resulting in a greater sense of confidence on the part of members. From this common base (but not necessarily without difficulty) members can proceed together to recapitulate the process of maturation, moving unconsciously from infancy toward adulthood, developing new mappings, new relations, and new ways of coping that are more appropriate to their actual situation. It is through such a cognitive and affective experience that a group with a sense of "we-ness" develops. Of course, when common ground is not found, when instead rifts and incompatibilities are discovered, then the individuals may disperse or, if they cannot, will likely experience deep splits both psychologically and between each other.

Meanwhile, through the normal processes of interpersonal communication, involving outward projections of inner thoughts and symbolic expressions of latent feelings, portions of current unconscious images and representations become more explicit and recognizable so that members have the opportunity at least to become aware of their content and of their part in governing the group. For example, members may share a latent assumption that the group is a mother who should nurture and care for members, though this might retard individual initiative on a difficult task. Presumably insight into such assumptions better enables the group to become free of unconscious limitation and to replace assumptions with those that correspond more closely to the way the group has come to define current reality.

Within the psychoanalytic model, group life tends to oscillate between regression in the search for common ground and progression toward both an awareness of latent group process and an ability to work constructively together.

Two brief points should be mentioned about the psychoanalytic models within the context of the present chapter. First, analysts since Freud have extended his original formulation not only to be more easily applied to a wider range of group situations but also to connect those situations to the earliest interpersonal experiences of the individual. Second, there is clear recognition in the literature of the difference in scope of psychoanalytic models and of more comprehensive sociological models. Forty years ago Redl said that "groups are phenomena containing so many different ingredients that the attempt to bring them into any one formula by the technique of psychoanalytic exploration must remain futile."[15] Instead, psychoanalytic models "single out only one of the aspects of group life, the emotional and instinctual relationships between persons who constitute a group."[16] Thus quite consciously these models are designed to complement but not to supplant the other models described in this chapter.

THE SYMBOLIC INTERACTION MODEL[17]

The group is like a set of actors on stage in search of the meaning of what they say and do. We can imagine them asking: Who are we as actors? What roles are we playing? What is the point to the drama we find ourselves enacting? What of it is real and what is make-believe? After all, the meaning of the drama we are born into is not given; it must be discovered.

The central idea in this model is that the ongoing search for meaning—the interpersonal processes involving signs, language and behavior—is the ontological core out of which emerge the elemental images of the self, the other, the group, and even the larger society. The images that appear not only orient action but through interaction become subject to examination and modification by others. In this sense the search is simultaneously personal and social. Images described by one member may be altered and enriched by others, leading eventually to sets of definitions that are part of the group culture. Members are able to experience the idea that this is what I am, this is what you are, this is what we are, and this is our situation. Such images are working copies of the world and its objects, including the group itself. Cooley, one of the originators of the model, suggests that essentially the group is a relation among the images in the heads of members: A group is the set of notions that members have of one another as a unit.[18]

Although this model appears in a number of different versions, the common themes, according to Meltzer, Petras, and Reynolds, are (1) that meanings emerge from social interaction, (2) that humans act toward objects on the basis of the meanings those objects have for them, and (3) that meanings are modified and dealt with through an interpretive process used by persons when responding to things encountered.[19] These processes are made possible by what Mead called the human's abilities to "take the role of the other," to use symbols and to create significant symbols; that is, symbols when used in the social context call up in the minds of the various individuals meanings sufficiently alike to permit joint action.[20] While the identity of a given group is a composite of constructions generated in the minds of members (and of others with whom the group deals), personal identities are mental constructions built up through experiences in one group setting after another.

Groups vary in the degree to which their meanings are fixed by the surrounding culture. Some groups such as tellers at a bank have group meanings supplied for them, even imposed upon them; others, for example a jazz group, are free to discover their own meaning. Groups also vary in the degree to which their work is routinely ordered. Flight crews are quite tightly programmed; exploration teams set their own program. Since the time of Mead and Cooley, the symbolic interaction model has been extended to accommodate some of these variations. Blumer recognized that the surrounding culture's dictionary is often vague and its template for group structure often unclear; he emphasized that the concrete situation itself must be explored by the actors involved and appropriate meanings conjured up through their own initiative.[21] Turner, pointing to rapidly changing contexts, noted that individuals must do more than simply take the role of the other or internalize the pattern "out there." Instead, they must often at some risk try out new roles, possibly signaling to others that they are doing so, read responses, and make appropriate changes. They must create out of ambiguous cues and an uncertain design workable relations and courses of action.[22] Through these and similar processes new patterns with new meanings emerge. Out of the ongoing process there emerges not only Cooley's "looking glass self" (a reflection of self through the eyes and actions of others) but the self singly as innovator of roles and the group collectively as creator of new forms.

We mentioned in the Introduction two derivatives of the symbolic interaction model. The first derivative was the expectation theory advanced by Berger and others who abstract from the complex symbolic process those conscious and unconscious anticipations that are precipitates of previous interaction, and that govern current action in specifiable and testable ways (see pages 15-16). The second derivative was exchange theory which attempts to model the conditions under which the ongoing process is a source either of gratification or of a sense of deprivation (see page 15). A third example is Erikson's conception of process-as-ritual through which images of a situation are formed and capabilities are either enhanced or undermined for effectively handling the major crises in the life cycle.[23]

With the symbolic interaction model investigators must make direct contact with those they study, for the meanings sought are in the minds of the actors themselves, singly and collectively. Clearly to use the model the investigator must enact it in relation with the group members: empathize with them, take their roles, read their symbolic representations, and test out interpretations of the symbols. Only then can the investigator reconstruct the cognitive framework the group employs.

Ideally, the investigative categories are replicas of the categories of meaning being used by the actors themselves. Indeed, the investigator is warned by some adherents (Blumer, for one) against importing one's own *a priori* definitions for they may not coincide with the group's definitions. What is authentically "cooperative," for instance, is not what fits a stranger's criteria but what members themselves define it to be. These latter criteria can only be inferred by the investigator through observations of interaction and the attribution of meaning to interaction. You will recognize the difference between this position and the approach of the problem-solving model described later, where, for instance, actions might be classified as interfering with problem resolution despite group members' belief otherwise.

The latter point is a source of criticism of the symbolic interaction model. While the model takes into account the creation and change of meanings, its scope tends to be restricted to local meanings, to the exclusion of other possible meanings, implications, and consequences. For example, family members may interpret their behavior towards a disturbed child as normal and natural, yet others may recognize that those actions contribute to the child's illness. Though local meanings may be necessary for predicting responses, they are not sufficient for determining system consequences.

If the model identifies the group as a set of actors in search of meanings then that search would seem to be enough of a challenge for both actors and investigators. Who has yet been able adequately to identify all the myriad meanings of mind, self, group, and society? Yet investigators must be prepared for more: There are unconscious meanings as well as conscious ones; there are feelings and emotions as well as definitions; there are other plays, other stages, and other authors; there are other viewpoints, such as that of the critic whose scope of understanding may extend beyond that of the actors and yet be quite relevant to a comprehension of the drama they enact.

THE PROBLEM-SOLVING MODEL

The group is a problem-solving team. In response to universal personal needs, universal conditions of communication, and standard requirements of the problem-solving process, the team generates a series of actions each of which can be classified according to its main function. One act with its function stimulates (with a certain probability) another act with its function, which in turn is the stimulus for a subsequent act, and so on. A question, for example, stimulates an answer which calls forth an evaluative response. Since acts are classified as functions they are essentially unchanging (one occurring early in group life is equal to one occurring later on) which may be added up and otherwise arithmetically manipulated in a representation of the group's operation.

According to this model, group interaction follows universal and unchanging laws. Group behavior is like a game that is played over and over again so many times that one knows both the game and the players well enough to predict what will happen next. General laws apply to such features as who will tend to speak, to whom they will speak, trends in types of behavior from the beginning to the end of the meeting and so on. Bales, particularly in his earlier work, sought to discover these laws and to construct coherent models from them.[24] His models emphasize the importance of the problem-solving situation. Although they acknowledge that some role is played by other factors, such as the larger society to which the group belongs, the group's own purpose, the variety of personalities in its membership, and the type of problem being faced, that role is minor compared to the intellectual problems and the emotional forces that are brought into play when a number of individuals face a problem that must be solved. From this viewpoint the immutable core of the small group is the lawfulness of interaction when persons confront a problem together.

The aim of sociologists using this type of model is to discover the invariant and universal systematics in groups. The procedure is to construct a tentative model, observe a sample of groups, check the fit between model and observation, and—where the fit is poor—alter the model so that it applies to the greatest number of cases. The researcher's interest is not in differences between groups but in similarities. The model is improved until it states a set of universal principles.

Such models are valuable because they assert that our interpersonal processes are far more ordered and far more systematic than common sense leads us to believe, or the doctrine of the uniqueness of the individual (or the family, the club, or the nation) would have us assume. Observed differences are often obvious (and comforting), while similarities are more subtle (and often offensive). Although these models have led and may well continue to lead to discoveries of regularities that sociology needs to know and understand,[25] they are subject to two considerable limitations: one of substance and one of application. First, except for laying down the criteria of regularity and lawfulness, they contain no independent standard of what is relevant and important for sociology and group members. It is an elementary error to equate relevance with uniformity—as we are reminded by the study of language, where it has been found that more often than not it is just those properties least important to its service as a medium of communication that seem to behave lawfully.[26] Second, in its application, a model of selected processes often substitutes for apprehension of the total process: As more data are collected to substantiate the model, less knowledge is gained about the aspects that are excluded until the excluded aspects become vague and are forgotten.

THE EQUILIBRIUM MODEL

The group is a system in equilibrium. Any disturbance, whether from inside or out, tends to be counteracted by opposing forces so that the system returns to the state prior to the disturbance. The clearest statement and application of this model to small groups has been made by Bales, who proposes that a push toward achieving the group goal disrupts solidarity and consequently tends to be followed by efforts to pull the group together again—and that, since this reconsolidation deflects energy from goal achievement, it tends to be followed by a renewed push toward the goal. And so it goes, until a point of equilibrium is reached between the pushing and pulling tendencies; or, more accurately, a moving point, because both the distance from the goal and the solidifying mechanisms may alter in the process.[27] Bales's model includes more group elements than both Festinger's theory of dissonance, which refers to cognition,[28] and Heider's balance theory, which includes affective and evaluative processes,[29] yet all three conceive of their respective processes as operating according to an equilibrium principle. A disturbance, dissonance, or imbalance creates strain or tension, which tends to be followed by an attempt, successful or not, to restore the system to a state of integration, consonance, or balance.

The value of the equilibrium model is that it simply and coherently organizes highly complex and interdependent phenomena. Yet because of its simplicity, it must be applied with circumspection and restraint. Perhaps most important, one must specify the sector of the total system to which it is being applied, distinguishing it from sectors where it is not applicable.[30] To illustrate the point, let us take the experience of a young couple having a baby.

The wife's becoming pregnant, the birth, the addition to the household—all these are changes which "disturb" the previous arrangement shared by a young married couple. If we were to apply the equilibrium model, with the discipline and naïveté required in using theoretical models, we would expect, on the basis of the model alone, responses to the arrival of the third party which would tend to return the system to its previous state. This would involve reducing the triad to a dyad—in other words, getting rid of the baby! Now it is true that one often finds traces of such a tendency (such as fantasies of infanticide), but the emphatic tendency, of course, is not for the couple to act on such fantasies, but instead to transform themselves on the baby's behalf. The man becomes a father as well as a husband; the woman a mother as well as a wife; while together they become parents of a child. The parties respond to birth by fundamentally reconstituting their group.

Although application of the equilibrium model is nonsensical in this case because one "knows" it should not be used for *that* part of the system, misapplication is not easy to detect in less familiar settings. The problem is a general one, for while one may find a sector of a group that operates according to the model, one can usually find sectors that do not; and, while a group in its totality may follow the model for a brief period, since members do die and most small groups dissolve it is unlikely that any group as an over-all system always follows the model. Consequently its users need to specify both the sector and the duration for which the model is thought to hold.

Another lesson in the preceding illustration is the model's bias in viewing major events, particularly external influences, primarily as disturbances to be avoided or, failing that, as the causes of damage to be repaired. In doing so it overlooks those external influences which are perceived by insiders as good, helpful, and therefore welcome. The baby symbolizes these, but the list is long: news about the outside world; visitors such as a neighbor, the doctor, or a friend; a new technique or a new art form; and so on. Groups respond to such welcome intrusions by increasing their receptivity so that they can benefit, rather than by reverting to some previous state. When one wants to predict direction of system-change in such cases, it is just as important to know the positive or negative value placed upon the "disturbance" as it is to know the system's previous state.

THE STRUCTURAL-FUNCTIONAL MODEL

The group is a goal-seeking, boundary-maintaining system whose survival is problematical. It is a mutable and transitory arrangement of actions, norms, ideas, and techniques devised (though seldom entirely consciously) to meet the demands of personal, social, and environmental realities. It is subject not only to constant change, but to a cessation of functions or even disintegration unless real demands are adequately met. At each moment the group (through its agents) must exercise intelligence and ingenuity, mobilize its resources, and act positively in meeting changing demands. Parsons, Bales, and Shils separate demands, and capabilities for meeting them, into four areas:[31]

(1) *Adaptation*—when external resources are cut off, the group must be able to find new ones; (if it is to handle the problem); when current techniques become obsolete or ineffective, it must invent new ones.

(2) *Goal attainment*—when obstacles appear before the goal, it must be able to circumvent them; when members become confused or frustrated or distracted, it must be able to reorient them and remobilize their resources.

(3) *Integration*—when one part of the group threatens to destroy other parts, the group must be able to check, protect, and coordinate them; it must bridge differences between the strong and the weak, the competent and the inept, the active and the passive, and so on; it must create concepts or symbols of itself as a collective unit that unites its parts.

(4) *Pattern-maintenance and change*—in the face of contrary pressures, the group must be able to sustain its standard procedures, reinforce members' feelings and affective relations, enforce its rules, confirm its beliefs and affirm its values; and in response to internal and external necessities it must be able to alter patterns without falling apart.

The model assumes that members will be gratified as the group progresses toward its goal. Moreover, it assumes that some group members (or some part of each of them) will serve as group agents whose purpose is to assure the group's survival so that it may continue to gratify members through pursuit of its goal. The functions of agents are at each moment: (1) to observe what is happening; (2) to assess the effects of events upon goal-attainment and survival; and (3) according to this assessment, to take action. To "take action" means to redirect a process when it is likely to miss the group goal; to reinforce it when it is headed toward the goal; and, simultaneously, to counteract any negative effects that goal effort might have upon adaptation, integration, and pattern-maintenance, but to support them when their effects are positive. In addition, the agents' function is to learn from this experience and to infuse this learning into the group's culture. In short, in response to the four sets of demands, group agents act and learn on behalf of the group— learning how to achieve the collective goal, and how to assure the group's survival.

Depending upon the skill of its agents, a group tends toward a balance or oscillation between the multiple demands of adaptation, goal-attainment, integration, and pattern-maintenance. Change is determined by the interplay of these demands and by accumulated learning and the effective use of that learning. The model acknowledges the fact that many groups fail to achieve their goals and that some groups do not even survive. Achievement of goals and survival depend upon the adequacy of techniques and learning relative to actual demands, so that determining the likelihood that any specific group will survive or achieve its goals requires empirical investigation.

The model makes several important contributions to the sociology of small groups. First, it acknowledges the role of learning and consequently the role of culture. Group culture evolves through the assessment and reassessment of how the group meets demands. And while the model acknowledges the fact that many groups replace ineffective ways with more effective ones, it escapes the assumption that progress, or evolution toward attainment of goals, is an inevitable process. Its second contribution is to link motivation of the individual member to group survival. The group must gratify its members; it must attract and sustain their interest; it must fulfill, or hold a promise of fulfilling, certain of their needs. Promise of gratification ties the individual to the group, and the members' investment in the group provides it with motivational energy. This is an important contrast to the interaction models, which implicitly assume the source of energy to be outside the system.

Contrary to the views of critics of structural-functional analysis,[32] the model does afford systematic treatment of group disintegration: when requirements for survival are correctly identified but groups do not fulfill them, then groups disintegrate. Confusion on this issue arises through misuse of the model. When in the name of structural-functional analysis sociologists assume that all observable events and structural arrangements have a positive effect upon survival and goal-attainment, they are misusing the model. For the model requires that before investigators draw conclusions about the functional significance of group properties, they must determine independently what is and what is not a positive function.[33] As critics have correctly noted, this is often difficult to do when dealing with larger societies, not only because they are complex but also because most of them survive despite failure in attaining goals. Such is not the case in the study of small groups, for application of the model is more direct and since each day relatively large numbers of small groups fail to survive (marriages, friendships, partnerships, small businesses, rock groups, and so on) comparisons are possible and tests can be made of those necessary conditions that were not met. However even when this analysis is done well, special attention must be paid in distinguishing between the operation of determining what is dysfunction and evaluating the desirability or undesirability of the breakups themselves. Some critics who perhaps think primarily in terms of larger societies seem to be confused on this point.[34] In terms of certain values (e.g., therapeutic) the breakup of one family might be desirable whereas the breakup of another undesirable. Clearly two levels are involved. The structural-functional model does not assume that existing structures coincide perfectly with the values of the evaluators of the system, whether they be inside the unit or outside.

Another criticism is more justified—namely, that the model has a conservative bias. Not that it favors the status quo (a group that holds together so that it can learn more effectively how to pursue its goal is not necessarily a group that seeks to preserve the status quo), rather, conservative in the sense that survival is a conservative criterion. Groups may survive while exacting the high price of pain, confusion, and frustration from their members; they may survive while operating at a fraction of their potential. While helpful in establishing basic requirements, the standard of survival is simply not enough when one is dealing with groups capable of far more than maintaining themselves—groups capable of growth and advancement. As we shall see, the next model shifts emphasis from survival to growth, from simply meeting existing demands to meeting a wide range of possible demands, and from pursuing a given goal to developing abilities for achieving a variety of goals. Compared to such a model, the structural-functional dependence upon the criterion of survival is conservative.

THE CYBERNETIC-GROWTH MODEL

Human groups are information-processing systems potentially capable of increasing their capabilities. Like the structural-functional model of Parsons, Bales, and Shils, the cybernetic model of Deutsch assumes the existence of group agents who observe, assess the situation, and act with consequence upon the situation they observe.[35] When in the face of either internal or external demands these operations are unsatisfactory or inadequate, the group suffers impairment or, in the extreme, destruction. On the other hand, when conditions are favorable and the operations are effective, the group not only survives but becomes capable of monitoring itself, altering its direction, determining its own history, and learning how to learn to determine its history—with the consequence that it accumulates and expands its capabilities, or grows.

Self-determination and growth depend upon three orders of feedback of increasing complexity and importance. The first is goal-seeking feedback, which is assumed in the structural-functional model and exemplified in Deutsch's terms by the homing torpedo. With a collective goal in mind, group agents determine by observation whether current actions are taking the group toward or away from the target. When the reading is positive, the agents may do nothing. When it is negative, they attempt to decrease the error by altering the way the group acts on the environment—whereupon they read the effects of their intervention and if necessary again redirect operations in order to minimize the error. Through observation, intervention, and observation of the effects of intervention group agents learn how to operate to achieve collective goals.

The second order of feedback is more complex, for it involves a rearrangement, or a reconstitution, of the group itself. Let us suppose for the moment that feedback processes are all at the conscious level. When agents observe a basic incongruence or incompatibility between the habits, customs, beliefs, techniques, and so on, of the group and the group's external realities, they first consider how rearrangement of the group might improve the fit; secondly they attempt to alter the internal components of the group; then they assess the effects of these attempts; and finally they learn from a series of attempts effective ways of accomplishing internal rearrangements. In Strauss's terms these rearrangements are newly "negotiated orders."[36] We can return to the example of the birth of a baby to illustrate incongruity and internal rearrangement. Were the relation between husband and wife to remain unchanged upon the arrival of a baby, that relationship would be incongruent with reality. But as they acquire the new roles of father and mother—as they learn to become parents—their arrangement more nearly fits reality. Their reconstitution as parents is what is meant by *second order feedback.* (Further examples are the constant alterations of their conceptions of the child as he or she matures, their ways of responding to and teaching the child.) The third order of feedback is *consciousness*—a process through which a system gains greater (though never complete) awareness of itself. People contribute to their consciousness when in addition to acting they observe and formulate ideas about themselves as actors. A group contributes to its consciousness when in addition to responding to demands, its members formulate and communicate ideas about its character as a system that meets demands. Consciousness is gained by adding to the function of acting the functions of observing, comprehending, and articulating comprehension about the system that is acting.

All three orders of feedback are necessary for self-determination. They are used in combination: For example, in professional football coaching staff and players try to maximize their options and take advantage of their team's strengths. Assistants in the stands and on the bench, the quarterback and other players on the field, all serve as observers reading the action and funneling information to the head coach who combines it with his own knowledge as he attempts to read the weaknesses in the other team's defenses and to capitalize on those weaknesses (goal-seeking in the most literal sense). Unforeseen circumstances may lead him to abandon the pregame player assignment and force him to try out one alternative combination after the other (internal rearrangement). Meanwhile, using information from up in the stands, the bench and the field players are selected and put into position and new readings are taken on the results, all a part of the process of *putting a clearer comprehension into action* and of *gaining deeper comprehension from the action* (the two-way process of generating consciousness). To the degree that the coach and players can act on their ideas—observing the effects of this action and therefore, testing them—they are in a position to learn how to learn to create strategy. Through self-monitoring, self-steering, and testing these processes they are able to increase their capabilities for self-determination.

The developmental processes tend to increase the potential for group growth. Self-monitoring shows both what the group is and what it is not, which resources are utilized and which are not, what its goals are and what they are not. Self-steering, and monitoring the steering operation, shows where the group is going, its flexibility in changing directions, and, by implication, where else it might go. Consciousness introduces knowledge about unrealized potential, and notions of alternative goals. Consciousness tends to expand the group's conception of its possibilities (as well as clarify its disabilities and limits). By feeding these ideas back for test, and by acting upon the appropriate responses, the group gains a capacity for growth.[37]

But what specifically is meant by growth? Not an increase in membership for the group certainly, but an increase in capabilities for meeting a wider range of possible demands. Using the structural-functional classification of demand areas, we suggest the following set of indicators of group growth:

INDICATORS OF A SMALL GROUP'S CAPACITY TO GROW

1. *Adaptation*
   a. "... an increase in openness—that is, an increase in the range, diversity, and effectiveness of a [a group's] *channels of intake* of information from the outside world. ..."[38]
   b. Capacity to extend the scope of the group's contacts and obligations beyond current boundaries
   c. Capacity to alter the group's customs, rules, techniques, and so on, to accommodate new information and new contacts
2. *Goal-attainment*
   a. Capacity to hold goal-seeking effort in abeyance while alternative goals are being considered
   b. Capacity to shift to, or add, new goals
3. *Integration*
   a. Capacity to differentiate into parts while maintaining collective unity
   b. Capacity to export resources without becoming impoverished and to send emissaries without losing their loyalty
4. *Pattern-maintenance and extension*
   a. Capacity to receive new members and to transmit to them the group's culture and capabilities
   b. Capacity to formulate in permanent form the group's experience and learning and to convey them to other groups and to posterity

These few indicators are perhaps enough to suggest the important advance of the growth model over the survival model. Groups oriented toward survival attempt to maintain their boundaries while obtaining gratification, while growing groups penetrate and extend their boundaries. Growing groups are increasingly receptive to new signals, new possibilities, new responsibilities; they are increasingly confident both in admitting strangers and in spawning new groups; and they cross the boundaries of space and time by putting their experience in communicable form for others. From the viewpoint of the cybernetic-growth model of Deutsch, small groups are a source of experience, learning, and capabilities, rather than just recipients.

Group growth does not occur automatically but depends directly upon members who are both capable of personal growth and committed to group development. Since each individual is an information-processing system, the model can be applied to himself as well as to the group as a whole. He may employ the three orders of feedback: process information from his external world, from his past, and from his present state; develop ability to self-monitor and self-govern; and acquire the ability to grow. In fact, unless he or some other member is committed to group development, no advance in the group's capabilities can be expected. In other words, all information processes we have attributed to the group are actually performed by and through individuals as essential components of the collective system. Whether viewed from the personal or the collective perspective, the capabilities of the persons as parts place a ceiling upon the capabilities of the collectivity. The application of the cybernetic-growth model to small groups presumes its simultaneous application to individual members. In this sense then it is a model of both personal and group growth. Though space is not available for a detailed application, the following outline suggests indicators of personal growth, using a male for illustration.

INDICATORS OF A PERSON'S CAPACITY TO GROW

1. *Adaptation*
    a. Receptivity to a wider range of information about himself, others, his groups, his and other societies, and the physical environment
    b. Receptivity to new freedoms, responsibilities, and obligations—to new roles
    c. Flexibility in modifying his ideas, beliefs, personal norms, and emotional attachments without loss of intellectual or moral integrity
2. *Goal-attainment*
    a. Capacity to postpone immediate gratification, and to conceive of and evaluate an increasing number of avenues for gratification
    b. Capacity to decommit himself from one goal, and to recommit himself to new and additional goals, and to learn how to attain them
3. *Integration*
    a. Capacity to perform in an expanded repertoire of roles and variety of social relations without suffering diffusion of his identity
4. *Pattern-maintenance and extension*
    a. Capacity for deeper emotional involvement with others without surrendering his self
    b. Increasing ability to convey his experience, learning, and capabilities to others

The cybernetic model is not complete unto itself as a small group model. It refers to some, but not all, sectors of human systems. It refers to the information processing sector—but not to the sector of human drives, nor to the directions drives tend to take. One must go outside the model to understand what motivates the system—what pushes, pulls, or drives it; one must go outside to discover channels of feelings, their network, and the emotions that flow through them; and one must go outside to define the way biological and sociological realities structure the demands that must be met and set limits upon system change (e.g., physical and emotional needs of the infant; personality structure and types of members; the structure of sex, age, and kinship relations). Note for example that in specifying personal and group growth it was necessary to call upon the structural-functional model both for a classification of demands and for a bridge between personal motivation and information processing. This is just one indication that for a more complete model of small groups, sociology needs a composite of several models: Deutsch's cybernetic-growth model; the structural-functional model of Parsons, Bales, and Shils; and a model of emotional processes as suggested by the psychoanalytic models discussed before.[39]

Among the cybernetic model's contributions, two stand out. First, the model directs the outside observer's attention to the concrete moment of action and to the information that is contained in and relevant to that moment—the present state of the system, its past, and the relation of the system to its environment. This is an important step in a theoretical model because it is precisely the realities of the concrete moment of action that confront the member of the group and that he or she must manage. Furthermore what is relevant information for the insider is precisely the information that is useful to the outside observer. Consciousness on the part of insiders (ideas about the nature of the system) corresponds to the substantive and professional aim of the outside observer (a sociological comprehension of the nature of the system). What the member learns about his or her group is relevant to the sociologist, and vice-versa. Under advantageous circumstances, advances in consciousness increase the capabilities of both. The model assumes an inherent collaborative relation between group member and observer and perhaps anticipates a convergence of their viewpoints. (Yet note that though viewpoints converge, responsibilities need not, for while the member's feedback responses alter the group, the sociologist's feedback responses alter his or her sociology.)

The model's second contribution is its provision for growth. Not only does it accord with the easily observed facts that both persons and groups learn and grow, but it becomes a useful analytical tool when the sociologist encounters persons and groups who are interested in more than survival and immediate gratification; whose vision for the group includes new ideas, techniques, and goals; who are willing to assume responsibility for maximizing the general capabilities of the group; and who experience gratification when the group progresses toward that end. With a flexible model of growth the sociologist can keep in step with processes in the group; without one his or her sociology becomes irrelevant to groups that advance in capabilities.

SUMMARY

The models sketched in this chapter are relatively simple, abstract formulations of selected dynamic processes in groups. They help organize and guide the sociologist's thinking. To perform that function as knowledge and circumstance change they must be on the one hand tentative and modifiable, and on the other constantly examined, tested, and when necessary modified according to observations of actual groups. For a lively and growing science there needs to be active interchange between model and findings, and sufficient flexibility both for new models and for new sources of data. There also needs to be a productive working relation between investigator and group being studied. Sociologists need to develop not only an intellectual viewpoint that transcends the boundary separating insiders from outsiders but also the capacity to "become stranger to the familiar" while empathizing with those being studied. The next two chapters concern that relation, first, as an observer, then as an experimenter.

NOTES

1. R. D. Laing, *The Politics of the Family and Other Essays* (New York: Pantheon, 1971), p. 6.
2. See Walter Buckley, *Sociology and Modern Systems Theory* (Englewood Cliffs, N.J.: Prentice-Hall, 1967); Grahm S. Gibbard, John J. Hartman, and Richard D. Mann, eds., *Analysis of Groups: Contributions to Theory, Research and Practice* (San Francisco: Jossey-Bass, 1974); and Cary L. Cooper, ed., *Theories of Group Process* (London: John Wiley, 1975).
3. Herbert A. Simon, *Models of Man: Social and Rational* (New York: John Wiley, 1957).
4. For a variety of current approaches, see A. Paul Hare, Edgar F. Borgatta, and Robert F. Bales, eds., *Small Groups: Studies in Social Interaction* (New York: Knopf, 1955), pp. 54–187.

5. A reference by Calvin Hall and Gardner Lindzey in their "The Relevance of Freudian Psychology and Related Viewpoints for the Social Science," in Gardner Lindzey and Elliott Aronson, eds., *The Handbook of Social Psychology* (Reading, Mass.: Addison-Wesley, 1968), 2nd ed., p. 275, to Sigmund Freud, *Group Psychology and the Analysis of the Ego* (New York: Liveright, 1949).

6. Norman O. Brown, *Love's Body* (New York: Random House, 1966), pp. 3–89.

7. Fritz Redl, "Group Emotion and Leadership," *Psychiatry*, 5 (1942), 573–96; reprinted in Hare, Borgatta, and Bales, eds., *Small Groups*, pp. 71–87.

8. Melanie Klein, *New Directions in Psychoanalysis* (London: Tavistock, 1955).

9. Helen E. Durkin, *The Group in Depth* (New York: International Universities Press, 1964), p. 75.

10. Freud, quoted by Durkin, ibid.

11. Ibid., p. 77.

12. Ibid., p. 79.

13. Leroy Wells, Jr. "The Group-as-a-Whole: A Systemic Socio-Analytic Perspective on Interpersonal and Group Relations," in C. P. Alderfer and C. L. Cooper, eds., *Advances in Experiential Social Processes*, Vol. 2 (New York: John Wiley, 1980), 165–99.

14. Henry Israel, "A Psychoanalytic Approach to Group Treatment," *British Journal of Medical Psychology*, 23 (1950), 59–74. Also see James Gustafson and others, "Cooperative and Clashing Interests in Small Groups II, Group Narratives," *Human Relations*, 24 (May 1981), 367–78.

15. Redl, "Group Emotion and Leadership."

16. Ibid.

17. See Sheldon Stryker, "Symbolic Interactionism: Themes and Variations," in Morris Rosenberg and Ralph H. Turner, eds., *Social Psychology: Sociological Perspectives* (New York: Basic Books, 1981), pp. 3–29, and Sheldon Stryker, *Symbolic Interactionism: A Social Structural Version* (Menlo Park, Calif.: Benjamin/Cummings, 1980).

18. Stryker, "Symbolic Interactionism," in Rosenberg and Turner, eds., *Social Psychology*, p. 6.

19. M. Meltzer, J. W. Petras, and L. T. Reynolds, *Symbolic Interactionism: Genesis, Varieties and Criticism* (London: Routledge & Kegan Paul, 1975).

20. George H. Mead, *Mind, Self and Society* (Chicago: University of Chicago, 1934).

21. Herbert Blumer, *Symbolic Interactionism: Perspective and Method* (Englewood Cliffs, N.J.: Prentice-Hall, 1969), pp. 1–60.

22. Ralph H. Turner, unpublished papers referred to by Stryker, "Symbolic Interactionism," in Rosenberg and Turner, eds., *Social Psychology*, pp. 20–22.

23. Erik H. Erikson, *Toys and Reasons: Stages in the Ritualization of Experience* (New York: W. W. Norton & Co., Inc., 1977), pp. 67–118.

24. Robert F. Bales, "The Equilibrium Problem in Small Groups," in Talcott Parsons, Robert F. Bales, and Edward A. Shils, *Working Papers in the Theory of Action* (New York: Free Press, 1953), pp. 111–61.

25. For one sample of empirical generalizations, see Bernard Berelson and Gary A. Steiner, *Human Behavior: An Inventory of Scientific Findings* (New York: Harcourt Brace Jovanovich, Inc., 1964).

26. Joseph H. Greenberg, "Language and Evolution," in Betty J. Meggers, ed., *Evolution and Anthropology: A Centennial Appraisal* (The Anthropological Society of Washington, 1959), pp. 61–75.

27. Robert F. Bales, "Adaptive and Integrative Changes as Sources of Strain in Social Systems," in Hare, Borgatta, and Bales, eds., *Small Groups*, pp. 127–31; and Robert F. Bales, "The Equilibrium Problem in Small Groups," in Parsons, Bales, and Shils, *Working Papers in the Theory of Action*, pp. 111–61.

28. Leon Festinger, *A Theory of Cognitive Dissonance* (Evanston, Ill.: Row, Peterson, 1957).

29. Fritz Heider, "Attitudes and Cognitive Organization," *Journal of Psychology*, 21 (January 1946), 107–12.

30. For discussion of the limitations of the equilibrium model see David Easton, "The Limits of the Equilibrium Model in Social Research," *Behavioral Science*, 1 (April 1956), 96–104; Theodore M. Mills, "Equilibrium and the Processes of Deviance and Control," *American Sociological Review*, 24 (1959), 671–79; and Jean P. Codal, "Social Norms and the Pattern of Equilibrium," *Annee Psychologique*, 24, no. 1 (1974), 201–18. Also see Mike Robinson, "The Identity of Human Social Groups," *Behavioral Science*, 26 (April 1981), 114–29.

31. Parsons, Bales, and Shils, *Working Papers in the Theory of Action,* pp. 63–109; 179–90. Also see Robert K. Merton, *Social Theory and Social Structure: Toward a Codification of Theory and Research,* rev. ed. (New York: Free Press, 1957).

32. Ralf Dahrendorf, "Out of Utopia: Toward A Reorientation of Sociological Analysis," *American Journal of Sociology,* 64 (September 1958), 115–27; also David Lockwood, "Some Remarks on 'The Social System,'" *British Journal of Sociology,* 7 (June 1956), 134–46.

33. For a discussion of various applications and a critique of functional models see Francesca M. Cancian, "Varieties of Functional Analysis," in David L. Sils, ed., *International Encyclopedia of the Social Sciences,* 6 (New York: Macmillan, and Free Press, 1968), 29–43.

34. Irving M. Zeitlin, *Rethinking Sociology: A Critique of Contemporary Theory* (Englewood Cliffs, N.J.: Prentice-Hall, 1973), pp. 103–107.

35. Deutsch, *The Nerves of Government* (New York: The Free Press, 1963), pp. 75–142.

36. Anselm Strauss, *Negotiations: Varieties, Contexts, Processes and Social Order* (San Francisco: Jossey-Bass, 1978).

37. Brogdan Wojciszke, "Evolution of Cognitive Explanation in Contemporary Social Psychology: Theoretical Implications for the Problem of Consciousness," *Przeglad Psychologiczny,* 23, no. 2 (1980), 281–308.

38. Deutsch, *The Nerves of Government,* p. 140.

39. Paul Butkovich, Jim Carlisle, Robert Duncan, and Mervin Moss, "Social System and Psychoanalytic Approaches to Group Dynamics: Complementary or Contradictory?" *International Journal of Group Psychotherapy* (January 1975), pp. 3–31.

CHAPTER 2
OBSERVATION

For the essentials in building a science, the eminent physiologist L. J. Henderson suggested three ingredients: first, intimate contact and habitual, intuitive familiarity with the phenomena; second, means for systematically collecting and ordering data; and third, an effective way of thinking about the phenomena.[1] The relevance of his proposal for widely separated fields is apparent when, for example, we compare astronomers and sociologists of groups.

First, astronomers, through search, scanning, and repeated observations, soon acquire a "feel" for the heavens and cognitive maps of its particulars: objects, dimensions, relations, movements, and so on. Although at any one time they may not be able to reproduce all of its particulars, their maps are of enormous service in locating where they are, in allowing them to concentrate in a selected area without losing touch with other areas, and, of course, in helping them to sense immediately any new and strange object. A comparable "feel" and "map" is acquired by sociologists through direct and repeated contact with groups, through observation of a wide variety of groups, and through active participation in them. In time, and as figure and ground separate, they become sensitive to what is and is not happening in a group, to what the group is forgetting or avoiding, to shifts in rules, to changes in direction, and to conflicts before they become otherwise apparent.

As for the second ingredient, both astronomer and sociologist make systematic observations. While the astronomer takes readings on mass, density, rotation, speed, and direction of movement, the sociologist observes and records indicators of what group members do, say, feel, and think. Both use such readings as working data.

Third, both attempt to construct conceptions of their phenomena—abstract, simplified models, or theories, which account for or help to explain a proportion of the facts. The heliocentric theory of the solar system is an example from astronomy; the boundary-maintaining system that tends toward a state of equilibrium (referred to in Chapter 1) is a theory from sociology.

In short, although astronomy and sociology are clearly different in subject matter, refinement of techniques, and theoretical sophistication, they are comparable in the types of procedures by which they make science out of their respective inquiries. Both require intuitive familiarity with the phenomena, systematic data, and an effective way of thinking about the phenomena.

Despite these similarities, however, an important procedural difference remains. Since sociology is human studying human it is highly reflexive. As human beings, sociologists cannot exclude themselves from their inquiries, nor can they ignore the reciprocal influences between them and those whom they study. The investigative process affects each party and the parties influence and alter one another. Sociologists can exclude themselves from the study, of course, but to do so is, as Cooley suggested,[2] to discard one of their strongest assets—namely, their affinity with their object of study, their capacity to empathize with their subjects, their opportunity to talk with and to learn from them. As Shils suggests, sociologists and their subjects are "part of the vast, unorganized collective effort of the human mind to understand itself as a collectivity."[3] In this sense, the observers' experiences are part of what they are trying to understand and the theory to which they contribute "is not just like any other theory; it is a social relationship between [the observer and the observed]. It is a relationship formed by the sense of affinity."[4] Because of this affinity and because of the reflexivity of sociology, we are obliged to add to Henderson's list a fourth ingredient: a collaborative exchange between the investigator and the investigated. We know that, aside from surreptitious observation, even the most rudimentary description of a group requires a reciprocal relation between sociologist and group; the sociologist must contact the group and the group must open at least part of itself to the investigator. And, as the frontiers of our knowledge expand horizontally and vertically, we can expect such growth to call for even more skillfully devised social relationships where groups permit the investigator to become increasingly familiar with their operations, where systematic data may be collected not only on obvious and public matters but over an increasingly wide and deep range of phenomena, and where the ideas in the minds both of group members and sociologist about how groups operate may be exchanged, applied, tested, and reformulated. Because other procedures are contingent upon this relationship between observer and observed, this chapter begins with a consideration of the dynamic relation between observer and group; because the long-range growth of the sociology of groups depends upon the quality of interchange between group and investigator, the chapter ends with a six-step scale of interchange, ranging from the rudimentary to the optimally productive. In between, the questions of what is observed and how it is observed are discussed. Chapter 3 introduces the special problems that arise from experimentation, and the remainder of this book deals with the problem of developing an effective way of thinking about groups.

THE OBSERVER AND THE GROUP

Many scientists, as we know, use special instruments to bring their phenomena closer to them. The microscope and the telescope are common examples. As the worlds these instruments open become familiar, the scientist senses additional realms, and often devises new instruments (such as the electron microscope and the radio telescope, to maintain the example) to reach these new realms. In such instances, technology and the investigator work together to both increase the intimacy of contact and extend the realm of phenomena about which the investigator is learning.

Much the same may be said for social scientists, whose concern with groups leads them to find ways to be brought into ever closer and broader contact with group processes. But the technology through which this is accomplished is of a special kind. Because group processes occur within and among persons, and because both persons and groups surround themselves with boundaries which regulate access to these processes, the barriers separating groups and their investigators are more social, emotional, attitudinal, and cultural than they are physical. Consequently, the barriers must be transcended by social, psychological, and cultural means, the extent depending, of course, on the issue under investigation. Some issues, such as who in the family purchases what items, may require simple strategies compared to other issues such as the actual decision-making process or the emotional relations across generations. The special technology (and the first technical procedure) in the study of groups is to devise that quality of social relation between investigation and group which allows the degree of familiarity appropriate for the research issue.

Since effective construction of such a relation depends upon a comprehension of the boundary that separates the group from the investigator, and more generally upon an understanding of the dynamics between insiders and outsiders, and since comprehension of these dynamics comes best through actual contact with groups, let us imagine an apprentice, a young woman, who in beginning her career as a sociologist will require close relations with her subject, and trace the highlights of her experience in confronting groups.

THE DYNAMICS OF FAMILIARITY

The apprentice's training program may take her to any of a number of different settings; the wardroom of a ship, a nursery school, a group therapy session, a training seminar for senior military personnel, a family conference in a living room.[5] Wherever she goes to work one of her first discoveries is that she is in direct and immediate contact with unique, concrete, unrehearsed, and largely unpredictable human processes. Events are disorderly and often incoherent, appearing to her in raw form, unfiltered by anyone else's interpretation of their meaning. Although she may be confused by lack of order and pattern, she can sense the possibility for independent observation and analysis. Her first discovery, then, is that the opportunity exists to become intuitively familiar with the phenomena—Henderson's first requirement.

Soon, the apprentice is surprised by the extent to which people under observation reveal themselves.[6] She finds that they are not always on guard, and as a consequence she inadvertently becomes privy to information that, in certain circumstances, could seriously affect their lives. A military officer's castigation of a commander could ruin the officer's own career; a corporation executive's offhand admission of illegal tax procedures could lead to imprisonment; wives' intimate talk in group therapy could estrange their husbands; a young psychiatrist's ineptness in a training group could destroy patients' faith. The apprentice learns that, to be sure, some guards are up, but many others are down.

The apprentice finds this experience of discovering the unexpected affects her personal composure. When she sees more than she expects to and more than members intend to reveal, and when there are no limits on what she should see or on what she should do with what she sees, she feels uneasy and embarrassed, as though she were stepping out of bounds—as if she were some sort of transgressor. (Such doubts about the right to observe were reflected in the dream of one observer following his first day with a therapy group: dressed in a doctor's white coat, he was in a courtroom being tried as a Peeping Tom before a greatly oversized microphone, which as the dream progressed seemed to him in his state of confusion to represent the judge.) Seeing too much violates childhood taboos and associates oneself with the spy, the snooper, or the voyeur—or with lonely persons who are neither entirely inside or outside. And not only the right to observe, but one's motivation in observing comes into doubt. One could even come to see oneself as a pervert or a blackmailer and become further upset by the jokes about observation laboratories and about those who work in them—jokes that play on voyeuristic potentials. Anxiety over precisely this matter causes some apprentices to leave the role of observer altogether. Others, of course, overcome such occupational hazards and become perceptive observers of human processes.

Our apprentice sociologist stays to discover that group members attribute superhuman powers to her. As the group imagines it, the observer misses no signals and forgets nothing. She is an all-seeing, all-knowing judge, and frequently is thought to be in collusion with the authority figure in the group and aligned with those who have jurisdiction over the group. Members often warn their fellows against the power of the observer, as in the following quote of a military officer in which the ostensible reference to someone at a distant base turns out to be a comment on the observer who is present in the room: "The important thing to remember here is that Sherril is just a spy, no more. He can't do anything—can't produce anything solid. He's just going around getting the dope and sending it over his hot line up above. Everybody should realize that he can make or break anybody on the base. A snooper like that can tear an organization apart." Is not this officer's concern generally shared by those being observed? (What is being done with the information about me? Can it be used against me? How safe are we? Who controls the observer? Until we know, we either close ranks against him, or risk falling apart.)

One interpretation of these disturbances is that observation confuses traditional notions about boundaries. Whereas the observers' sitting on the side and being excluded from group activity affirms the existence of a boundary, their access to inside information denies the boundary. Although they are outsiders, they want inside information and want it without becoming insiders. And, while privy to the group, they remain outside its jurisdiction. In all these ways and more, their presence implies a privileged position, with the right to take away information without giving anything in return, and to be above the group while it is "subject" to them.

The apprentice discovers a curious fact that groups both define the observer as being above them, and feel she takes something away from them. The mechanism is somewhat as follows: if she is the observer, then we need not make observations of our own; if she is a superior observer, then we'd better not make our observations; if she is the judge—a superior judge—then we'd better not make our own decisions. The observer acts as a catalyst for dependency. Members tend to delegate to the outsider their own responsibilities, perhaps in the hope that she will oblige by performing them—for to observe, judge, and predict what happens is indeed a difficult task. However when (in keeping within the limits of propriety recognized by the well-trained observer), she does not accept these responsibilities, they tend not only to resent the observer but in the meantime may have allowed their own capabilities to atrophy. The observed have become more watchful but less observant, more critical but less evaluative, more controlled but less committed. They often attribute their loss of these powers to the presence of the outside observer. The maneuver is defensive, for there is no technical reason why group and observer cannot make independent observations, judgments, and decisions.

The apprentice next discovers that the group wants to observe her—a discovery sometimes made when it is least expected. For instance, on one occasion, a training group in a laboratory stopped abruptly and announced that it would go no further until the several observers were brought out from behind the mirrors, identified, and given the opportunity of explaining their real purposes in being there. This was a first step in "getting to really know the observers." Group members want to contact the observers—to have the observers respond and reveal themselves—partly, of course, so that the group can correct their vague and oversized image of the observers, and partly to find out about themselves and to detect the standards they use in judging the observers, but also, we suggest, to bring the observers into the group and under its jurisdiction.

Should it surprise us that in the meantime the apprentice discovers within herself a desire to join the group? Increasingly she wants to express her feelings toward members—her warmth toward some, coolness toward others, admiration for some, distaste for others. Increasingly she empathizes with the leader, wanting to prompt or advise the leader or discuss the philosophy of leadership. Increasingly her emotional state follows the emotional swings of the group. In the extreme, she may cross over the boundary, "go native," and identify with the group to the extent that she comes under all the influences it is under—as, for example, in becoming converted to their religion or in taking the same experimental drugs the group is taking.

In other settings the apprentice may discover feelings disturbing to the scientist, as Malinowski did when he was among the Trobriand Islanders, or Turnbull among the Ik in Africa, or Chagnon among the Yąnomamö along the Orinoco River in South America. Malinowski wrote in his diary, "What is terrible is that I am unable to free myself completely from the atmosphere created by foreign bodies."[7] As he became aware of his deepening aversion to the natives and their culture he reported in his diary "moments of frightful longing to get out of this rotten hole."[8] Turnbull dedicated his book to "Joe" who helped him learn not to hate a people who had become totally devoid of human affection.[9] Chagnon's only course of adaptation as an observer among "a fierce and filthy people" was to become equally fierce in his relations with them—a course he found painfully difficult to stomach.[10] Whether our apprentice enacts these or other experiences either in the laboratory or the field, she is likely to be challenged not only by the boundary issue mentioned above but by the love-hate relations that will be developing, howsoever inadvertently, between her and those she studies, for in entering the role of sociological observer, the apprentice presents herself as a candidate for a niche in an affective structure that she can seldom full anticipate.

Simultaneously, she becomes subject to a special way of interpreting what is happening in the group, a way that differs from that used by the members themselves, at least if she and the members follow the general trends indicated by recent research. Jones and Nisbett, with considerable empirical data to support them, have suggested that while the outside observer in search for explanations tends to look to an actor's dispositions ("the reason John left is because it's not like him to fight back") the member inside the group tends to look for the special circumstances of the moment, with its situational demands and constraints ("the reason John left is that it was the end of the session"). While the outsider looks for explanatory motives, the insider looks for situational influences.[11] This difference in observation-set should not surprise us, wrote Jones, for among other differences, the observers and the actors differ both in the information they process and in their perspectives. Actors take a longitudinal view of their actions, while observers take a cross-sectional view.[12] By this Jones means that actors who know their own personal history of acting in a variety of situations look to the special circumstances in the current one to account for why they do what they do. In contrast, observers, without comparable knowledge of the life histories of the actors but probably familiar with the demands of the observation setting, look to the special features of particular actors for their explanations. As indicated in our introduction, research is now being done to understand more fully the apparently contrasting sets used by the actors and the observers in their *attributions* of causes and responsibilities.[13]

In short, our apprentice has entered a working role that is problematical, politically, emotionally, and intellectually. In the first instance the presence of the observer contradicts the traditional notion of the boundary separating insider from outsider: The observer, to repeat, is an outsider wanting inside information without becoming an insider. The group might either solidify its boundary, sealing itself off from the observer, or extend its jurisdiction around the observer trying to incorporate and control her. In either case science would lose, for in both instances our apprentice would vacate the position of independent scientific investigator. Emotionally, the feeling of being neither clearly in, nor clearly out, may seek resolution by, as we said, identifying with the group ("going native") or, in the other extreme, experiencing revulsion, wanting "to get out of this rotten hole." In either case, how can she achieve accurate, insightful, and balanced interpretations?[14] Finally, the gap between observer and observed is intellectually problematical, for if one is drawn toward motivational explanations and the other toward situational ones, then what interchange is necessary in order to obtain a balanced view?[15]

This all suggests forces on several levels that tend to move the investigator out of the role of scientist. The technical problem is to counteract these forces. The solution, in general terms, is to help reconstitute the group boundaries so that they may be both maintained and transcended: maintained through mutual respect for the legitimate and distinct purposes, first of the group's development, and second of respect for scientific observation; and transcended through mutual appreciation of the essential kinship between the observer and the observed arising from their affinity as members of the human community. How this is to be accomplished will vary from one circumstance to another, but note that a solution is critically important to the sociology of groups. On the one hand, if the boundaries are not transcended, the group will repel the investigator, and if the boundaries are not maintained the group will incorporate the investigator; on the other hand, if the boundaries are both transcended and maintained, then entrance into one area of inquiry is likely to improve the chance for further inquiry.[16]

THE SYSTEMATIC COLLECTION OF DATA

For our apprentice who emerges from the phase of open, unstructured observation into a new phase where she formulates ideas about how groups tend to operate and seeks evidence against which to check these ideas, Henderson's second procedure is to devise methods for taking disciplined readings of phenomena.[17] The range of phenomena has increased enormously through the experience of observers and researchers over the past 60 years. As stated earlier, the ongoing group process is like the coaxial cable carrying thousands of messages to be unscrambled by carefully devised methods of detection and selection. Action-carrying messages range from facial expressions (wrinkling the brow, blinking the eyes, pursing the lips), exchanged glances, body movement (crossing the legs, leaning forward, folding the arms), moving toward or away from or keeping one's distance from others, pitch and timbre of speech, timing of words and phrases, patterns of exchange (assisting, interrupting, alternating, paralleling), content of what is spoken (explicit and implicit, connotative and symbolic), impact of action upon others—not only is this list incomplete but under any of these categories you can readily imagine finer distinctions.[18] The trick for the apprentice is to select the set of ongoing phenomena appropriate for her clearly stated and theoretically relevant research problem so that in the end the stream of concrete events is linked to social system theory. Weick has suggested that "if an observer wants to increase precision—without sacrificing naturalness, he should choose dependent variables that are plausible response measures within the setting, discriminable from other behaviors, easy to observe and score, compatible with other measures, defensible in terms of . . . canons [of measurement], sensitive to variations in the independent variables, and valid indicators of psychological [and in our case, sociological] processes."[19]

Methods of measurement and techniques for collecting data, if they are to be of more than transitory interest, derive from a conception of which facets of group phenomena are relevant and important both to the immediate group and to the general universe of groups. As an introduction for the apprentice, few methods better connect a clear conception of group dynamics with a systematic method for collecting data than does Bales's *Interaction Process Analysis*.[20]

Interaction Process Analysis

Each overt act that occurs in a group is classified in one of 12 categories shown in Table 1. The reduction of all possible ways of interpreting group events into this set is a product of a highly ordered conception of group processes; some main features are paraphrased as follows:

1.   The small, face-to-face group is one instance of a more general type of system (the social system) which includes organizations, communities,

societies, and nations. As such, the small group possesses many features comparable to features found in social systems, such as an organization of activities, differential contact among members, division of labor, norms and means of social control, power structure, sub-groups, ideology, ceremonies, and patterned means for coping with both internal and external problems.

2.   The origin of these features and their dynamic relation may be studied easily in the small group, not only because groups are relatively easy to observe but because the structural features (such as a division of labor or a given power structure) are solutions to issues arising out of a specific context of interaction. Through detailed study of the interaction process one is able to identify such issues, to specify the group's response to them, and consequently to account for the structural features of the system. The more detailed the analysis of process, the clearer it becomes that the structural features and interaction process are simply two aspects of the same phenomenon.

Table   1   Bales's Set of Categories

TASK AREA:	*POSITIVE REACTIONS:*
	1. Shows solidarity
	2. Releases tension
	3. Agrees
4. Gives suggestion	
5. Gives opinion	
6. Gives orientation	
7. Asks for orientation	
8. Asks for opinion	
9. Asks for suggestion	
	NEGATIVE REACTIONS:
	10. Disagrees
	11. Shows tension
	12. Shows antagonism

Adapted with permission from Robert F. Bales, "A Set of Categories for the Analysis of Small Group Interaction," *American Sociological Review*, 15 (1950), 257–63.

3.   A wide range of interpersonal encounters can usefully be conceived as problem-solving. When people meet, there are differences to be ironed out and decisions to be made—whether the occasion is an argument among roommates, a family at dinner, a community meeting, a university seminar, a board of directors' meeting, or a council of war.

4.   If a group is to solve its problems and arrive at its decisions, certain basic functions must be performed at a minimum level of proficiency: (a) *communication:* through exchange of information, members must arrive at a common definition of the situation they confront; (b) *evaluation:* through exchange of ideas and opinions, they must arrive at a more-or-less shared attitude toward the situation; and (c) *control:* in the face of competing alternatives, they must choose and decide upon a single course of action.

5. Meanwhile, freedom to work on the problem depends on certain inter-personal processes: There must be a periodic feedback from members, indicating whether movement of the group in a particular direction is acceptable or unacceptable; the tension level within and between members must not get too high; and the group must be held together.

6. Finally, Bales suggests that the instrumental functions in 4 above, and the socio-emotional functions in 5 above, are dynamically related: attempts to solve the task tend to break up the group, thereby necessitating rein-tegrative activity; and attempts to pull the group together tend to weaken task efficiency, thereby requiring renewed emphasis upon the task.

The scoring procedure is simple: The observer (1) gives each group member an arbitrary number; (2) screens each act or gesture to determine to which of the functions it is most directly relevant; (3) records the act by placing it in the appropriate category, indicating both the number of the person initiating it and the number of the person to whom it is directed; and (4) continues this procedure as acts occur, keeping scores in an order corresponding to their occurrence (and often using as an aid a machine with a moving tape).

With training and considerable practice, and after having scored process in a given set of groups, the apprentice may arrange data in order to answer the following types of questions:

1. Does interaction follow an ordered sequence—for example, from the beginning to the end of a meeting? Bales and Strodtbeck suggest a general, and ideal, sequence wherein instrumental emphasis shifts first from problems of communication to problems of evaluation, and finally to problems of control.[21]

2. Is there a dynamic relation, or covariation, between task activity and socio-emotional activity? Again Bales and Strodtbeck suggest that as the group moves through problems of communication, evaluation, and control, "red-light" activity will increase, and that after the point of decision and as a manifestation of consolidation, "green-light" categories will increase.[22]

3. Is there a pattern in the distribution of interpersonal interaction? Is the communication network structured? Bales and associates have collected evidence suggesting a tendency to each actor to distribute his or her action among others according to their output, resulting in a network wherein the relative frequency of acts between any two parties can be estimated by their total output relative to other members.[23]

4. How do members divide among themselves the performance of the various behavioral functions represented by the categories? Slater and Bales find a tendency, under certain conditions, for one active member to push toward solving the problem while the other active member attempts to hold the group together—a division of functions corresponding to the major distinctions among the categories and, accordingly, to the basic functional problems outlined in Bales's original formulation.[24]

5. Conceiving of the interaction process as a more-or-less ordered system changing through time, what variables affect the characteristics of this system? Here the apprentice may be led in any one of a number of directions. For example, consider the effect that the following factors would have: the kind of problem the group is working on; the personalities of

the members, taken individually and as a configuration; the size of the group; sex, age, and social class of members; age of the group; relation of the group to other groups, and its relation to the observer. One could extend the list, but the question remains essentially the same—namely, if we view the overt interpersonal behavioral process as the result of the convergence of a number of forces at particular time and place, what factors affect those forces which, in turn, alter in a determinate way the interaction process?

Other Dimensions of Group Process

The value of Bales's method to our apprentice goes beyond the data produced. First, it sharpens her eye and disciplines her to attend to each event that occurs. Though she may score only one aspect of each act, she leaves out no acts. Second, the method introduces a conception of the ongoing interaction system, the problem-solving aspect of which is clearly formulated and rationally connected to the scoring operation. The good scorer employs this conception and, as she improves her scoring, tends to refine her own conception of the system. With the conception of the system on one hand and the appearance of an event on the other, the scoring operation is, in the end, a judgment about what each event does to the system. In making such judgments the apprentice tends to become more keenly aware of the intricate patterns and ordered sequences that characterize interaction. Like the student of music who learns an orchestral score, she begins to comprehend the design underlying interaction; the sensing of a "score" by the apprentice tends to open to her a new world of interpersonal process. Third, Bales's method does not try to capture the richness of all these processes. From the full score, as it were, it abstracts one line: It selects the problem-solving relevance of activity, leaving other dimensions, or other lines in the score, to other methods. (We refer to this "line" as the goal-seeking level in Chapter 4.) The value to the apprentice is that what is picked up is clearly and unambiguously formulated. As might be expected, Bales's method threw into sharp relief untouched dimensions of group process. Subsequently, special methods have been devised to cover a number of them.[25] Among the dimensions are the following:

1. The substantive content of statements; the ideas and images that are conveyed.
2. The intent of the actor; the aim, purpose, or motivation behind actions.
3. Feelings experienced by others, as well as the actor, while someone is acting.
4. Thoughts in the minds of members stimulated or evoked by the action, such as: Is what is going on good or bad, appropriate or inappropriate, effective or ineffective, desirable or undesirable?
5. Images in the minds of members stimulated or evoked by the action, such as the group melting or exploding.

With separate methods tapping distinct levels, they may be applied simultaneously. A single scorer may score multiple levels, as is done with SYMLOG, or the investigator may use a bank of observers, each employing a method that taps a separate dimension: One may classify content; another, problem-solving relevance;

another, feelings; another, the relationship between activity and rules; yet another, the relation between activity and group values. With independent but simultaneous readings on these analytically distinct dimensions, the investigator will be able to study an even more general sociological issue—namely, the dynamic principles that relate (1) interaction, (2) cultural content, (3) emotional processes, (4) rules and norms, and (5) beliefs and values. First, are there such principles? If so, are they uniform from one group to another, or are there different sets of principles for different types of groups? Are such principles constant throughout the life of a group, or do they alter as the group forms, develops, performs its purpose, and then disbands? This issue parallels major theoretical and empirical concerns of historians, sociologists, and anthropologists who study the dynamics of larger organizations, societies, and nations. The strategic advantage of studying these dynamics in the small group setting is precisely that these systematic data on processes can be gathered and empirical tests can be made. Through empirical tests many vague and fanciful ideas about social systems can be culled—all the more reason for developing methods for collecting data on configurations of covert thought, group norms (the appropriate and the inappropriate) and values (the desirable and the undesirable), thereby extending the range of empirical tests.

In addition to collecting systematic data on observable group processes, investigators often take readings on the state of the group, for example, at the end of each meeting. By means of questionnaires, tests, individual or group interviews, the researcher elicits *ex post facto* responses from members about their thoughts and feelings and attempts to piece together a picture of the covert processes in group experience.[26] All postsession responses are influenced by the fact that they are given to an outsider. Although not enough is known about this influence, from the viewpoint of an analysis of what happens in the group, it must be assumed to be an error factor until demonstrated otherwise.

In summary, there are practical methods for collecting systematic data on the more overt dimensions of group process, such as interaction, content, and certain feelings; and there are techniques for eliciting members' postsession responses. Sociologists are attempting to achieve a more comprehensive analysis through developing workable techniques for detecting and assessing the continuous but largely covert emotional, evaluative, and ideational processes.

COLLABORATION BETWEEN OBSERVER AND GROUP

To Henderson's three ingredients of (1) intuitive familiarity with the phenomena, (2) systematic collection of facts, and (3) an effective way of thinking about the phenomena, we have added a fourth that seems necessary for the making of a science of human groups; namely, a collaborative relation between the observer and the group being studied.[27] If our apprentice's first step was to gain access to the group without either undermining it or losing scientific perspective, and if the second step was to learn a set of reliable and valid methods for analyzing the various dimensions of group process, then her third step is to arrange a working relation with reciprocal feedback between her and the group.[28] For example, she reports her observations to the group and re-interprets their meaning by judging its reaction to them. What is accepted, what is denied, what seems strange, what seems clear—all these are taken as new readings about the nature of the group and, of course, may be fed back immediately for another round of reactions. Meanwhile, the group judges the viewpoint and the perceptivity of the observer through what she selects, misses, emphasizes and minimizes and in view of their assessment, instructs her further on the experience as they see it. Through such an exchange the different viewpoints are brought to light, the relation between group and observer is clarified and an additional framework for interpreting the original observations appears. Such a relation would promise not only to increase the relevance of sociology to existing groups but also to extend the degree of intimate contact with group phenomena and the range of phenomena on which data can be collected systematically. This seems basic at the present stage in the development of the field.

NOTES

1. Lawrence J. Henderson, "Procedure in a Science," in Hugh Cabot and Joseph A. Kahl, *Human Relations, Concepts and Cases in Concrete Social Science,* Vol. 1 (Cambridge, Mass.: Harvard University Press, 1953), pp. 24–39.

2. Charles H. Cooley, "The Roots of Social Knowledge," *American Journal of Sociology,* 32 (July 1926), 59–65; reprinted in Cabot and Kahl, *Human Relations,* pp. 60–71.

3. Edward Shils, "The Calling of Sociology," in Talcott Parsons and others, eds., *Theories of Society,* Vol. II (New York: Free Press, 1961), p. 1418.

4. Ibid., p. 1420.

5. On the observer's relation to groups in the field see Musafer Sherif and Carolyn W. Sherif, *Reference Groups* (New York: Harper & Row, Pub., 1964); William F. Whyte, "Observational Fieldwork Methods," in Marie Jahoda, Morton Deutsch, and Stuart W. Cook, eds., *Research Methods in Social Relations,* Vol. II, 1st ed. (New York: Dryden, 1931), pp. 493–511; and E. Rosenfeld, "The American Social Scientist in Israel: A Case Study in Role Conflict," *American Journal of Orthopsychiatry,* 28 (July 1958), 563–71.

6. These highlights are drawn from experience observing and supervising observers over the past thirty years at laboratories at Harvard, Yale, and SUNY Buffalo, at group conferences and in the field.

7. Bronislaw Malinowski, *A Diary in the Strict Sense of The Word* (New York: Harcourt Brace Jovanovich, Inc., 1967), p. 163.

8. Ibid., p. 201.

9. Colin M. Turnbull, *The Mountain People* (New York: Simon & Schuster, 1972).

10. Napoleon A. Chagnon, *Yąnomamö, The Fierce People* (New York: Holt, Rinehart & Winston, 1968), pp. 1–17.

11. Edward E. Jones and R. E. Nisbett, *The Actor and the Observer: Divergent Perspectives of the Causes of Behavior* (New York: General Learning, 1971).

12. Edward E. Jones, "How Do People Perceive the Causes of Behavior," *American Scientist,* 64 (May–June 1976) 300–305.

13. For a summary of subsequent research on attribution see John H. Harvey and Gifford Weary, *Perspectives on Attributional Processes* (Dubuque, Iowa: Wm. C. Brown, 1981).

14. On observer bias see Karl L. Weick, "Systematic Observational Methods," in Gardner Lindzey and Elliott Aronson, eds., *The Handbook of Social Psychology,* Vol. II (Reading, Mass.: Addison-Wesley, 1968), 428–35.

15. There is some experimental evidence that actor and observer are each able to shift

perspective to the other's viewpoint—see M. D. Storms, "Videotape and the Attributional Process: Reversing Actor's and Observer's Points of View," *Journal of Personality and Social Psychology*, 27 (1973), 165–75; and evidence that through the passage of time actors alter their viewpoint toward a set closer to observers—see Bert S. Moore and others, "The Dispositional Shift in Attribution over Time," *Journal of Experimental Social Psychology*, 15 (Nov. 1979), 553–69.

16. The issues for an observer of small groups are paralleled in the general sociologist's relation to societies. They are discussed in the latter context by Shils, in "The Calling of Sociology," in Parsons and others, eds., *Theories of Society*, Vol. II, 1405–1448.

17. Dorothy S. Thomas, *Some New Techniques for Studying Social Behavior* (New York: Columbia University Press, 1929). For an excellent discussion of scope, content, and technical issues in modern techniques see Weick, "Systematic Observational Methods," in Lindzey and Aronson, eds., *The Handbook of Social Psychology*, Vol. II, 357–451.

18. See R. G. Barker, ed., *Nonverbal Communication* (New York: Oxford University Press, 1979), 2nd ed.; E. T. Hall, *Beyond Culture* (New York: Doubleday, 1976); George F. Mahl and G. Schulze, "Psychological Research in the Extralinguistic Area," in T. A. Sebeok, A. S. Hayes, and Mary C. Bateson, eds., *Approaches to Semiotics* (London: Mouton, 1964); and Albert E. Scheflen, *Communication Structure* (Berkeley: University of California Press, 1972).

19. Weick, "Systematic Observational Methods," in Lindzey and Aronson, eds., *The Handbook for Social Psychology*, 2nd ed., Vol. II, 380.

20. In our illustration we refer to the initial version of the categories. For subsequent developments see Robert F. Bales, *Personality and Interpersonal Behavior* (New York: Holt, Rinehart & Winston, 1970). Also see Borgatta's revision in line with later information on peer rating and task requirements: Edgar F. Borgatta, "A New Systematic Interaction Observation System: Behavior Scores System," *Journal of Psychological Studies*, 16 (1963), 24–44.

21. Robert F. Bales and Fred L. Strodtbeck, "Phases in Group Problem Solving," *Journal of Abnormal and Social Psychology*, 46 (1951), 485–95.

22. Ibid.

23. Robert F. Bales and others, "Channels of Communication in Small Groups," *American Sociological Review*, 16 (1951), 461–68.

24. Robert F. Bales and Philip E. Slater, "Role Differentiation in Small Decision-Making Groups," in Talcott Parsons and others, *The Family, Socialization and Interaction Process* (New York: Free Press, 1955), pp. 259–306; for examples of the application of Bales's method see George A. Talland, "Task and Interaction Process: Some Characteristics of Therapeutic Group Discussion," *Journal of Abnormal and Social Psychology*, 50 (1955), 105–109; George Psathas, "Phase Movement and Equilibrium Tendencies in Interaction Process Analysis in Psychotherapy Groups," *Sociometry*, 23 (June 1960), 177–94; and H. Lennard and A. Bernstein, *The Anatomy of Psychotherapy: Systems of Communication and Expectation* (New York: Columbia University Press, 1960). For the application of interaction analysis to families of schizophrenic families, see Elliot Mishler and Nancy Waxler, *Interaction in Families* (New York: John Wiley, 1968).

25. For a review of content analysis see Ole R. Holsti, "Content Analysis," in Lindzey and Aronson, eds., *The Handbook of Social Psychology*, 2nd ed., Vol. II, 596–692. Also see Theodore M. Mills, *Group Transformation* (Englewood Cliffs, N.J.: Prentice-Hall, 1964), pp. 19–41; Philip J. Stone and others, *The General Inquirer: A Computer Approach to Content Analysis* (Cambridge Mass.: M.I.T. Press, 1966); Robert F. Bales and Steven P. Cohen, *SYMLOG: A System for the Multiple Level Observation of Groups* (New York: Free Press, 1979). For methods for inferring and recording emotional states, see R. L. Birdwhistell, *Introduction to Kinesics* (Louisville, Ky.: University of Louisville Press, 1952); George F. Mahl, "Exploring Emotional States by Content Analysis," in Ithiel De Sola Pool, ed., *Trends in Content Analysis* (Urbana: University of Illinois Press, 1959), pp. 89–130; A. T. Ditman and

Lyman C. Wynne, "Linguistic Techniques and the Analysis of Emotionality in Interviews," *Journal of Abnormal and Social Psychology,* 63 (1961), 201–204; Robert E. Pettinger, Charles F. Hockett, and John J. Danely, *The First Five Minutes: A Sample of Microscopic Interview Analysis* (Ithaca, N.Y.: Paul Martineau, 1960); and Richard D. Mann, Graham S. Gibbard, and John J. Hartman, *Interpersonal Styles and Group Development* (New York: John Wiley, 1967) and Richard D. Mann and others, *The College Class Room: Conflict, Change and Learning* (New York: John Wiley, 1970).

26. For a discussion of various types of sociometric (and related) questions, their application, and ways of analyzing the data they provide, see Gardner Lindzey and Dawn Byrne, "Measurement of Social Choice and Interpersonal Attractiveness," in Lindzey and Aronson, eds., *The Handbook of Social Psychology,* 2nd ed., Vol. II, 452–525; also see A. Paul Hare, *The Handbook of Small Group Research,* 2nd ed. (New York: Free Press, 1976), pp. 152–78; for the use of projective devices see Michael P. Farrell, "Collective Projection and Group Structure: The Relationship between Deviance and Projection in Groups," *Small Group Behavior,* 10 (Feb. 1979), 81–100; and, for earlier applications, see William E. Henry and Harold Guetzkow, "Group Projective Sketches for the Study of Small Groups," *Journal of Social Psychology,* 33 (1951), 77–102; M. Horwitz and Dorwin Cartwright, "A Projective Method for the Diagnosis of Group Properties," *Human Relations,* 6 (1953), 397–410; and Theodore M. Mills, "Developmental Process in Three Person Groups," *Human Relations,* 9 (1956), 343-54; for the long-term development of a member-rating checklist see Bales and Cohen, *SYMLOG,* pp. 241–99; regarding interviews see Eleanor E. Maccoby and Nathan Maccoby, "The Interview: A Tool of Social Science," in Lindzey, ed., *Handbook of Social Psychology,* 1st ed., Vol. 1, 449–87; for a comparison of the use of the interview and questionnaire see Claire Sellitz and others, eds., *Research Methods in Social Relations,* rev. ed. (New York: Dryden, 1959), pp. 236–68; for a discussion of factors affecting collaboration between interviewer and interviewee see Charles F. Cannell and Robert L. Kahn, "Interviewing," in Lindzey and Aronson, eds., *The Handbook of Social Psychology,* 2nd ed., Vol. II, 526–95.

27. For an attempt to maximize the value of interchange between actors and observers see Theodore M. Mills and Michael P. Farrell, "Group Relations and Science: The Question of Compatibility," *Journal of Personality and Social Systems,* 1, no. 2 (Oct. 1977), 11–31; and, Theodore M. Mills, "Seven Steps in Developing Group Awareness," *Journal of Personality and Social Systems,* 1, no. 4 (Sept. 1978), 15–29. For a classical story of an observer's relation to a group see William F. Whyte, *Street Corner Society: The Social Structure of an Italian Slum,* 3rd ed. (Chicago: University of Chicago Press, 1981).

28. For a six-point program to develop such a relation, see Theodore M. Mills, *The Sociology of Small Groups,* 1st ed. (Englewood Cliffs, N.J.: Prentice-Hall, Inc., 1967), pp. 38–41.

CHAPTER 3
EXPERIMENTATION

The experimental method enjoys a definite advantage over observation and description. Through an example, this chapter notes this advantage, points to certain dynamic effects of manipulating group variables, and, following the lead of the previous chapter, suggests an optimal working relation between experimenter and groups. But before we get deeply into our discussion, let us consider a few simple facts.

Obviously the discovery through observation (in any discipline you might care to mention) that one variable is associated with another may be considered a gainful advance in that field of knowledge. However, the question remains as to whether change in one of the variables is both a necessary and a sufficient condition for change in the second. For example, suggesting associations between such things as altitude and barometer readings, climate and malaria, business activity and suicide, frustration and aggression, and democratic leadership and satisfaction is no proof of what causes the barometer's change, malaria, suicide, aggression, and group satisfaction. If, while holding other things constant, one were able to alter one variable and observe change or lack of change in the other, then one could begin to determine "causes." And if, through a series of tests, one were able to alter one variable after the other, one might eventually discover variables or sets of variables to which the second variable is most sensitive—the study of malaria being a case in point.

We begin to see that compared to observation and description, the experimental method is highly efficient both in eliminating apparently reasonable but inadequate hypotheses, and in indicating those hypotheses that cannot easily be rejected. Experimentation proves particularly valuable in such special circumstances as dealing with two theories where one predicts an opposite outcome from the other, for then the experiment tests an entire body of thought.[1] Though attractive because of its efficiency and potential power for resolving theoretical issues, the experimental method is not practical or even possible for many investigators. For example, modern astronomers still cannot shift heavenly bodies at will in order to observe the effects of such shifts. Instead they must wait for an eclipse, or for the visit of a comet, to conduct their experiments. Only recently have astronomers been able to take readings from beyond the earth's atmosphere and to plan experiments within the solar system. The struggle to obtain more accurate readings of the heavens and to be able to introduce known variations has been going on since ancient times. We see that physical realities continue to limit the use of the experimental method in this particular science, and much the same applies to other fields. The astronomer's counterpart in social science is limited more frequently by the realities of moral restraints and of human sensitivities.

To experiment on communities or nations—for example, to test the effects of a change in technology, or a change in the legal structure, or a change in the form of government—requires the unusual freedom to "play with" individual and collective life.[2] Traditionally, that freedom is granted only to those who assume political responsibility both for their own acts and for the society on which they act. The implicit rule is: "Whosoever exercises power over us must do so—or we must have reason to believe is doing so—primarily for *our* sake. Life and society are too precious to be risked simply for the sake of a scientist's abstract ideas." Perhaps the rule was felt stronger in those societies where traditions were not threatened by rapid changes of circumstances. In many societies during the last century it has become increasingly clear that traditions, including ways of learning about the self and society, are inadequate and that leaders, whether of nations or of very small groups, need better information and a clearer grasp of social processes. Partly because of the possibility that social science can evaluate our folk-beliefs about how groups should operate by examining and testing how they do operate, the moral restraint on experimentation has gradually lessened, although recent calls for restraint suggest counter-swings, if indeed the long-term trend is downward. Then, too, the restraint is undoubtedly less for small groups than for societies, and probably even less for individuals than for groups. In any case, the twentieth century in social science has been marked by a rapid increase in experimentation. People such as Kurt Lewin have hoped that we might be able both to locate specific causes of group phenomena and to test beyond reasonable doubt some of our basic ideas about groups.

Because of Lewin's influence, Lippitt and White were aware of the possibilities of experimentation when they tested the effects of leadership styles upon groups of boys.[3] In one set of groups an adult took the part of an autocratic leader; in another, the part of a democratic leader; while in a third, the part of a *laissez-faire* leader. After a period in one group, leaders shifted groups, and in some cases shifted their leadership style. By comparing measures of a number of variables covering the boys' reactions when dealing with a particular leader-style, the investigators were able to examine systematically the effects of the three styles. Since these styles are related to folk-beliefs about how groups should be led, the experiment has implications for our ideology as well as for the researchers' hypotheses. Quite apart from the results, this experiment demonstrated the feasibility of training persons to act a certain way, of introducing them into groups, and of testing the effects of their performance upon other processes in those groups.

Another feature was controlled and varied by Bavelas and his associates.[4] It is common knowledge that not everyone in organizations has equal access to information—that information is channeled through a network, with some persons at certain intersections receiving and giving more than others. With the supposition in mind that a relationship must exist between the pattern of such networks and the capability of organizations to solve problems, Bavelas set up laboratory groups of five persons each in which he varied the configuration of communication channels (for example, from the "circle" pattern where each person can get in touch with his two neighbors but with no one else, to the pattern where four persons can communicate with a central person but not with each other), gave the groups identical problems to solve, then measured the speed and accuracy of their solutions. Later, by varying the types of problems (from those requiring an accumulation of information to those requiring insight), the investigators suggested a three-way relation between type of network, type of problem, and degree of efficiency.[5] Again, apart from the results, the experiments demonstrated that it was possible to establish in the laboratory, and to alter with relative ease, such a complex group feature as the network of interpersonal communication.

Though these and other experiments of the period inspired an impressive list of laboratory tests, some social scientists doubted their value. "Yes," it was said, "experiments are *possible,* but are they relevant? To what extent can findings obtained in the artificial world of the laboratory from *ad hoc* groups that work on unrealistic problems be generalized to the real world outside?"[6] Though we cannot detail the debate in this book, it should be noted that the problem common to all experimenters, regardless of their field of science, is precisely to spell out the circumstances where results obtained in one context can be usefully applied in another. The readings on an ammeter in the lab and lightning in the heavens are an example. While everyone sees the obvious difference between the movement of a needle and a lightning bolt, it takes a leap of imagination to recognize that each are indicators of electric charge. A theoretical concept of electrical charge is required, and an appreciation of the enormous range of charges, from very small to very large. When the analytic concept and the empirical knowledge are furnished, quite precise transposition equations can be written linking the indications in the lab and in the sky. In the study of groups theoretical concepts (such as value conflict or cohesion and the models of which they are part) help make comparable connections, although our measurements are relatively crude. We must also note that the social scientist has a responsibility to construct those equations that link phenomena observed in the laboratory to phenomena outside. Yet we suggest that bridging the gap intellectually is complicated by the fact that rather than simply observing group processes the experimenter *acts on* the group. Norbert Weiner, a pioneer of cybernetics, said more than once in public lectures that the study of human groups is like trying to find out what makes a watch tick when the only way to open it is with a sledge hammer. In moving from observation to experimentation, investigators shift from passive to active: from simply observing a change to inducing a change; from taking groups as they are to introducing actors into them; from observing existing groups to creating them for their own purpose. Their dilemma is that the more they do to the group, the less they know what it would be, do, or become without interference. By experimenting, not only do they perform functions which are ordinarily performed by members themselves, but the tighter the controls and the more careful the investigator's manipulation, the less the opportunity for the group to develop on its own—and consequently, the greater the difficulty in transposing findings from such groups to more autonomous groups outside.

In Weiner's terms, how can we open the group to tests of relations within it without taking a sledge hammer to it? The present chapter presents a strategy developed toward a solution of this basic problem. First, experimenters, as professionals, must reexamine their relation to the groups they study, including the meaning they have to members, what they and the group want from each other, the goals and values they do and do not share, and the impact of manipulations on both parties. Second, experimenters must devise types of collaborative relations with groups that enable the experimenter to learn "what makes groups tick" without violating their individual and collective integrity. Since experiments differ not only in the sensitivity of the issues they raise, but also in the degree of manipulation they require and in the intrusiveness of their measures, appropriate working relations between the experimenter and particular groups also vary. Rather than deal with all of these variations, the discussion of strategy in this chapter focuses on those settings that make maximum demands upon both the group members (e.g., in terms of sensitivity) and the experimenter (e.g., in terms of involvement with the group). We hope these strategies will enable experimenters to test hypotheses that are important and relevant to both parties.

Just as we argued in the previous chapter that familiarity depends upon the observer's social relation with the group, it is argued here that extending experimentation to cover more autonomous groups depends upon a relationship where the group voluntarily grants the scientist the right to manipulate it while the experimenter grants the group the freedom to maintain or to develop its independence. To illustrate our strategy let us imagine an apprentice experimenter, a young man, beginning his career as a sociologist and facing for the first time the issues of why and how experiments are done.

THE ORIGIN OF AN EXPERIMENT

For several months our apprentice sociologist has been observing a group of 10 male students who meet for discussion two hours each week to improve their understanding of group process, particularly in their own group. Previous topics have included: "What Is the Group's Real Purpose?"; "'Masking,' 'Passing,' and 'Authenticity' in Presenting Oneself to Others"; and "The Moral Issues in Civil Disobedience."

Thirty minutes before the end of a session, the observer is surprised to see John, an active and articulate member, rise from his chair, say, "Well, I have to leave," and then go.

HARRY: Good luck, John!
  BOB: Where's he going?
HARRY: Being interviewed for medical school.

The observer recalls that before the departure the group was discussing "silences," and from his notes he traces the following sequence:

PHIL: There are more sudden silences here than in other groups. . . .

HARRY: Here you don't feel obligated to talk. Other places you have to fill in immediately to avoid the pain.

BOB: But when heavy talkers leave off, we fill in, don't we?

PHIL: Here, if you break a silence you know breaking it will be analyzed.

JOHN: Silences are uncomfortable, like disagreements. I don't feel comfortable when there is a disagreement. I try to work them out. When there's a silence, I want to jump in to fill the gap; keep it going to make everyone feel good.

A short silence follows.

PETER: Yeah!

(General laughter)

ALLEN: You're looking for confirmation. You make a point and you want a response, not just a blank. It was that way with me last week. . . .

JOHN: It's like having an argument with your girl. You say something nasty, and you want her to say something in return. . . .

PHIL: To take the sting out. . . .

JOHN: To take the sting out. Instead, she'll cry or walk out of the room or something. In a case like that, who's manipulating whom?

It was at this point that John left.

An attempt by several individuals to draw out a silent member is interrupted by Peter, who asks: "Are we the same group now that he's not here—now that John's gone?" An active response to this question includes such comments as: "Everybody has a functional role, and when someone leaves, someone else takes it over"; "We all take part of it; we all become more dominant"; "We change more when someone leaves than when someone is absent"; "But, there were traces of you here last time."

In the midst of the discussion Phil turns to Peter and says: "You actually inherited John's departure and have been talking ever since!" Laughter around the table is spotty and restrained and Harry murmurs, "Every time someone leaves we get on this goddam subject!"

PETER: This time there was a special reason. I felt insecure. It reminded me of last time, when a lot of you weren't here. I wasn't sure we were a group.

ALLEN: Yes. There are certain roles to be performed. It's the group's identity. When someone leaves, his role has to be taken over, if. . . .

BOB: By whom? Now, it's Peter taking over John's?

DICK: Oh, you see! We have no way of talking about this! We have ruined it by talking about it! If you had only waited to see what would happen . . . but now, after two seconds, we say, "Peter has John's role."

While Dick is speaking, Peter picks up his papers and with a broad smile moves into John's chair. Harry, next to him, jokingly suggests that he put one foot up on the table as John often does. Others watch the moves carefully. Finally, with a flourish, Peter strikes John's pose.

ALLEN: What's going on here?
PETER: Oh, well! I can't quite fill his role.
HARRY: You're right! You're so right! In losing John I feel like I have lost the king of the mountain—being alone on this side of the table. I felt I had to hold up this side of the table. You get security when someone is next to you.

"Well," says Bob to Peter, "now say something!"

Later, the apprentice reviews the sequence: discomfort over silences; analysis of the person who breaks them; the less-active filling in when talkers are quiet; breaking a silence is like settling a disagreement; "Is the group the same without John?"; functional roles and group identity; Peter's bodily move in taking John's place; and Harry's comfort in having a companion.

The observer recalls similar occasions: Members daring someone to sit in the leader's chair when the leader was absent; the father's instruction to the son: "Take care of the family while I'm away"; the daughter's excitement in playing mother while the mother is away; a hockey team whose star is in the penalty box; the loss of fellow soldiers on a patrol. Clearly, when a group member leaves, others tend to fill the gap. But how general is this gap-filling phenomenon? How can it be explained? What about groups can be learned by the way they manage departures?

The apprentice formulates a first explanation of the gap-filling phenomenon as follows: Groups are in problem-solving situations. They must perform certain functions to meet situational demands. Through trial and error, members allocate among themselves activities so as to perform these functions. A departure results in a functional void, and the void incapacitates the group. To counteract this, other members, either singly or in concert, alter their own behavior. The gap is filled and the function is performed. The use of phrase, gesture, and stance of the absent person is simply a more noticeable indication of the less obvious gap-filling.

On reflection, this hypothesis is so reasonable to the apprentice that he abandons it—that is, until he is challenged by a fellow student during a seminar report. "How," he is asked, "do you know what is cause and effect? You observe the gap-filling *after* the member departs. How do you know the member does not leave because his role is being taken over? In your illustration, John said that the friend left because he had been nasty; and remember: just before he left, he asked, 'Who is manipulating whom?' I would argue that members, being possessive about their own functions, feel undermined when they sense others are usurping their functions, and will, if they can, leave the group before it becomes obvious that they are being displaced. By your example you can't prove that departure precedes gap-filling. Maybe being displaced precedes departure."

"But," replies the apprentice, "this can be tested experimentally: we can set up groups and pull members out according to a pre-arranged plan unknown to group members. If gap-filling follows, then there is little question."

A second student agrees to the test but suggests another reason for the gap-filling phenomenon. "Your hypothesis," she argues, "assumes that solving a problem is the primary concern, as though the most important loss to the family when the mother is away is housekeeping. The mechanism may not be so cold, rational and goal-oriented. Group members become emotionally attached to one another. When someone departs, others naturally feel an emotional loss and try to reduce it by bringing him back, by acting as he would act and by saying what he would say. I think others will fill the gap when they are fond of the person, regardless of how effective he is. I predict gap-filling when others are fond of the person, while you predict gap-filling when he is effective."

Still another view comes from a third student: "Whether the phenomenon is rational or non-rational, instrumental or affective are secondary issues. The primary point is that groups tend to maintain a state of equilibrium. Accordingly, the disturbance of a departure should be followed by a reaction tending to return the group to the state prior to his departure. While gap-filling fits this in general, the specific reaction should be in proportion to the extent of the disturbance. This means that gap-filling is correlated with the activity rate of the person who leaves. Only if he has been active—as John was in your example—will gap-filling occur. If he had been silent or passive it would not have occurred. Suppose John had been a silent member, would you expect others to be silent as a means of filling a gap?"

To complete the circle, a fourth student contends that everyone is being constrained by a single illustration. "Before you go on, consider two points. First, think of all the possible factors that might effect your dependent variable, the gap-filling phenomenon. How about group size? The smaller the group, the greater the disturbance, loss, functional void, or what-have-you. How about solidarity? The more cohesive the group, the greater the loss. Just two conditions in a long list that could include personality of members, their age, their class membership, the sex composition of the group, and so on. To what universe of groups are you trying to generalize? You must take into account the variables that differentiate groups if you are to be scientifically serious about it.

"And, second," he continues, " if you want to be genuinely theoretical, why restrict yourself to departures? The general issue is change in group boundaries. You should consider the arrival of a newcomer, or at least the re-entry of the person who leaves. What mechanism operates then, and why? The newcomer, as we know, must undergo initiation in order to belong. It's just as true that the person returning must pay a readmission price, bring a gift, give a party, or present some token, even if it is no more than to tell of his travels. How do groups react to the one who returns? Do they fill him in on what has happened in his absence? Note this second type of gap and this second type of gap-filling; namely, filling each other in on all that has happened to the two parties during separation. Both gaps are associated with change in boundary. You need an hypothesis that accounts for both departure and readmission, one that specifies the necessary and sufficient conditions both for taking the absent person's place and for bringing parties up to date after separation. Unless you cover both, the more general theoretical issue of boundary change is not covered."

AN EXPERIMENTAL PLAN

Feeling that the issue is becoming too involved for open discussion, the apprentice goes home, works alone, and later returns with the following plan:

1. Groups with six members each meet for five two-hour sessions to work on

a series of tasks including playing chess against the experimenter, debating the moral issues in civil disobedience, building a model town, interpreting a play, and inventing an automatic door-latch and release.

2. The sessions are videotaped with a back-up sound tape. At the end of each session, members rate each other on usefulness in solving the problems, and indicate whom they like and dislike.

3. Early in the fourth session the experimenter pulls one member out on a pretext, and asks the group to continue on their tasks.

4. During an intermission in the fifth session, the experimenter asks the member who was pulled out to return.

   The apprentice explains that the purpose of the experiment is to test the relative effects of two factors—*instrumental usefulness* and *libidinal attachment*—upon the gap-filling phenomenon.

5. There are four types of experimental groups, and a set of control groups. In control groups the experimenter pulls out no one. In experimental groups people are pulled out according to other members' ratings of them, and their classification into four types: (1) useful and liked; (2) useful but disliked; (3) not useful but liked; and (4) not useful and disliked.

6. Each member's activity during the entire series is categorized by both Bales's *Interaction Process Analysis* and a content analysis scheme, such as *The General Inquirer.*[7] Two observers classify nonverbal behavior, one isolating on the person to be pulled and the other observing the remaining five. Activity before the departure is compared with activity after the departure. Changes in members' activity toward the departed person's type of activity is designated as *gap-filling activity.* In control groups, comparisons are made with persons randomly selected, since, of course, no one is pulled out.

The apprentice argues that if gap-filling activity is more frequent in experimental than in control groups, then at least departure can "cause" *gap-filling,* though of course it is still possible that displacement could cause departures. Further, he argues that if *usefulness* makes a significant difference, but libidinal attachment does not, then gap-filling is primarily an adaptive mechanism—a means of coping with the external demands; whereas, if *attachment* makes a significant difference, but not usefulness, then gap-filling is primarily an integrative mechanism—a means of reducing the group's emotional loss. If both *usefulness* and *attachment* make a difference, then gap-filling is a compound mechanism.

The equilibrium hypothesis, the apprentice continues, can be examined after the experiment, simply by testing the correlation between rate of activity of the person who is pulled out, and the volume of gap-filling activity. Finally, by asking the person to return to the group, he can compare management of readmission with response to departures, and further explore the general issue of boundary changes.

If, when pretested, members do not naturally fall into the four desired categories, then the apprentice will train role-players to act out the four parts, then pull them out. If that works, then he will eventually extend his experimental program to test the effect of other factors mentioned above.

Before describing the apprentice's experience in conducting the experiment, let us review the steps in the procedures so far.

1. During unstructured observation, and quite by accident, he saw one member move into the chair of another who had departed.

2. The act brought together previous observations. Could it be part of a more-or-less universal mechanism? He called it "the gap-filling phenomenon."

3. The apprentice formulated a tentative explanation for it.

4. Following discussions with fellow students who presented alternative hypotheses and certain methodological and theoretical problems, he reexamined the formulation.

5. Two of the hypotheses mentioned were of interest. Since the choice between them could not easily be made through uncontrolled observation, he decided to test them by an experiment.

6. He designed one that would not only test these ideas but would allow the exploration of the related question of readmission.

7. In short, from a chance observation the apprentice planned a major experimental program on a simple but interesting theoretical issue.

THE DYNAMICS OF MANIPULATION

The time is some months later and the scene is the university laboratory. The occasion is the first run of the apprentice's experiment. Since drawing up the plan, the apprentice has reviewed the relevant literature, established more precise measures of the gap-filling phenomenon, selected statistical tests to evaluate results, and circulated questionnaires throughout the university, seeking volunteers and information on their social class, family background, personality trends, attitudes, values, intelligence, peer-group associations, and so on. He has already pretested the experimental plan and, as feared, has had to change it. Since few persons in the pretest were both effective and clearly disliked, and few were both clearly ineffective and liked, he has decided to use role-players. The apprentice has trained four associates to perform roles in groups so that they will be rated by others in one of the four classifications. A second change has arisen because not enough students have volunteered. As a result, the experimenter is obtaining subjects through large introductory courses which require a minimum number of hours' service as an experimental subject.

As the first group gets underway, the apprentice senses the dramatic nature of experimentation.[8] The laboratory seems a separate theatre world; the first run like opening night. The subjects under bright lights are the actors, and the observers in the dark behind the one-way mirror are the audience. The apprentice knows what it is to be producer, playwright, and director for this is his show; he has screened and selected the actors, composed the groups, constructed the tasks, designed the questionnaires, prescribed the observations to be made and the measures to be taken. He has brought people together and will send them away. From beginning to end he has written the script—except for those few vacancies to be filled in by indicators of the dependent variable. How subjects will respond is part of the drama; a larger part is whether the experiment will work, for now it is the experimenter who is being judged. It is the experimenter who is now watchful, careful, and anxious.

If the session goes poorly, he is likely to discard the run, tighten up controls, and start over again. If, on the other hand, the results are clear and positive, and other groups follow suit, then the experimenter is likely to discover the strangest fact of all. On the intellectual level he will want, naturally, to check against artifacts, sleeper variables, alternative interpretations, and so on. But beyond and beneath that the apprentice discovers that *success creates a growing doubt about the reality of what has happened.* Is it, he wonders, too good to be true? Are the findings authentic? Or, with the doubt put in a more familiar way: How do the results apply to real groups in the real world outside? Might the whole production be just a play? Are the groups real or artificial; am I a scientist or a magician?[9]

The source of the experimenter's disorientation lies not so much in the laboratory's relation to the outer world as in the experimenter's relation to the group. Contrast, if you will, this relation with the relations of our apprentice observer in the previous chapter. With established groups, she was guest; here, he is host. She went to the hospital or to the school; he brings subjects to the laboratory—at best a strange and mysterious place. She observed persistent groups; he deals with one group after the other as they are ushered in and out. She observed a type with internal ties of affection and undercurrents of hostility, with both a tradition and the power to set its own rules, one with both a purpose and the power to establish its own agenda, one with both boundaries and the power to admit and to exclude on its own; in short, an autonomous group—or at any rate autonomous enough to get along without her.

In contrast, the experimental group is almost wholly dependent upon the experimenter for its substance, form, and direction. Now, it is the experimenter who admits and excludes, assembles and dismisses, announces the purpose, sets the agenda, prescribes the rules, shifts direction, shields against outside influence, and so on—all in order properly to achieve comparable groups, standard procedures, and a reduction in experimental error. The point of the comparison is that while our observer encountered groups that performed their own executive functions, now it is the experimenter who performs those functions for the group. The group literally does not know what it is until the experimenter assembles it, nor does it know what to do until they are told.

In these circumstances the experimenter's feeling of unreality is a real response to a real contradiction—namely, that while in actuality he performs executive functions for the group and is therefore sociologically inside the group, according to scientific tradition he conceives of himself as outside, detached, and disinterested. Though in actuality the experimenter is the group's creator, goal-setter, programmer, lawmaker, paymaster, and judge, he thinks of himself as having no role at all within it. More than this, he believes he should not have a role in it. Consequently, although an insider, the investigator must pose as an outsider. He impersonates an outsider; he is in masquerade. As a result, he is not sure *where* he is, nor *who* he is, and things begin to appear unreal and artificial.

The use of deception ("Would you come with me, Mr. Brown—someone wants you on the phone.") is another part of the same theme. In proclaiming that something *is* A when it is *not* A (and in having this believed), experimenters inject existential propositions into the group cultures. Their word sets the group definitions of that part of reality, much as in giving task instructions they set goals and procedures. Another elaboration on the theme is the use of role-players, for to proclaim, or to imply, that these persons are in the group when they actually are not is to set a definition of group membership.[10]

In the meantime, what has happened to the group? As already implied, it has become a phantom, compared to what it might have become under more favorable conditions. One could present new tasks, change the rules, proclaim a new purpose—

and again it would not matter, for it has become infinitely responsive, pliable, and obedient. It has become this way because when it was formed each person became committed to the experimenter rather than to fellow members and, basically, because the experimenter needs subjects who are willing to commit themselves primarily to the scientist.

This phantom group is in fact the experimenter's own creation. By being playwright, producer, and director (and, we might add, by conforming closely to the prevailing practices of journeyman experimental scientists), the apprentice usurps just those functions and prerogatives that the subjects themselves need if they are to develop into a genuine group. Oddly, with one hand the experimenter creates the potential for a group, but with the other takes away its means for becoming one. Quite precisely, in forming the group the apprentice gives it a form; he creates the character of his experimental subject.

This act of creating one's own subject may be peculiar to the group situation. To be sure, in recruiting someone for an experiment, a new social relation between that person and the experimenter is created, but we would not say a new person is created. However, for groups we can say just that. By bringing people together, the experimenter creates a group. Although it is young, indistinct, and illusive, it is nonetheless a new unit with a potential for development. If this point be granted, then we may suggest that the manner in which persons are brought together—the way the group is conceived, if you will—makes a difference in what it can and cannot become.

To summarize: The first illusion is that the experimenter is outside the group, whereas sociologically the experimenter functions within it; the second is that the assembled aggregate is a group, whereas it is only partial, its government and executive powers having been taken over by the experimenter. In short, the grand illusion is that experimenter and group are *separate* systems, whereas in actuality they are *one*. They are a *single* system in which functions are divided: controlling and being controlled, setting rules and conforming to them, giving directions and obediently following them, being in charge and complying with the one in charge, being the authority and being the subordinate. Though their functions differ, the two parties constitute a single unit, a single system masquerading as two. Neither one, let us recognize, can get along without the other.[11]

COLLABORATIVE RELATIONSHIP BETWEEN EXPERIMENTER AND GROUP

As intimated above, a strategy to solve this elemental problem is, first, to reexamine, sociologically, the relation between experimenter and group and second, to arrange, or shall we say invent, a working relationship between experimenter and group so that they may be both autonomous and interdependent. They should be *autonomous* so that the investigator can experiment more freely for the sake of science and so that groups have the opportunity to develop their capabilities without in any way being incapacitated. They should be *interdependent* in the sense that groups become prepared to give up voluntarily part of their autonomy for the sake of experimental knowledge about themselves (as well as about themselves for others); and in the sense that the experimenter becomes prepared to give up some controls for the sake of learning about groups with more substance. The development of such a relationship is not only desirable for the advancement of experimental sociology, it is critical to that advance. Without it, the investigator is reduced to testing ideas within phantom contexts. With it, there is promise not only of a wider range of groups open to experimentation but of the infusion of the experimental notion into groups so that they are more willing to experiment on themselves.[12]

SUMMARY

An increased realization of the power of experimentation, along with an apparent trend toward the relaxation of traditional restraints upon experimenting with people, have contributed to a rapid rise in the number and variety of experiments on groups. At the same time, researchers have become more acutely aware of some of the problems in such a program—in particular, the fact that the more experimenters control groups, the less opportunity groups have to develop on their own and, therefore, the more difficult it is for investigators to bridge the gap from the laboratory to more autonomous groups. A two-step solution to this problem is suggested: First, a fuller understanding of what experimenters do to groups when they experiment on them; and second, a collaborative relation between experimenter and group, who jointly work out appropriate degrees of latitude in group development and of freedom to experiment.

Our review of the apprentices' experiences, one as observer and one as experimenter, suggests a number of forces which tend in the first instance to press the apprentice out of the role of independent, scientific observer, and in the second instance prevent the experimented-upon group from becoming self-governing. Those forces tend to retard the sociology of groups. One means of counteracting them and advancing the field is to conceive of and to engineer social relations between investigator and group which reinforce their affinity and permit productive interchange.

NOTES

1. On the logic of experimentation see Claire Sellitz and others, eds., *Research Methods in Social Relations,* rev. ed. (New York: Dryden, 1959), pp. 80–143; on the strategy of laboratory experimentation see Leon Festinger, "Laboratory Experiments," in Leon Festinger and Daniel Katz, eds., *Research Methods in the Behavioral Sciences* (New York: Holt, Rinehart & Winston, 1953), pp. 138–72; on experiments with groups in the field, see John R. P. French, Jr., "Experiments in Field Settings," in Festinger and Katz, eds., *Research Methods in the Behavioral Sciences,* pp. 98–135; for types of experiments, see E. Greenwood, *Experimental Sociology, A Study in Method* (New York: King's Crown, 1945); for functions of experiments see Abraham Kaplan, *The Conduct of Inquiry, Methodology for Behavioral Science* (New York: Harper & Row, Pub., 1964), pp. 126–70; and for a review of recent experiments on some of the problems mentioned above in our introduction see Philip B. Bonachich and John Light, "Laboratory Experimentation in Sociology," in Ralph H. Turner, James Coleman, and Renée C. Fox, eds., *Annual Review of Sociology,* Vol. 4 (Palo Alto, Calif.: Annual Reviews, 1978), pp. 145–70.

2. Henry W. Reicken and others, *Social Experimentation: A Method for Planning and*

Evaluating Social Intervention (New York: Academic Press, 1974); and Harvey A. Hornstein and others, eds., *Social Intervention: A Behavioral Science Approach* (New York: Free Press, 1971).

3. Ronald Lippitt, "An Experimental Study of the Effect of Democratic and Authoritarian Group Atmospheres," *University of Iowa Studies in Child Welfare,* 16 (1940), 43-195, condensed version published as Ronald Lippitt and Ralph K. White, "An Experimental Study of Leadership and Group Life," in Guy E. Swanson, Theodore M. Newcomb, and Eugene L. Hartley, eds., *Readings in Social Psychology,* rev. ed. (New York: Holt, Rinehart & Winston, 1952), pp. 340-55.

4. Dorwin Cartwright and Alvin Zander, eds., *Group Dynamics,* 2nd ed. (Evanston, Ill.: Row, Peterson, 1960), pp. 669-82.

5. Swanson, Newcomb, and Hartley, eds., *Readings in Social Psychology,* rev. ed., pp. 108-25.

6. See Henri Tajfel, "Experiments in a Vacuum," in Joachim Israel and Henri Tajfel, eds., *The Context of Social Psychology: A Critical Assessment* (New York: Academic Press, 1972) p. 106; Guy E. Swanson, "Some Problems of Laboratory Experiments with Small Populations," *American Sociological Review,* 16 (1951), 349-58; and Lewis A. Coser, "The Functions of Small Group Research," *Social Problems,* 3 (Winter 1955-56), 1-6.

7. Philip E. Stone and others, *The General Inquirer* (Cambridge, Mass.: M.I.T. Press, 1966).

8. On the interpersonal dynamics in experimentation see Martin T. Orne, "On the Social Psychology of the Psychological Experiment: With Particular Reference to Demand Characteristics and Their Implications," *American Psychologist,* 17 (1962), 776-83.

9. On the consequences of the experimenter's orientation to subjects and to findings see Robert Rosenthal, *Experimenter Effects in Behavioral Research* (New York: Appleton-Century-Crofts, 1966); and his "Interpersonal Expectations: Effects of the Experimenter's Hypothesis" in Robert Rosenthal and Ralph L. Rosonow, eds., *Artifact in Behavorial Research* (New York: Academic Press, 1969), pp. 182-277.

10. Herbert C. Kelman, "Deception in Social Research," *Transaction,* 3 (July-August 1966), 20-24.

11. On this interdependence see Neil Friedman, *The Social Nature of Psychological Research: The Psychological Experiment as a Social Interaction* (New York: Basic Books, 1967); and Ernst Timaeus, *Experiment and Psychology, On the Social Psychology of Psychological Experiments* (Göttingen: Hogrefe, 1974).

12. For a six-point program to develop such a relation, see Theodore M. Mills, *The Sociology of Small Groups,* lst ed. (Englewood Cliffs, N.J.: Prentice-Hall, Inc., 1967), pp. 53-56.

CHAPTER 4
LEVELS
OF GROUP PROCESS:
BEHAVIOR
AND EMOTION

This and the following three chapters present a sociological way of thinking about groups. As a first step, the present chapter divides complex interpersonal processes into five levels which have been recognized by sociologists to be different and distinct: behavior, emotions, norms, group goals, and group values.[1] It asks the reader to consider the elements on each of these levels as organized into systems, or sub-systems, each with its own features and its own principles of organization. On occasion, it also asks the reader to imagine the experiences of a pair of individuals—one, male; the other, female—who enter a group as totally naïve newcomers but who learn, through progressive stages, to operate on one level after the other until they assume responsibility for the group as a whole and, in that capacity, operate on all five levels simultaneously. We propose that as the newcomers participate on the more advanced levels their subjective experience with the group changes, and that both the demands upon them and their potentials for contributing to the group also change. A thesis of this and the following three chapters is that as they shift from the relatively primitive levels of behavior and emotion to the more sophisticated levels, which involve a comprehension of the group's culture and purpose, both the potential for their growth as individuals and the potential for the growth of group capabilities increase.

Again, but this time more by way of definition, the five levels are as follows:

1. *Behavior:* How persons overtly *act* in the presence of others
2. *Emotions:* The needs persons experience, and the *feelings* they have toward one another and about what happens[2]
3. *Norms:* Ideas about how persons *should* act, *should* feel, and *should* express their feelings
4. *Goals:* Ideas about what is most desirable for groups, as units, to *do*
5. *Values:* Ideas about what is most desirable for groups, as units, to *be* and to *become*

Levels one and two are discussed in this chapter; levels three and four in the next; and the fifth level is discussed in Chapter 6.

At the outset, it is important to recognize that a number of different viewpoints can be taken in interpreting group phenomena. The most common is the viewpoint of the single individual who must confront the group and in some way work out satisfactory relations with the other members. This lone actor is one with whom we can all identify, not only as one from whom we can learn, but also as one whom in our imagination we can counsel and teach. Less common but nonetheless critical for the understanding of sociology is the viewpoint of one who seeks to understand what is happening to the group as a whole. What are the interpersonal dynamics? What is the course of the history of the group as a totality?

While it is true that the elements on the levels listed above are all "within the skin" of the individual or are produced by the individual (elements such as a drive, a feeling, an idea, or an act), it is equally true that these elements may be conceived of both as arrangements among individuals, and as constituting a social system. More specifically, one element on a given level may be considered in its relation to another element on the same level. For example, the act of one person may be considered in relation to acts of other persons, hence the conception of *interaction;* the feelings of one person may be considered in relation to the feelings of others, hence the conception of a structure of affective processes, or, using Redl's term, *group emotion*;[3] one member's idea about what member x should do under certain circumstances may be considered in relation to the ideas that other members have, hence the conception of group *norms* and (with all such ideas about all members in all circumstances) the group's *normative system*; and so on. From this viewpoint, elements on each level are conceived of as being arranged into sub-systems with dynamics of their own quite apart from the dynamics within individual persons who happen to participate in and contribute to them. From this viewpoint, the general question is how the whole complex operates. The sub-systems are as follows:

1. On the level of behavior, the sub-system is the *interaction system*, which is the organization of overt action among persons over time.
2. On the level of emotion, the sub-system is composed of the feelings members experience, consciously or unconsciously, including the emotional responses to events that occur and the configuration of feelings among members which we call the *affective (under)structure.*
3. On the level of norms, the sub-system is the *normative system*, which is the organized, and largely shared, ideas about what members should do and feel, about how these should be regulated, and about what sanctions should be applied when behavior does not coincide with the norms.
4. On the level of goals, the sub-system is the *technical system*, which is the set of ideas about what the group should accomplish, and the plans about how it is to be accomplished.
5. On the level of values, the sub-system is the *executive system*, which consists of the interpretations of what the group *is*, the ideas about what would be desirable for it to become, and ideas about how it might so become.

These five systems are empirically interrelated, for certainly our feelings are affected by what we and others do, our actions are influenced by our ideas, and our rules often change with a change in our goals. And relations among the five are asymmetrical in the sense that under ordinary circumstances interaction patterns are governed by the norms of the group, more than the reverse; the norms, in turn, are governed by the practical demands of the task; task activities are governed by values insofar as one task or goal is chosen over others; and, of course, all of these features can be overridden by feelings, as illustrated by the dissolution of the group through members' lack of commitment. A clear understanding of this complex inter-dependence among the sub-systems is, however, not to be expected until the student of sociology encounters more advanced problems in the study of group dynamics. A first step is to conceive of the sub-systems separately and to comprehend the particular, and perhaps different, principles according to which each respective system operates.

A second advantage of this sequential study of systems regards individual members in the group. Although a group as a whole, or only some of its members, may operate upon all five levels, this does not mean that all of its members must do so. A clear example is our newcomers, for although they may quickly interact with others and immediately have an emotional impact upon them, they cannot operate effectively on the other levels until they have the opportunity of learning what the group's norms, goals, and values are. It is instructive, in fact, to use the newcomers' experience as a general model for suggesting both the principles according to which the sub-systems operate, and the changes in subjective experience as one enters one sub-system after the other. Without suggesting that group entry is always neat and invariable, we trace the newcomers' progress into the group as though it occurs in four clearcut phases: (1) entry into interaction and group emotion—what is done and what is felt; (2) entry into the normative system—what should be done and what should be felt; (3) identification with the group goal; and (4) identification with other members and with the group as a whole in what it might become.

To recap a little: of the five levels, this chapter describes processes on the first two, behavior and emotion. We consider the newcomers' orientation to the group, and the group's reaction to them during this first phase. Other levels, and the new-comers' experiences as they operate on those levels, are considered in following chapters.

BEHAVIOR AND THE INTERACTION SYSTEM

Order

Observations of patterned animal behavior, ranging from traffic control and courting rituals to pecking orders, are well known among ants,[4] bees,[5] fowl,[6] ba-boons,[7] gorillas,[8] and other species. Human behavior is also patterned. Partly be-cause we are properly trained to look beyond the surface of overt behavior in order to infer what a people mean by what they say, or what they want by what they do, we tend to overlook the design that exists on the surface of interpersonal behavior. We tend therefore to underestimate the extent to which humans in general and humans in groups either follow or create an ordered, often ritualized way of interacting. This is gradually being corrected by applying systematic methods of observation like that of Bales described in Chapter 2.

With a set of categories which considers how one act is related to the next, our apprentice observer of the previous chapter is able to record the dynamic relations of interaction. She is able to study the dynamics of the interaction system in its own right. For example, employing a set of categories labeled with letters of the alphabet our observer records in one group the sequence *A B A B A B A B* . . . ; and in another group she records *F K T A G S L W D Q* . . . . The first is *ordered* but the second is *unordered*; she might designate the first "an *A B A B* system" and the second "a random system." Whether the *A B A B* system in question involves a witness replying to a lawyer's questions, or a vendor handing over produce in exchange for money from buyers, the observer can distinguish an ordered system from a random one. And quite apart from the nuances of the action, its causes, its subjective meaning, and its consequences, she can characterize interaction by its formal characteristics. (The question of *why* order occurs in one case but not in another can be reserved for and answered by research on the other four levels.)

Let us say that in another comparison the observer records a sequence in one group that is first *ordered*, then *disordered* (*A B A B A B F T C L K R D* . . .), while in the second group she records a sequence that is first *unordered*, then *ordered* (*D K C R L T F B A B A B A* . . .). Under what conditions, she will be led to ask, does an ordered system lose that order? Under what conditions does an unordered system gain order? What are the differences between groups that exhibit the two types of series?

To carry the observations one step further, let us say that she observes one group wherein a previous order is lost but then regained, and another group wherein a new order appears following a disruption. What are the conditions, she will be led to ask, which differentiate a group that returns to its previous pattern, from a group that shifts to a new order? Whether the first case represents an unsuccessful revolution and the second a successful one, the point is that the systematic features of the sequence of interaction can be recorded and summarized as basic data on the group. Phases from one period to another within a single group may be compared, and sequences in one group may be compared with those in other groups. Order, or lack of order, in act-by-act sequences is an elementary feature of interaction systems; methods for detecting it are relatively simple to devise, and easy to apply.

Distribution of Action
Among Participants

A second feature of interaction systems is the distribution of activity among members. Bales and his associates recorded the frequencies with which each member directed action toward each other member in a series of groups ranging in size from three to 10 persons. A summary of 18 six-person groups is shown in Table 2. Results were obtained by (1) ranking members in each group according to their total output; (2) constructing a matrix with both rows and columns ordered according to rank-order of output; (3) entering into matrix cells the frequencies of actions from each member so ranked to each other member (as well as to the group as a whole); then (4) adding together the 18 matrices.

Table 2   Aggregate Matrix for 18 Sessions of Six-Person Groups

Person Originating Act	To Individuals						Total to Individuals	To Group as a Whole 0	Total Initiated
	1	2	3	4	5	6			
1		1,238	961	545	445	317	3,506	5,661	9,167
2	1,748		443	310	175	102	2,778	1,211	3,989
3	1,371	415		305	125	69	2,285	742	3,027
4	952	310	282		83	49	1,676	676	2,352
5	662	224	144	83		28	1,141	443	1,584
6	470	126	114	65	44		819	373	1,192
Total Received	5,203	2,313	1,944	1,308	872	565	12,205	9,106	21,311

From Robert F. Bales, and others, "Channels of Communication in Small Groups," *American Sociological Review*, 16, no. 4 (August 1951), 463.

Note the gradations throughout the matrix. Once members are ranked by output (and the rows ordered according to that rank), then other totals fall in order: note the column totals, the cell entries in each column, and the cell entries in each row. Also note that with few exceptions, interaction tends toward higher ranks; for example, rank two speaks to rank one more than rank one speaks to rank two (1,748 vs. 1,238), and so on throughout the matrix. All in all, the matrix exhibits a remarkably systematic distribution. It suggests that the way group members tend to interact with one another can be stated in a set of simple principles. The suggestion would be stronger, of course, had each individual group (or a majority of them) exhibited the tendencies before being lumped together.

As a follow-through to these findings, Stephan and Mishler recorded outputs and receipts of students in 36 college discussion groups varying in size from two to 12 members.[9] They discovered that the percentage of contributions of students in a given rank-order could be adequately estimated by the following simple exponential function: $(P_i = ar^{i-1})$, where P_i is the estimated percentage for students ranked i in output, r is the ratio of any rank to the percentage for the next higher rank, and a is the estimate for students ranked highest. When applied to an estimation of receipts, the function served almost as well. (In neither case did their estimates include the instructor.) Their findings are additional evidence that tendencies in the systematic distribution of action among group members can be stated in simple, formal principles.

These observations are of tendencies and are not absolute, as illustrated by Tsai's test of the Mishler model (as modified by Hovrath) where an analysis of the minutes of an United Nations council showed lack of fit between model and actual process.[10] In fact, departures may prove to be as frequent as pure cases, if for no reason other than the influence of such factors as: (1) formal status differences among members (e.g., children in the presence of adults or guests in the presence of their host); (2) the goal of the group and the procedures required to attain the goal (e.g., a teacher instructing students, in contrast to patients reporting to their therapist; or a supervisor clarifying a new directive, in contrast to elders advising the chief); (3) sub-group formations (e.g., a split jury or a group with cliques that have their respective representatives); and (4) personality characteristics of members—and, of course, other factors.

In any case we see that by (1) defining the unit of action, (2) identifying the actor and the one to whom the actor is speaking, and (3) counting acts one can easily characterize a configuration of the interaction system based on activity output. Activity output—ranging from hyperactivity to silence—turns out to be one of the more important variables in determining the structure of the interaction system. Bales and associates factor-analyzed tens of thousands of readings of interaction in a wide variety of groups to find three factors that accounted for most of the variance. Members could be placed along the first dimension, the active and involved at one end and the passive and withdrawn at the other; along the second, the open and friendly at one end and the hostile and independent at the other; and along the third, the hard worker at one end and the "expressive-irresponsible" at the other.[11] Setting aside the last dimension (instrumental vs. expressive) for discussion in the next chapter, the first two dimensions (dubbed "up-down" and "positive-negative" by Bales) form the axes of a plane; any given member can be represented at an intersection of these two variables. These operations provide a simple-yet-powerful representation of the behavorial roles of respective members. The distribution of the points over the plane suggest features of the structure of the interaction system, such as degree of differentiation and location of negativity.

Group Size

The number of persons in a group affects both the distribution and the quality of interaction. Stephan and Mishler confirmed the original observations of Bales and his associates and clarified the effects of group size when they discovered that the parameter a in the function given above changes regularly with group size. They propose that: $a_n = 234/(n + 4)$ for outputs and that: $a_n = 157/(n + 4)$ for receipts. This is to say that, leaving the teacher aside, as classes increase in size, participation becomes flatter—adjacent ranks become more alike both in output and in receipts.

Slater found the quality of action to vary with group size.[12] After using Bales's method to score 24 groups ranging from two to seven members, he devised an "index of inhibition," which consisted of the ratio of "safe" acts to impulsive, aggressive acts (Bales's categories 3, 7, 8, and 11 to categories 1, 2, 4, 10, and 12). Comparing the ratios in groups of various sizes over four discussion sessions, he found (1) that as group size increases, the index of inhibition decreases; and (2) that as members become better acquainted through the course of the meetings, inhibition drops more for larger groups than for smaller ones. For the types of groups he observed, he suggests that as size increases, "the consequences of alienating a single member becomes less and less severe. . . ."

> In the larger group, physical freedom is restricted while psychological freedom is increased. The member has less time to talk, more points of view to integrate and adapt to, and a more elaborate structure into which he must fit. At the same time he is more free to ignore some of these viewpoints, to express his own feelings and ideas in a direct and forceful fashion, and even to withdraw from the fray without loss of face.[13]

Restricted Channels of Interaction

The above studies show that even when interaction is free and open, a systematic pattern tends to appear. Apparently there is an "economy" of interaction, an economy which is modified by a number of variables including group size. As mentioned in Chapter 3, Bavelas considered the causal chain from the other direction. Instead of asking how members tend to order and restrict their own interaction, he asked what effects a fixed or restricted pattern of interaction might have upon the group. What effects might various networks of communication have upon, let us say, satisfaction and effectiveness of the group in solving given problems? In Chapter 3 we described how Bavelas and his associates experimentally established and varied the channels of communication among five members in order to test the effect of such patterns upon group efficiency and member satisfaction.[14]

In a follow-up study, Leavitt tested the effects of four patterns: the circle, ⬠ ; the chain, o–o–o–o–o ; the wheel, ⟠ ; and the "y," ⤙ . He found that speed and accuracy in solving a problem were greater in the last two centralized networks but that, in general, satisfaction was greater in the others.[15] Heise and Miller found that problems requiring an accumulation of information could be better solved in open networks, while problems requiring synthesis and insight could be managed more easily in the centralized ones.[16] Shaw found that persons could better distinguish relevant from irrelevant information in open networks than in others.[17]

In an interesting and important variation, Cohen and Bennis tested the effect of a change in network.[18] One set of groups worked first with the wheel, then with a completely open situation; a second set worked with an open situation on both occasions. They found that whereas the groups having first worked in the wheel tended to remain centralized rather than to shift to a more open and more gratifying network, the groups having first worked in the open network tended to keep channels open rather than to shift to the more efficient, centralized networks. Twenty years later, follow-up studies were conducted on Bavelas's original experiments. Burgess ran an experimental reevaluation,[19] and Mackenzie, using graph theory, reanalyzed the networks, coming up with a superior index of centrality and a decomposition of the original networks into sub-networks that suggested new consequences for the relations between position in a network and behavior.[20] Clearly the evidence indicates that restricted interaction channels affect both member satisfaction (an element in group affect) and problem-solving efficiency (an element of the technical system).

Summary

The few studies reported above suggest certain elementary features of the interaction system. They show both that interpersonal behavior tends to become ordered, and that situational factors affect the characteristics of that order. These are probably indications that future discoveries will show that human interaction is both highly complex and systematic. Presently enough is known to say that our newcomers entering a group are likely to be cast into particular behavioral roles and to enact them whether they and others are aware of it or not. The male is likely to be cast into a stereotypic masculine role and the female into a stereotypic feminine one. These roles are likely to affect their views of the group, what they can learn, what they can and cannot do, and how they feel about themselves and others. Changes in the system will involuntarily alter their roles; and, in turn, what they do or do not do in their roles, particularly as they change, cannot help but affect the rest of the system to some extent.

FEELINGS AND THE AFFECTIVE (UNDER)STRUCTURE

In their study of adolescent groups, Sherif and Sherif reaffirm an important point about groups:

> Individuals do not form groups of their own choosing just to be, mechanically, one of a set, or because of any inherent tendency to conformity, or because they want to regulate their behavior in this or that direction. They come together and interact with strongly felt urges and with desires experienced as their own, whether these be desires to be accepted as a person in one's own right, desires to gain social distinction, sexual urges, wishes for desirable objects and instrumentalities, desires for exciting leisure-time activities, searches for recognition, or desires to prove themselves. . . . Individuals come together . . . and stay together because they experience *some* strong motivational basis. . . . [21]

When in the presence of others, human needs, desires, wishes, and feelings of fear, frustration, estrangement, pleasure, affection, satisfaction, and solidarity are the ingredients of affective processes in the group. No one ingredient exists in isolation, rather they all are in some sort of interdependent relationship. What a person in a group does makes a difference to other members; how one feels has a contagious effect upon the feelings of others; and one's needs, or signs of those needs, arouse emotional responses in others. There is perhaps constant interplay among the emotional experiences of persons in groups.

Interplay often results in a structure of emotional relations among members which can quite easily be ascertained, formulated, and confirmed, as in the following two cases described by Redl:

> There is a group of sixteen-year-old girls in a class of a girls' high school. In charge of them is a male teacher—young, attractive, but narcissistic enough so that they are not too greatly frightened sexually from the outset. It is known that in some such cases "the whole class falls in love with him." From that moment on, they will act like a group. . . . Despite their infatuation for him, it would not be surprising if the teacher complained that he had trouble with discipline—that these girls did not obey him or follow his wishes without pressure. [22]

> In a coeducational class of approximately sixteen-year-old children, there is one especially pretty girl, rather narcissistic. In similar situations one frequently finds a whole cluster of boys loving and adoring her in various ways, but equally unsuccessful insofar as their wish for exclusive possession goes. The girl is equipped with special skill for keeping them all equidistant and yet equally near. Symptoms of dense group formation may sometimes be observed among these boys. They seem very close to each other, and yet their relationship is not genuine friendship. . . . This becomes evident when the girl ultimately decides in favor of one of her suitors. The other boys then begin to hate

him as their rival, with the exception perhaps of the one or two who may move even closer to the successful colleague and, thus, enjoy some of the satisfactions denied to them. . . .[23]

"There is no doubt," explains Redl, "that the teacher (in the first example) and the girl (in the second example) are playing the role of central person without whose presence this type of group formative process would not have been evolved."[24] The mechanism of group formation is: "The children choose one and the same person as an object of their love, and on the basis of this similarity they develop group emotions between each other."[25] There is no doubt, one can add, that the emotional orientations of the persons in both cases are arranged in a clear and ascertainable structure.

Bion observed an interesting phenomenon in his therapy groups. He found that his patients interpreted the purpose of the group to be his healing them. They assumed that they had no work to do themselves, rather that he was to do it all. They were surprised and puzzled, then later angered, by his assumption that *they* were the ones who had to work if they were to get well. Their assumption of being dependent upon him polarized their emotions towards him, and his contrary assumption that they work to understand themselves polarized his feelings towards them. Consequently, the affective processes in this case were structured around two opposite poles.[26]

Whereas both Redl and Bion suggest mechanisms according to which a group forms, Freud describes a hypothetical affective (under)structure that substantially precludes group formation. We refer to his famous description of the primal horde.[27] The value of the formulation is not its correspondence to the life of earliest humans (although Freud seemed convinced of its plausibility, others have dismissed the formulation as a "just so" story because of the lack of supporting evidence); instead, its value is in its correspondence to the unconscious emotional relations among members—or, in our present terms, affective (under)structure—that is likely to exist in any small group where one person has unquestioned superior power over others.[28] The following are highlights of Freud's formulation.

The father (and chief) is omnipotent and absolutely narcissistic. His personal wants are served without respect to others. He leads a band of impotent sons who are dependent upon him for protection yet who are deprived of all sources of gratification, including sex. The chief preempts all of the women for himself. He is both revered and hated by the sons. Their desire to kill him is immobilized first by the fear of retaliation in case they do not succeed, and second by the fear of being murdered by the strongest of the brothers in case they do succeed. The women (hardly mentioned by Freud) apparently respond to the power and superiority of the chief. Fear, reverence, hatred, attraction, omnipotence, impotence, self-indulgence, total deprivation—these are the emotions which in a particular arrangement constitute the primal horde. Narcissistic omnipotence on the one hand and narcissistic impotence on the other are its central features.

The Concept of Affective (Under)Structure

As the examples above suggest, the elements of group emotion include (1) the needs and drives which serve in the first place as causes of group formation; (2) feelings of satisfaction or frustration resulting from actual group experience; (3) interpersonal attachments and animosities; and (4) feelings of attachment to, or alienation from, the group as a whole. In general, the concept of group emotion refers to the configuration of those conscious or unconscious instinctual and emotional elements and processes occurring within and among persons which affect what the aggregate of members can and cannot do, say, believe, and think, or affect the likelihood of what is done, said, believed, and thought. If we conceive of a field of forces operating at each moment and affecting what does and does not happen in the group; and if we select those forces which originate in members' drives and feelings; and, finally, if we conceive of those particular forces together, as a differentiated and organized arrangement of forces—then that arrangement is what is meant by the affective (under)structure.

Can individual emotions be conceived of collectively? Since a group *per se* cannot think, is it not fallacious to use the notion of "group mind"? Since emotions are internal, individual processes, and not group processes (in the sense that a group might "feel" something), is it not fallacious to refer to feelings in group terms?

An analogy may help to suggest the usefulness of the notion of collective group phenomena. Consider iron filings distributed at random over a surface.[29] (By "random" is meant that if one photographed a number of scattered inch-squares on the surface and compared the distribution of filings in the various photographs, one would be unable to identify by the distribution of the filings the location of the area photographed.) Next, assume that a magnetic current is passed through the field. The filings alter their orientation and line up in some characteristic pattern. The current, as a vector passing through the field, has organized the filings. Patterns in photographs of selected areas would now reveal the location of those areas, for they are simply parts of a larger, organized field. Although the vector does not appreciably alter the individual character of each filing, it does alter the relationship among the filings. By passing first one, then another vector through the field, one may observe and compare the different types of relationships resulting from the various vectors. One may meaningfully refer to structures of relations among individual elements.

In the human situation, instinctual and emotional processes occurring within individuals correspond to the filings. Events which arouse, evoke, alter, or transform those processes are vectors corresponding to the electrical current. When such events either arrange or rearrange into a recognizable pattern the set of emotional processes among a number of group members, we may meaningfully and legitimately refer to a structure of affective processes.[30] Here are three examples of vectors that alter the affective (under)structures: (1) The presence of an outside observer usually alters the emotional state of members; they feel vulnerable and, as we saw in Chapter 1, seek, perhaps unconsciously, either to incorporate or to expel the observer. (2) The attractiveness and narcissism of the girl in Redl's second example above is a vector: it evokes both love for her and, among those who love her, a sense of being in the same group. (3) The dominance of the chief in the primal horde.

Formulating the Dynamics of Group Affect

Although many persons operate effectively with an intuitive sense of interpersonal dynamics, the step from *familiarity with* to formulating an effective way of *thinking about* emotional processes is a large and difficult one. Aside from ancient and durable observations such as the function of the scapegoat and the solidifying effects of an external enemy, the more advanced attempts at formulation have been made by practitioners, clinicians, teachers, and consultants who have had the opportunity to observe a variety of long-term groups and to identify those formations and dynamic changes which tend to be common or to recur.

For example, Bion, in addition to identifying the group's assumption of dependence upon him (mentioned above), identified three formations: (1) mobilization of group energy for either attack against a target (fight) or for an escape *en masse* from the field (flight); (2) turning to one another for intimate contact and gratification (pairing); and (3) rechanneling instinctive processes into joint work.[31] Semrad, a psychoanalyst, group therapist, and group trainer, proposed that a necessary condition for the development of a working relationship among members is that the leader enter intentionally the role of scapegoat, thereby absorbing the hostility arising from various sources, and freeing members to deal more easily with one another and with the group's task.[32] Redl identified 10 mechanisms whereby orientation toward a central person results in group formation. One was referred to above. Others include: (1) the case when members love their leader, identify with the leader in their ego-ideal (what they would most like to be) and, with this in common, are then able to identify with one another—a mechanism first formulated by Freud in *Group Psychology and the Analysis of the Ego*; (2) the case when members fear their leader, identify with the leader in their "super-ego," become subject to joint constraint and, although together, lack comradeship; and (3) the case when members who might be overcome by guilt feelings and fear of their own drives are saved and brought together by a person who, being free of their conflicts, easily does what they dare not do.[33]

From a different viewpoint, Whitaker and Lieberman have clarified otherwise confusing episodes in therapy groups by identifying the underlying and largely shared conflict that members are experiencing and attempting to resolve. A "focal conflict" exists, for example, when, countering the wish of each member to be specially favored by the therapist, is the fear that the therapist will punish them for such a demand. One attempt to resolve the conflict is for members to become more alike.[34] The combination of the wish, the fear, and the mirroring of similarities constitutes one dynamic through which affect becomes structured.

Though sociologists historically have tended to neglect study of emotions and their social configurations, recent attempts have been made to extend the boundaries of theoretical models to include them. The works of Kemper and of Heise are important cases in point.[35]

Research on Affective Processes

As we indicated, systematic empirical research on emotional processes creates difficult technical problems. For one thing, emotional processes cannot be directly observed, but instead must be inferred from indirect manifestations. Since there are many modes through which a given feeling is made manifest, and of course similar modes reflecting different feelings, a sizable sample of episodes is required before one is well-enough understood for the observer to infer reliably one's emotional state. Consequently, there is a lag between the emotional experience and its assessment—a lag that is considerable when only one person is being assessed, and so of course much greater when the experiences of all members are being considered. Indeed, as the number of persons to be understood increases, the interrelations increase at a geometric rate, and in short order the problem can become overwhelming. Finally, since these interrelations are configurational rather than atomistic, and systemic rather than additive, adequate assessment requires information on first-, second-, and third-order relationships—and this, of course, extends the lag even further. In fact, few persons (if any) have been able both to trace the course of changes in affective structures in a given group, and clearly tell others how it is done.

In spite of these difficulties, researchers have tried to assess processes related to group emotion.[36] Mahl, for example, has attempted to devise a technique for assessing feelings of individuals.[37] Birdwhistell's early work on "coding" body movement and gestures for the feelings they might express has been followed by an expanding effort on the part of researchers in various disciplines to interpret nonverbal communication.[38] Moreno's pioneering work on interpersonal bonds and preferences has been followed in a similar fashion by efforts to obtain reliable and valid data on their underlying structures.[39] Using another approach, Horwitz and Cartwright used projective techniques to bring out latent group processes.[40] The latter technique is based on the assumption that just as dreams, interpretations of ink blots, and stories told in response to pictures provide clues to an individual's emotional processes, a group's mythology, rituals, and artistic creations, including joint stories told in response to projective pictures, provide clues about the latent emotional issues among its members. In an exploratory study they found a correspondence between the content of group stories and features of the group as estimated by other means—for example, between the frequency of hostile acts by characters in the story and freedom of expressing hostility in the group, and between positive acts by characters in the story and a sense of solidarity in the group.

Using a similar technique, Torrance asked 71 eleven-man bomber crews to tell joint stories about two pictures, one of a group in a working situation and the second of a group during off-hours. In comparing crews rated on effectiveness by their superiors, he found that effective crews told stories about working groups that were both more successful and more solidary, and that effective crews were more emotionally expressive in response to the informal picture, including more conflict, more friendship, more discord, and more pleasure.[41] Mills used projective pictures to estimate changes both in members' feelings toward the person in charge, and in members' emotional relationship with one another, over a six-week period.[42] Selecting the "authority figure" as a critical focal point in affective structures, Mann and associates devised an empirical method for screening every act and every statement for indications of how members orient themselves emotionally toward that authority.[43] More recently Bales and associates have devised an empirical method to "get at" the underlying feelings of group members by identifying and interpreting the images they use in their speech.[44] For example, comments such as "This seems to be a friendly group" and "It was a suffocating experience" are taken to reflect feelings being experienced by those who make them. Moreover, the researchers visualize the images acting in a three-dimensional space comparable to the space used to locate interaction (referred to on page 75 above) so that "friendly group" is to be scored as *upward* and *positive* and "suffocating experience" scored *downward* and *negative*. Their work and the studies mentioned above suggest the possibility that both the latent emotional relations among members, and the emotional orientation of the group as a whole, can be inferred from a careful analysis of what is done and of the content of what is said in the group. including what is said about outside objects, events, groups, and so on.

Summary

The major points about affective processes in groups are as follows:

1. Persons do not shed their instinctive drives, their desires, their wishes, or their feelings when they come into contact with one another; instead, their confrontation with one another is in large part in the service of those drives and feelings.
2. In the interpersonal situation, a given person's feelings rarely exist in isolation; instead, they both influence the feelings of others and are affected by the feelings of others.
3. This interplay of drives, feelings, and emotions (conscious and unconscious) results in more or less complex configurations whose characteristics and consequences cannot be fully explained with reference solely to the experiences of individual members; those configurations, as they form and change—sometimes kaleidoscopically—are affective (under)structures.
4. A given person's part in the configuration is that person's *primordial role,* examples being "the person everyone loves," "the one who can heal us all," and (on the negative side) "the black sheep" and "the scapegoat."
5. Affective (under)structures differ in their effect upon group capabilities. For example, a group based upon fear and suspicion of its leader tends to be more edgy and less venturesome than one based upon respect for and trust in its leader.
6. Primordial roles differ in their effect upon individual capabilities. For example, "the darling" of the group tends to be kept just that while "the instigator" is egged-on.
7. The overall growth of the group and its various members is affected either positively or negatively by the affective (under)structure.
8. Of the theoretical models sketched in Chapter 1, the psychoanalytic model provides the most direct access to thought about affective processes and their social configurations.
9. More systematic research is required in order to advance beyond the suggestions made above about these structures to the stage where we have a working knowledge not only of the dynamics of given structures but also of how changes on the level of feelings and emotions affect, and are affected by, changes on other levels of group process.

TWO LEVELS: BEHAVIOR AND EMOTIONS

Early in the study of groups it was not uncommon for observers to assume that overt behavior reflected directly underlying feelings experienced by group members. Thus, the member who initiated more negative acts (as per the categories on page 50) than positive acts was taken to be more hostile than friendly; and the group that exhibited more negative behavior than positive was more disorganized and less cohesive than those where the ratio was the reverse. It soon became apparent that one-to-one correspondence between behavior and emotion (and between interaction structures and affective structures) was easily disproved. For example, the fact that married couples showed more disagreement than strangers meeting for the first time did not mean that they were less friendly, less cohesive, or less emotionally attached; the fact that a boss acted friendly, and to whom others acted polite and friendly, did not mean that he was not feared and they not mistreated; the fact that hyperactive group members were given more attention than others did not mean that others did not discredit and reject them. Evidence accumulated that the interaction level is both analytically and empirically distinct from the level of personal and interpersonal affect. One simply cannot infer the structure of underlying feelings from the patterns of overt behavior (although there are of course indirect linkages). Realization of this led to multiple scoring of the ongoing group process, for example, scoring simultaneously both the problem-solving relevance of action and the content of what is said. The most recent case in point is *SYMLOG*, the method of Bales and others referred to earlier. *SYMLOG* stands for "System for the Multiple Level Observation of Groups." One level scored is interaction: Does the act "move" in the *up* (assertive) or *down* (deferential) direction? Does it "move" in the *positive* (friendly) or the *negative* (unfriendly) direction? Does it move *forward* (toward task accomplishment) or *backward* (toward the satisfaction of personal needs)? The second level is symbolic—interpreting the image used "as a picture of an emotionally laden focus of attention." Does a given picture reflect feelings of moving *up* or *down*? *positive* or *negative*? *forward* or *backward*? By applying the same dimensions to the two different levels, the *SYMLOG* model promises the possibility of more efficient tests of the dynamic relations between levels, at least along those dimensions.

A Summary for the Newcomers

In the beginning newcomers characteristically find themselves adjusting to existing patterns of behavior and seeking a secure position from which to operate. They look to others for guidelines and usually respond by doing what others call on them to do. Our pair is no exception. She surveys the females and the males, wondering how her own gender will affect her experience. He scans the group to locate those who make him uncomfortable and seeks those with whom he feels at ease. Each becomes involved in working out a niche in the group. In being oriented toward patterns of action they act in behavioral roles; in responding to the needs and feelings both in themselves and others they experience their primordial roles.

Compared to later phases, their orientation is presymbolic, precultural, and prenormative. Although they follow patterns, they are not aware of the meaning the group gives to the patterns; although they experience emotional exchanges, they do not appreciate their significance to the group. This is because they do not yet know the ideas that exist in the minds of other members. While she may quickly sense (under)structures of feelings and he may detect differences in the way members act, they need more information and need to employ a higher order of thought processes before they can determine how members define what is going on and how they think about it. Only when they can infer such ideas (or are told them and can accurately assess what they are told) can they learn the group's culture, know what the values are, and know what the rules and norms are. Only then can they know the meaning–the local group meaning–of what they and others do and feel. Until they are able to infer ideas about action and about feelings, and to relate those ideas to their own ideas, they remain uncertain as to what, in terms of the local culture, those acts and feelings in fact are.

The length of time a newcomer remains at the behavioral and primordial levels varies from very short for the experienced and versatile person to a number of years for the infant, and to forever for members of the sub-human species such as baboons, gorillas, and so on. As indicated above, although such sub-human groups are ordered and organized, they are apparently incapable of using symbols and, therefore, are incapable of having an idea or of inferring an idea about how life should be ordered and organized. This means that they are unable to advance from the behavioral and the primordial levels to the normative level or to the other levels. In our discussion, we assume that the newcomers are able to symbolize, and consequently to advance to other levels.

NOTES

1. Talcott Parsons and Edward A. Shils, eds., *Toward a General Theory of Action* (Cambridge, Mass.: Harvard University Press, 1951), pp. 3–29, 53–76.

2. On feelings and emotions, see Magda Arnold, *Feelings and Emotions* (New York: Academic Press, 1970); on emotional relations among members see Carl W. Backman, "Attraction in Interpersonal Relations" in Morris Rosenberg and Ralph Turner, eds., *Social Psychology: Sociological Perspectives* (New York: Basic Books, 1981), pp. 235–68.

3. Fritz Redl, "Group Emotion and Leadership," *Psychiatry,* 5 (1942), 573–96; reprinted in A. Paul Hare, Edgar F. Borgatta, and Robert F. Bales, eds., *Small Groups: Studies in Social Interaction* (New York: Knopf, 1955), pp. 73–75.

4. Wilhelm Goetsch, *The Ants* (Ann Arbor: University of Michigan Press, 1957).

5. K. Von Frisch, *Bees, Their Vision, Chemical Sensors and Language* (Ithaca, N.Y.: Cornell University Press, 1950).

6. C. A. Murchison, *Handbook of Social Psychology* (Worcester, Mass.: Clark University Press, 1935).

7. S. Zukerman, *The Social Life of Monkeys and Apes* (New York: Harcourt Brace Jovanovich, Inc., 1932).

8. George B. Schaller, *The Mountain Gorilla, Ecology, and Behavior* (Chicago: University of Chicago Press, 1963).

9. Frederick F. Stephan and Elliott G. Mishler, "The Distribution of Participation in Small Groups: An Exponential Approximation," *American Sociological Review,* 17 (1952), 598–608; reprinted in Hare, Borgatta, and Bales, eds., *Small Groups,* pp. 367–79.

10. Tsai Yung-Mei, "Hierarchical Structure of Participation in Natural Groups," *Behavioral Science,* 22 (Jan. 1977), 38–40.

11. Robert F. Bales, *Personality and Interpersonal Behavior* (New York: Holt, Rinehart & Winston, 1970), pp. 3–21, 30–50.

12. Philip E. Slater, "Contrasting Correlates of Group Size," *Sociometry,* 21 (1958), 129–39.

13. Ibid., p. 135. For a summary of research on the effects of group size see A. Paul Hare, *Handbook of Small Group Research,* 2nd ed. (New York: Free Press, 1976), pp. 214–31.

14. See pp. 58–59. See also Dorwin Cartwright and Alvin Zander, eds., *Group Dynamics,* 2nd ed. (Evanston, III.: Row, Peterson, 1960), pp. 669–82.

15. Harold J. Leavitt, "Some Effects of Certain Communication Patterns on Group Performance," *Journal of Abnormal and Social Psychology,* 46 (1951), 38–50.

16. G. A. Heise and G. A. Miller, "Problem Solving by Small Groups Using Various Communication Nets," *Journal of Abnormal and Social Psychology,* 46 (1951), 327–36; reprinted in Hare, Borgatta, and Bales, eds., *Small Groups,* pp. 353–67.

17. Mark E. Shaw, "Some Effects of Irrelevant Information upon Problem Solving by Small Groups," *Journal of Social Psychology,* 47 (1958), 33–37.

18. A. M. Cohen and Warren G. Bennis, "Predicting Organization in Changed Communication Networks," *Journal of Psychology,* 54 (1962), 391–416.

19. R. L. Burgess, "Communication Networks: An Experimental Reevaluation," in R. L. Burgess and D. Bushnell, eds., *Behavioral Sociology* (New York: Columbia University Press, 1969), pp. 127-42.

20. Kenneth D. Mackenzie, "Structural Centrality in Communications Networks," *Psychometrika,* 31 (March, 1966) 17–25; and his "Decomposition of Communication Networks," *Journal of Mathematical Psychology,* 4 (1967) 162–73.

21. Muzafer Sherif and Carolyn W. Sherif, *Reference Groups, Exploration into Conformity and Deviation of Adolescents* (New York: Harper & Row, Pub., 1964), pp. 243–44.

22. Redl, "Group Emotion and Leadership," p. 79.

23. Ibid., pp. 79–80.

24. Ibid., p. 80.

25. Ibid.

26. W. R. Bion, *Experiences in Groups, and Other Papers* (New York: Basic Books, 1959), pp. 29–34, 77–86.

27. Sigmund Freud, *Group Psychology and the Analysis of the Ego* (New York: Liveright, 1949), pp. 90–100. For suggested links between Freud's image of the primal horde and political and social structures see Norman O. Brown, "Liberty," in *Love's Body* (New York: Random House, 1966), pp. 3–31.

28. R. Holmes, "University Seminar and the Primal Horde," *British Journal of Sociology* (June 1967).

29. From an example given by Paul A. Weiss in Roy R. Grinker, ed., *Toward a Unified Theory of Human Behavior* (New York: Basic Books, 1950), pp. 117–21.

30. Leroy Wells, Jr., "The Group as a Whole: A Systematic Socioanalytic Perspective on Interpersonal and Group Relations," in C. P. Alderfer and C. L. Cooper, eds., *Advances in Experiential Social Processes,* Vol. 2 (New York: John Wiley, 1980), pp. 165–99.

31. Bion, *Experiences in Groups,* pp. 77–113.

32. Elvin Semrad and others, "The Field of Group Psychotherapy," *International Journal of Group Psychotherapy,* 13 (1963), 452–575; also see Philip E. Slater, *Microcosm* (New York: John Wiley, 1966).

33. Redl, "Group Emotion and Leadership," pp. 86–87. Also see Graham S. Gibbard and others, eds., *Analysis of Groups* (San Francisco: Jossey-Bass, 1974).

34. Dorothy Stock Whitaker and Morton A. Lieberman, *Psychotherapy Through the Group Process* (New York: Lieber-Atherton, 1964), pp. 14–40.

35. Theodore D. Kemper, *A Social Interactional Theory of Emotion* (New York: John Wiley, 1978); David Heise, *Understanding Events: Affect and the Construction of Social Experience* (Cambridge, Eng.: Cambridge University Press, 1979); also see S. Schott, "Emotion and Social Life, A Symbolic Interactionist Analysis," *American Journal of Sociology,* 84, no. 6 (1979) 1317–34.

36. Warren G. Bennis and others, eds., Part I: "Emotional Expressions in Interpersonal Relationships," *Interpersonal Dynamics,* 3rd ed. (Homewood, III.: Dorsey, 1973), pp. 11–126.

37. For a discussion of this problem area and for references, see George F. Mahl and G. Schulze, "Psychological Research in the Extra Linguistic Area," in T. A. Sebeok, A. S. Hayes, and Mary C. Bateson, eds., *Approaches to Semiotics* (London: Mouton, 1964), pp. 51-124.

38. R. L. Birdwhistell, *Introduction to Kinesics* (Louisville, Ky.: University of Louisville Press, 1952); and for reviews of the expanded work see M. L. Knapp, *Nonverbal Communication in Human Interaction* (New York: Holt, Rinehart & Winston, 1977); and S. Wertz, ed., *Nonverbal Communication,* 2nd ed. (New York: Oxford University Press, 1979).

39. For reviews of research see Gardner Lindzey and D. Byrne, "Measurement of Social Choice and Interpersonal Attractiveness," in Gardner Lindzey and Elliott Aronson, eds., *Handbook of Social Psychology,* 2nd ed. (Reading, Mass.: Addison-Wesley, 1968), Vol. II, 452-525; and Dexter Dunphy, "The Measurement of Interpersonal Sentiments," in his *The Primary Group* (New York: Appleton-Century-Crofts, 1972), pp. 225-30.

40. M. Horwitz and Dorwin Cartwright, "A Projective Method for the Diagnosis of Group Properties," *Human Relations,* 6 (1953), 397-410.

41. E. P. Torrance, "Perception of Group Functioning as a Predictor of Group Performance," *Journal of Social Psychology,* 42 (1955), 271-82.

42. Theodore M. Mills, "Authority and Group Emotion," in Warren G. Bennis and others, *Interpersonal Dynamics* (Homewood, Ill.: Dorsey, 1964), pp. 94-108; also see Michael P. Farrell, "Collective Projection and Group Structure: The Relationship Between Deviance and Projection in Groups," *Small Group Behavior,* 10 (Feb. 1979), 81-100.

43. Richard D. Mann and others, *Interpersonal Styles and Group Development* (New York: John Wiley, 1967) and Richard D. Mann and others, *The College Classroom: Conflict, Change and Learning* (New York: John Wiley, 1970).

44. Robert F. Bales and Stephen P. Cohen, *SYMLOG: A System for the Multiple Level Observation of Groups* (New York: Free Press, 1979).

CHAPTER 5
LEVELS
OF GROUP PROCESS:
NORMS AND GOALS

In their study of adolescent groups in the Southwestern United States, Sherif and Sherif found that although a boy may be a skillful basketball player, he will not become a *bona fide* member of the gang unless he learns (1) that he should never criticize a fellow's performance while in competition; (2) that while in competition "it is O.K. for him to foul if he can get away with it" but that (3) it is not O.K. when practicing with fellow members (though he will find that the leader has a right to foul more frequently than do others).[1] He must learn many other rules, including (4) that stealing is permissible providing one uses common sense in not getting caught, that one has a clear plan, that one does not have too many persons involved, and that one takes other reasonable precautions; (5) that going with a new girl is permissible so long as it is announced to the group in case there are any objections; (6) that one does not trespass upon another's right to go out with a girl while he is exercising that right; and most important, (7) that one must protect the integrity of the group. The newcomer will be told truthfully that some boys have been expelled from the group because they "ratted" to parents or to the police, and others because they deserted the gang in a street fight. Thus, the prospective member learns that there are rules he must not violate if he is to be accepted in the group, and that he must demonstrate an ability to learn and to know rules, and to govern himself according to them. In general, it is through his response to group codes that the newcomer signifies his desire to be a full-fledged member.

NORMS AND NORMATIVE CONTROL

The Concept of Group Norms

Rarely can rules be inferred directly from behavior; they are ideas rather than patterns of behavior, and so must be learned as ideas. This fact is discovered by newcomers through typical object lessons. For example, young children find that they are prohibited from doing what they see others in the family doing; that what was rewarded in the past is now punished; that what is permitted on one occasion is prohibited on another; that there is not a general one-to-one correspondence between the type of acts children and others perform, and rewards and punishments. The new gang member's object lesson is similar when he discovers that while his fouling in practice offends the group, the leader's fouling does not. The obvious inference is that fouling has various meanings and that the principle that applies to him is not the same as the principle that applies to the leader. Still, in other instances, when he observes that some acts (such as "ratting") are disapproved of no matter who commits them, the obvious inference is that this principle applies to everyone equally. Thus, through experience he learns that the significance of an act is not in the act itself but in the *meaning* the group gives it. And he learns that this meaning may alter according to who commits it, and the circumstances under which it is committed. Fortunately for the student of sociology, though this variability in the meanings given to behavior is confusing to the newcomer, it is quite simply accounted for through the sociological concept of *group norms*.

Group norms are ideas in the minds of members about what should and should not be done by a specific member under specified circumstances.[2] Referring to the example above, a shared idea among members is that no one should foul a fellow member during practice, but that because of his position, the leader has a special privilege in this regard. It is a shared idea that one does not trespass on another's right to go out with a girl, though if there is to be an exception, it would be made for the leader. Finally, it is a shared idea that new members and the youngest members be given the disagreeable tasks. Because norms are ideas and are therefore subject to elaborate qualifications, they can specify the many fine distinctions necessary to accommodate different persons, times, occasions, and circumstances.

Classification of Norms

Norms, which have all too often been thought of as haphazard or random standards, actually help orient persons to each other, providing guidelines as to how certain universal interpersonal issues are to be managed by the parties in question. Parsons presents a classification of these issues and of the possible guidelines.[3] Norms in any society or group, he suggests, must provide answers to questions relating to at least four issues: (1) Are relations among members to be based upon the expression of the feelings they have toward one another, or upon the assumption that those feelings are to be suppressed and controlled (i.e., are affective processes to have precedence over normative control, or vice-versa)? (2) Is involvement with one another to be total and unbounded (as with parent and child), or is it to be restricted and specific (as with driving instructor and pupil)? (3) Is the significance of the other to be due to the unique relation one has with him or her (as brother, sister, cousin, or friend), or is it to be due to the fact that he or she represents a type, or a class, of person (a servant, a client, or an employer)? (4) Is the significance of the other to be due to his or her qualities (steady and wise), or is it to be due to how he or she performs (as a scientist, as an athlete, and so on)?

The norms across groups may be compared by reference to the answers their members give to these questions. Although various combinations of answers are possible, some are more likely than others, and with two combinations an easy contrast can be made between the traditional primary group and more technical groups—for example, between the family (where relations are based upon expression of feelings, unbounded involvement, unique ties, and personal qualities) and the surgical team (where relations are based upon suppression of emotions, restricted involvement, technical qualifications, and skill in performing the prescribed tasks).

Parsons's classification is useful for comparing different groups because it may be applied to all members alike in a given group, and may therefore be used to characterize the group as a whole. Another type of classification is helpful for analyzing the differences in privileges and obligations among members within the same group: Hohfeld's classification of bilateral legal relations is an example; though designed for more formal legal systems, the scheme has been applied to primitive societies by Hoebel, and is appropriate for small groups as well.[4] Briefly put, the four basic normative relations are as follows: First, person A has a *demand-right* while person B has a *duty*, meaning that according to the law (norms), A has a right to expect that B do (or refrain from doing) x for him, while B has a duty to do (or refrain from doing) x for A. Example: gang member John has a right to go out with his girlfriend without interference from other members; the other members have a duty not to interfere. Second, person A has a *privilege-right* while person B has *no demand-right*, meaning that A can do x without being subject to B's penalty, and that B has no redress if A does x. Example: John may sell his car to anyone he chooses without becoming subject to disapproval from another member, Pete, while Pete has no redress when John sells his car to whomever he wants. Third, person A has *power* while B is *liable*, meaning that A may voluntarily create new duties for B, and new demand-rights for himself. Example: in response to gang leader Harry's request for volunteers to do a special job, Pete volunteers. Harry may or may not accept Pete as a volunteer—that is his power; but if he does accept, Pete cannot renege—that is his liability. Fourth, A is *immune* while B has *no power*, meaning that A is not obligated to accept a new relation proposed by B, while B has no power to create the relation if A chooses not to do so. Example: in response to John's proposal that henceforth gang decisions be made by majority vote, the leader, Harry, announces that the question will be discussed later. Harry is free to accept or reject John's proposal; John has no power if Harry happens not to accept the proposal.

Norms vary in the ease with which they can be learned. Some (such as statements in bylaws and code books) are codified; some are easily recognized and verbalized by members; others are less explicit and become apparent only when they are violated; still others are unconscious, as in the case of some taboos which are in themselves unthinkable ideas. Whether easily learned or not, group norms are a set of statements about feelings and behavior. They are cognitive and moral statements which screen, evaluate, prescribe, and proscribe feelings and actions. As statements they are distinct from feelings and from behavior. They exist in symbolic form in the mind, and are elements of group culture. Their dynamics are cultural rather than emotional and behavioral, and it is for this reason that they are considered to be on a distinct level differentiated from the levels of behavior and emotion.

Deviance

In gangs reported by Sherif and Sherif, it is deviant to criticize a fellow player during competition; it is deviant to go with a new girl without clearance; it is deviant to "rat" to the police; and it is deviant to leave during a fight. The formal sociological concept is simple: An act is deviant when it violates a shared idea about what, on the occasion in question, should or should not be done.[5]

Of course, behavior may in some circumstances depart from tradition without being deviant. For instance, although a passive member may become highly active, such a change is not in itself deviant; it would be deviant only when the norms prescribed that he remain passive. Also, taking an unpopular position on an issue is not deviant unless there is a norm prescribing that all hold similar opinions. Correspondingly, although altering one's feelings toward another constitutes a change in group emotion, such a change is not deviant unless there exists a norm prescribing the former emotional relationship. Deviance, to repeat, refers to the formal relationship of action in violation of the norms.

Sanctions

Sanctions are acts in response to other acts. They carry at least two messages, either or both of which may be explicit or implicit. The first message refers to the relation of another act to the norms (such as, "What you have done was what should have been done," or "That act goes against the rules"). The second is a demand about future relations between actions and norms, either to reinforce a previous relation ("We should like to have you do more of what you have done") or to alter a previous relation ("You must cease and desist"). In the latter case, what must be changed in order to achieve conformity varies from altering a discrete act to altering the total relation of the member of the group. For example, negative statements may vary greatly in range, thus: (a) "*You* are accepted but that type of *act* is inappropriate"; (b) "Not only is that act unacceptable, but your attitude is wrong"; (c) "Your action, your attitude, and your relation to the group are all inappropriate"; (d) "Your membership in the group is to be terminated"; (e) "Your life is to be terminated." Of course, like all other actions, sanctions are themselves subject to norms, whether they be based on an accurate assessment of those norms, or an erroneous assessment. And they may be legal or illegal, legitimate or nonlegitimate—and, therefore, either conforming or deviant.

The Normative System

In larger societies the law of the land and the judicial system are familiar as explicit and formal parts of the normative system. Other components are less familiar. Although many societies and most small groups neither codify all their laws nor formalize all their judicial procedures, they nonetheless regulate their expression of feelings, and their interaction with reference to a more or less complex set of ideas about what should and should not be done. This set is designated *the normative system*. As a concept, the normative system refers to more than norms; it refers in addition to ideas about how norms themselves should be maintained, reinforced, and even changed. For instance, to assess the normative system of a group, one abstracts from the total group culture the following overlapping sets of ideas: (1) the norms; (2) by implication, the definitions of deviance; (3) the order of importance of the various norms; (4) by implication, the seriousness of deviant acts; (5) the boundaries of the norms (defining what is of group concern and what is of private concern, defining, in Hohfeld's terms, areas of immunity and no-demand right); and (6) the arrangement according to which norms, sanctions, and the boundaries of the normative system itself are to be legitimately altered. Altogether, the normative system refers to how social control *should* be exercised in the group. How control processes actually operate—in particular, whether they conform to or depart from stipulations in the normative system—is a question to be answered by empirical investigation.

Dynamics of Normative Control

How norms evolve, how they are learned and maintained, how they influence persons and events and, in turn, how they are modified by circumstances, are central problems in the sociology of groups.[6] The following sample of hypotheses and propositions only suggests the range of interest and viewpoints of those concerned with such questions. In 1951, Festinger and Thibaut hypothesized that the more cohesive the group (that is, the greater the total set of forces upon members to remain in the group), the greater the group pressures upon members to conform to the group norms.[7] A corollary is that the greater the attraction to the group, the greater the pressure to conform. Although Festinger cites evidence from a field study and a number of laboratory experiments to support the hypothesis, there remains a question of how cohesive groups in these studies actually were, and of whether factors in the situation other than cohesion might have contributed to observed differences in conformity.[8]

More recently, Walker and Heyns have argued that even if group pressure is greater in cohesive groups, such pressure alone would not be enough to cause a change in behavior toward the group norms.[9] A change depends specifically upon whether, for the person in question, conformity is a means of reducing personal needs. When need reduction is contingent upon conformity, then persons modify their behavior and attitudes. It is under these conditions that the principle "the stronger the need, the greater the tendency to conform" applies. Thus, if in a gang confidence is placed only in those who demonstrate their unconditional commitment to the gang by conforming, then the more a boy wants to belong, the more likely he is to alter his thought and style to coincide with the norms. "For social pressure to be effective in producing conformity," Walker and Heyns suggest, "the person must see conformity as an effective avenue to achieving the goal of acceptance of the group."[10]

In an intricately designed experiment which has been replicated by Emerson,[11] Schachter tested the hypothesis that when a member in a cohesive group deviates, others will first actively try to convert him to the norms and then, if they fail to do so, will reject him. He further suggests that both tendencies (to change and to reject him) are stronger as the group is more cohesive.[12] A paraphrase of this position is that tightly knit groups tend to be less tolerant of deviance than loosely knit ones.

In following Cohen's admonition that conformity and deviance be considered as two facets of the more general process of normative control,[13] Dentler and Erikson have considered the functions that deviance serves for the group. Contrary to the general assumption that deviance is bad and something we should have less of, their interesting conclusion is that deviance serves a positive function for the group.[14] First, since norms, as ideas in the minds of members, are often implicit and are rarely entirely obvious, the appearance of deviance (as an overt demonstration of what should not be done) makes the norms more explicit, thereby helping members to become more articulate about them. Instances of what should not be done clarify ideas about what should be done. Second, the group's emotional and behavioral reaction to deviance helps members apprehend what the group *is* and *is not*. For instance, to feel offended by an act and to see others similarly offended provides information about oneself and about the group, information that perhaps could be gained in no other way.

> Comparisons which deviance makes possible help establish the range in which the group operates, the extent of its jurisdiction over behavior, the variety of styles it contains . . . [which] are among the essential dimensions which give a group identity and distinctiveness. . . . A group is distinguished in part by the norms it creates for handling deviance and by the forms of deviance it is able to absorb and contain.[15]

For these and related reasons, Dentler and Erikson suggest that groups "will resist any trend toward alienation [total rejection] of a member whose behavior is deviant."[16]

To Dentler and Erikson's point can be added the argument that the exercise of legitimate sanctions is more than equilibrating. Rather than simply restoring a previous state, it increases group solidarity in two ways. First, for those who feel inclined to deviate but check themselves from doing so, public sanctioning of the actual deviant not only justifies their self-control, but affirms the fact that the norms which support self-control coincide with the norms which support group control. Consequently, the affinity of person with group is reinforced. Second, the overt sanction is an undeniable demonstration that members care enough about the norms (and the group) to act on their behalf and to attempt to maintain them. Consequently, commitment to the norms is both demonstrated and reinforced.[17]

The Normative Role

There is a distinction between behavioral, primordial, and normative roles: The first refers to action, the second to feelings, and the third to ideas about actions and feelings. For example (and as we have seen), how one responds to a command of a parent is an element of one's behavioral role; and how one feels about oneself and one's parent while responding in such a manner is an element of one's primordial role. The element of the normative role is the idea that in these circumstances children should obey their parents. The *normative role* is comprised of the total set of ideas which, for persons in a particular position in the group, stipulate how they should (and should not) behave toward others, and how they should (and should not) express their feelings toward them. In addition, it includes ideas about how they should control themselves, control others and, in general, act in order to maintain the normative system.[18]

While a person can perform behavioral and primordial roles by reading and responding to signals (that is, by observing and fitting into a pattern, or by redirecting one's response to avoid pain), one must be able to deal with symbols and with ideas to perform in the normative role. One must be able to formulate and to convey, to receive and to transmit ideas about, what is happening. One must be able to converse about what is being done, and to deal with messages about messages. For example, "What you said (a message) is x and not y (a message about a message)." This level of thought corresponds to the level of communication referred to by Reusch as *meta-communication*, or communication about communication.[19] For instance: "What I said was x; what I meant to say was $x + l$." "What I said was x, but I was only kidding. Don't take it seriously." "By the way you state your agreement, I gather that you actually disagree. Am I right?" When individuals think on this level, they arrive at private meanings about what is said and done; when group members openly discuss matters on this level, they arrive at public meanings about group processes. Past events are reviewed, defined, evaluated, and reinterpreted. Lessons are learned, and new rules are often formulated.

Through communicating about communication, newcomers acquire a new perspective on their group experience. For one thing, they become better able to conceive of what is going on, while still participating in the process. For another, their view of the group norms change. In the beginning, group rules are interpreted as both absolute and as constraints upon personal freedom. However, through talking over with others both what has been going on and what should have been going on, and, in particular, through taking part in changing the rules, the newcomer perceives them as less absolute and more flexible. In addition, they appear as guidelines as well as constraints. Our pair of newcomers become better able to conceive of norms as statements of the acceptable limits within which they are free to operate; they become less interested in what is prohibited and more interested in what is permitted. When they learn what is allowed, then they gain both a sense of assurance and a greater latitude in their behavior. Thus, through experience on the meta-communication level, the newcomers benefit from one of the positive functions of norms—namely, a conceptual vantage-point from which to interpret what is happening, and upon which to base their own choices of behavior.

GROUP GOALS
AND THEIR ACCOMPLISHMENT

Personal Goals and Group Goals

If a goal is a mental construct, how can a group, which has no mind, have a goal? F. H. Allport, an early social psychologist, would say that it cannot; to him the idea would be another example of the group fallacy. He argues that:

> . . . alike in crowd excitements, collective uniformities and organized groups, the only psychological elements discoverable are in the behavior and consciousness of the specific persons involved. All theories which partake of the group fallacy have the unfortunate consequence of diverting attention from the true locus of cause and effect, namely, the behavioral mechanism of the individual. . . . If we take care of the individuals, psychologically speaking, the groups will be found to take care of themselves.[20]

Sociologists would argue to the contrary: first, that groups as systems cannot be explained solely through knowledge of their constituent parts, and second that the classical position stated by Allport arises from a confusion between personal and group elements. An example will clarify the distinction between personal and group goals and suggest the utility of, and the necessity for, collective concepts.

Consider competitive games in general, and chess in particular. Each chess player plays to win—to win is the personal goal of each—and thus the goals of the two players are similar. Now, although the fact that both parties have similar personal goals is an interesting feature of this dyad (that is, of this particular pairing of two parties), it provides no information about the nature of their collective goal. It would be fallacious, for example, to conclude that since both parties aim to win, "to win" is the goal of the group: similar personal goals do not a group goal make.

To infer the group goal we must first conceive of the dyad as a unit (that is, we must think of the two parties as one party, group, unit, or whatever) and then ask what present or future state *of this unit* is thought by the parties to be desirable. Clearly, that state cannot be "to win," for the dyad as a unit is not a contestant and has no opponent; the dyad itself can neither win nor lose. Consequently, to refer to the goal of the unit as "winning" is meaningless. Do we conclude from this that the concept of a group goal is meaningless? On the contrary, there is an idea in the minds of the two parties which refers to a desirable state of the dyad: it is to have a high-quality contest which each party wants to win, wherein play is imaginative, in which superior play does win. The group goal, as distinct from personal goals, then, is to have a good contest.

The sociologist uses the concept of group goal because it helps explain phenomena that cannot be explained by personal goals, whether taken alone or in aggregate. For one thing, the rules of the game of chess are not devised primarily to supply a winner (though, of course, they provide for one); rather they are artfully constructed in order to create an absorbing and interesting contest. If we imagine the origin and development of the game of chess, we can see that the making of the rules is a means toward the end of a good game. For another thing, opponents are selected, or chosen by each other, not to assure that one party wins over the other, but rather to assure that the contestants are well matched. Thus the matching of players is another means toward the end of a good game.

Our suggestion is that the student conceive of two levels of goals in any formal contest, the first referring to the occasion as a whole and the second referring to the individual participants. The goal toward which all parties cooperate is to achieve a high quality contest, while the goal of the individual contestant is to win. Clearly, the two are interdependent, for the game must be well-designed to stimulate good play and participants must be motivated to make the game a good one. Still, the relationship between the two goals can be more clearly specified for there is an expectation that the party who enters the role of contestant will play to win. This is to say that the norms of the occasion demand that the individual contestants accept as their personal goal the desire to win, or at least that they play as though this were their goal. Otherwise, the overall goal of a good contest cannot be achieved. Sociologically speaking, the game norms demand certain personal goals: to play with no intention of winning is not only deviant in a formal sense but lets one's opponent down and tends to undermine the contest. Many contestants know on the one hand what little pleasure is derived from winning against opponents who do not care but on the other hand the satisfaction gained when, in a tight contest and in spite of excellent play on their own part, they lose. Clearly, satisfaction depends upon more than achieving one's personal goal of winning. So we see that setting up the rules of play, the process of selecting contestants and the conditions which provide satisfaction are examples of group phenomena which cannot be accounted for by personal goals but which are easily explained when we conceive of the goal of the occasion, or of the group as a whole.

Two points need emphasis. First, the group goal is not the simple sum of personal goals, nor can it be directly inferred from them. It refers to a desirable state for the group, not simply to a desirable state for individuals. As we have seen, the personal goal in chess is to win *over* one's opponent, while the group goal is to have a good game *with* one's opponent. The second point is that the mental construct of the group goal resides not in some mystical collective mind, but in the minds of group members. It cannot meaningfully exist anywhere else. It exists there along with other mental processes including personal needs, personal wishes, and personal goals. It may be shared by most or all members, but since many other ideas are shared, that is not its distinction. What sets the concept of group goal apart is that in content and in substance it refers to the group as a unit—specifically, to a desirable state of that unit. The concept resides in the minds of individuals; the referent of the concept is the group as a whole. There is no contradiction here, and there is no fallacy.

The Instrumental Role
and the Technical System

In his *Two Years Before the Mast*, Dana describes a scene aboard the ship *Pilgrim* as it sets sail from Boston's lower harbor.[21] As a new and wholly inexperienced hand, Dana stands to the side, out of the way, and is at some loss in giving his account. He does not understand the language of the officers, nor the relationship between the mate's orders and the men's reactions, nor how the men's movements change the positions of the booms, spars, rigging, and sails. "There is not so hopeless and pitiable an object in the world," he writes, "as a landsman beginning a sailor's life."[22] Still, he shares the excitement as the ship catches the wind and moves out. Weeks later, when again the *Pilgrim* sets sail, the scene is similar except for Dana, who this time moves quickly in response to an order and carries out his assignment. He knows what to do and how to do it, and takes pride in doing it well. In the interim, Dana has come to know the men and has learned the language and the ways of life aboard a merchant ship, and he feels at home. He has learned what has to be done in order to get a ship under way, and precisely how his particular assignment fits in with those of others so that together they accomplish the task. In sociological terms he has learned, and is operating in, an *instrumental role*.

In general, individuals enter the *instrumental role* in a group when they (1) conceive of the group goal, (1) accept it, (3) commit their personal resources, intelligence, skill, and energy toward accomplishing it, and (4) give its accomplishment higher priority than personal goals, the group's norms, and the existing pattern of emotional relationships among members, including their own popularity and personal comfort. They are committed to the goal and prepared to act on its behalf. They evaluate both their own performance and the performance of others more in terms of *effectiveness* than according to conformity to rules. Individuals aboard ship judge each other on many grounds, but a sailor is judged on seamanship.

For the officers and crew leaving Boston on the *Pilgrim*, the immediate *group goal* was to get the ship under way. Their *technical system* was comprised of: (1) their "know-how" in handling the ship and in coordinating the essential activities among the men; (2) their standards for assessing the *effectiveness* of any one activity in contributing to getting the ship under way; and (3) their standards for judging the total operation as a success or a failure. Dana's *instrumental role* is his specific assignment, plus the standards of effectiveness he and others applied to what he did in carrying it out. He had a target and was guided primarily by the standards defining what was and was not effective in reaching that target. He was primarily responsible for upholding standards of superior performance and for assuming his share of responsibility for actually reaching the target, and this responsibility took precedence over maintaining the norms.

Research on Group Effectiveness[23]

The most consistent (and perhaps the most obvious) empirical research finding in our area of discussion is that a group whose members know what to do in order to reach their target is more likely to approach it than a group whose members do not have the "know-how." The same is true for a group under a skillful and experienced leader (when compared with one under an inept and inexperienced head). Technical know-how is especially important when the goal is external—that is, when it involves a change in the environment (such as building a bridge) or a change in relation to the environment (such as finding one's way in strange territory).[24]

More interesting sociologically is the question of which factors account for differences in effectiveness among groups who are more or less equal in technical knowledge and skill. One such factor is the incentive system, otherwise known as the arrangement of rewards for performance. In a classical laboratory experiment, Deutsch demonstrated the differences between a cooperative arrangement and a competitive one.[25] He broke up a university class into 10 five-person groups which were to meet for a three-hour problem-solving session each week over a five-week period. Their participation substituted for class work. He divided the groups into two sets: cooperative and competitive. In the first set, the ratings, which were to be counted in the course grade, were based on the total performance of the five-man team, and all members were to receive the same rating. In the second, ratings were based upon the comparison of one team member against another, with the possibility that the better the performance of one member, the lower the ratings of others. A battery of measures, including a record of interaction, observers' ratings, and group members' reports, showed substantial differences between the two sets of groups. In the cooperative arrangement, members (1) were more concerned about completing their problems, (2) exchanged more ideas and reported less difficulty in communicating with each other, (3) coordinated their activity through dividing functions and pooling results, (4) expressed positive feelings among one another more frequently, and (5) showed (according to observers' ratings) clearer insight and better judgment in deciding their next steps. They also solved puzzles faster, and were superior in assessing human-relations problems that were presented to them. In all these respects, groups in the cooperative arrangement addressed themselves to the situation and managed their internal relations in a way superior to groups in the competitive arrangement.

It shoud be noted that in spite of this, when the productivity of separate individuals is considered, no significant difference in the two arrangements was found. But even so, evidence from the study shows that when the way to reach one's *individual* goal is through working with others in order to accomplish the *group* goal, then group effectiveness is superior to groups wherein rewards are granted to individuals irrespective of team performance. In the first case, accomplishing the group goal is a means toward individual goals, while in the second, personal goals are given priority over group ones.

A second factor is group cohesion—the degree to which members feel emotionally close to one another and share an emotional attachment to the group. Some studies show that cohesive groups are more productive than less cohesive ones. For example, Berkowitz found that in the absence of an outside superior, cohesive groups produced more than less cohesive ones.[26] Other studies show that effective groups tend to be cohesive. It is found, for example, that bomber crews who received superior ratings tended to associate with each other more frequently during off-duty hours than crews who received lower ratings.[27] Evidence in these and other studies suggest a general circular relation between effectiveness and group solidarity. Demonstrated competence seems to draw members closer together, while being close together seems to increase the likelihood of successful group performance. This circularity may be broken when group members are strongly committed to an important group goal. Nevertheless, under these circumstances, the effective group remains so even though its members do not become intimate, the case in point being bomber crews who felt beyond all else that they had critical missions to accomplish.[28]

Another factor affecting group productivity is the "fit" or, as the case may be, the "clash" between the personalities of its members. Schutz suggests that while some persons are most comfortable when they are close to their associates, others find such closeness disconcerting; that while some persons want to follow another's lead, others resent anyone in authority; and that while some want to lead, others are content to work along with those who lead.[29] Groups may be composed in such a way that these basic interpersonal orientations are either compatible or incompatible. When they are compatible, Schutz suggests, the group should be more productive than when they are incompatible. Schutz tested his hypothesis in a carefully designed experiment on 12 college-student groups meeting for 14 sessions over a six-week period. He found that both the groups composed of those who were comfortable when close, and the groups composed of those who wanted to keep their distance, were in general more productive on a series of tasks than were the groups which were mixed—that is, those where some wanted to be close while others wanted to keep their distance. The "clash of personalities" which appears to have interfered with group effectiveness was between those who wanted to be close and those who did not want to be close.

Other studies suggest factors that impair group effectiveness. Rosenthal and Cofer[30] found that the presence of a person who displayed disinterest and distaste for the task at hand undermined the entire group effort, or at least contributed to low productivity. In a study of 72 governmental and industrial conferences, Fouriezos, Hatt, and Guetzkow rated comments on the extent to which they expressed self-oriented needs of the speaker, and found that where the frequency was high, not only were members dissatisfied over procedures and decisions, but interpersonal conflict was high and fewer decisions were actually made.[31] These studies show that the presence of those who are committed to ends other than the group goal tends to undermine the effectiveness of the group as a whole. To these factors which impair group productivity can be added the example of the frequently observed practice of workers banding together and establishing a group norm to restrict output.[32] The basic factor in these cases is, of course, the conflict between the goal of the workers and the goal of management.

TECHNICAL SUCCESS AND THE FOUR LEVELS
OF GROUP PROCESS

In pursuing and accomplishing a goal, groups do not remain unchanged; rather they gain information, experience, and confidence. The technical system changes through the acquisition of new information, new techniques, new standards of evaluation, and so on. The affective (under)structure changes, usually through deeper commitment of members to the group and to each other. New coalitions may form while earlier coalitions shift. Patterns of interaction alter as practices are improved—obsolete norms tend to fade as governing factors. Some of these changes may permit greater flexibility in coordinating activities for a more effective performance. Empirical research shows that when more successful groups are compared with less successful ones, members in the more successful ones tend: (1) to commit themselves more fully to the group goal; (2) to communicate with each other more freely and more clearly; (3) to coordinate their activities more closely; and (4) to feel more friendly toward one another. For instance, Berkowitz and Levy found that during a break in problem-solving, bomber crews who were doing well on the problems continued discussion about the tasks and raised their aspiration level for the next ones, while less effective crews avoided talk about the tasks and actually lowered their aspiration level.[33] Shelley found that members in successful groups take a more favorable attitude toward their groups than do those in less successful ones.[34]

Returning to Deutsch's experiment on cooperation and competition: his results may be interpreted from the viewpoint of the consequences of success. It is reasonable to assume that over a five-week period, superior performance and higher productivity are themselves causal factors, inspiring enthusiasm, easing communication, creating friendliness, and allowing closer coordination. The various changes probably have reciprocal effects upon each other, or even a spiral effect whereby success increases both the amount of energy available for pursuing the goal and the information and skill in reaching it, while in turn, new energies and new social and technical skills increase the likelihood of success. This spiral relation, which is chiefly between the affective (under)structure and the technical system, may prove to be one of the more important principles of group dynamics.

The full set of dynamic relations among the sub-systems remains to be discovered. Sociologists need advanced techniques for taking simultaneous readings on the four levels. An important step in this direction has been taken by Bales and associates with their SYMLOG, mentioned in the previous chapter.[35] There we saw that estimates of the structure of the interaction system could be derived from their classification of *action* along the *up-down* and the *positive-negative* dimensions and that estimates of the affective (under)structure could be derived from scores of *imagery* along comparable dimensions. Here we add the point that the third dimension—*forward-backward*—is one on which the observer scores the actor's orientation toward or away from work on the group task and work in general. Since *SYMLOG* links the actor simultaneously to the interaction, the affective, and the technical sub-systems, it provides a method for tracing the dynamic relations among both the individual in his or her primordial, behavioral, and instrumental roles and among the group. Questions of how these sub-systems are related to the normative system and whether the "work" done is productive or not remain to be answered by other means. Meanwhile, Aldgren and Walberg found substantial validation of Bales's hypothetical dimensions in their study of 144 classrooms,[36] as did Solomon in his comparison of observer and actors' self-ratings.[37]

THE NEWCOMERS AND THE FOUR LEVELS
OF GROUP PROCESS

Newcomers rarely enter into all areas of group life at once. Nor do they progress from novices to fully responsible members by a smooth and gradual process. Instead—and perhaps like the parts played as people progress from infancy to old age—they enter the group by distinct steps, often marked by abrupt changes in behavior, in feelings, and in ways of perceiving others and in relating to them. These abrupt changes are important to the sociologist, for they signify the existence of distinctly different vantage points from which members orient themselves toward the group. Differences in these vantage points are due in part to the existence of distinct levels of group process: as one moves from one level to the other, one's vantage point and consequently one's entire perspective changes.

We have suggested that newcomers characteristically enter the group through four stages. During the first stage they operate within the behavioral and the primordial roles which are oriented respectively toward the existing interaction pattern and toward needs and their gratification. During the second stage they add a new role, the normative, which is oriented toward what should be done and what sorts of feelings should be expressed; this role alters the way they act and how they express their feelings. During the third stage they add still another role, the instrumental, which is oriented toward what the group as a unit should accomplish and which again alters their previous roles, since that accomplishment implicates actions, feelings, and norms. The fourth stage, of entering the executive role, is discussed in the next chapter.

New Demands

As the newcomers accumulate a repertoire of roles on additional levels, new demands are made upon them and new capabilities are required of them. In order to shift to the normative level, they must not only be capable of understanding the ideas about what should and should not be done, but they must also be capable of exercising control over themselves and others. In their normative role, then, they must both comprehend and participate in the normative control over group process. This means that they must operate according to a more complex feedback process than is required in the earlier stage. Steps in the new feedback process are as follows: given an act by some member, (1) does the act correspond to the group's ideas about what the act should have been? (2) if it does, then no response is necessary and attention is directed to other matters; (3) if, on the other hand, it does not correspond, then what sanctions are to be applied? (4) of the possible sanctions, which ones are, in terms of the norms, legitimate? (5) applying the sanction; (6) assessing the response to the sanctions, that is, reading its effectiveness in inducing the actor to conform to the norms; (7) altering the sanction to increase the likelihood that subsequent behavior will conform to the norms. In short, he or she assesses all that occurs in terms of the norms, and assumes responsibility for maintaining the norms.

Still other demands are made on the newcomers as they enter the instrumental role. They must be able to subordinate personal goals to the collective goal. They must be capable of conceiving the relation between the group as a whole and its environment. In addition, they must employ a still more difficult feedback process: given the group goal as a target and an act on the part of a member, (1) aside from the normative considerations above what are the act's consequences for moving the group toward the target? (2) when the act is judged effective, then how is it to be reinforced? (3) when the act is judged ineffective, then what can be done to improve its effectiveness? (4) acting in order to improve effectiveness; (5) assessing this attempt to improve effectiveness; and (6) altering both the ways of trying to reach the goal and one's attempt to influence the performance of others. One of the more difficult steps in the feedback process on this level is to read, moment by moment, the indicators of effectiveness. Since what is done usually has multiple effects, it is seldom obvious what the more significant ones are; and since goals are often more efficiently reached by indirect means, it is seldom clear whether a current direction is the best one. These difficulties are compounded when both the group and its environment are constantly changing. In this respect alone, assessments on the instrumental level require more information and are more demanding than are assessments on the normative level, where, as we have seen, the comparable question is how behavior corresponds to the norms.

New Latitude

It is interesting to note that as newcomers become more fully committed to the group's culture, including its norms and goals, they become less constrained by the demands of the group structure as it currently exists. This is because they become committed to what *should be* done rather than to what *is being* done, and to what *might be* accomplished rather than to what *is being* accomplished. Let us take the shift from the behavioral to the normative role to explain the point.

As indicated before, one of the positive functions of social norms is that they provide general guidelines to behavior. Before newcomers learn the norms, they can only adjust their actions according to directly observed patterns of behavior. In these circumstances, their behavior is immediately contingent upon what someone else does. Consequently, the newcomer expends energy, being constantly on the alert and remaining prepared to alter instantaneously responses according to someone else's next move. This dependence is illustrated by the young gorilla who must stop foraging and move elsewhere when the older gorilla chooses to move. The young gorilla's behavior is entirely contingent upon the behavior of the older one.

The newcomer's uncertainty is illustrated by the substitute football player who does not know the plays, or a new musician who has no score, or a new actress who has no script. To play at all would require great skill, flexibility, and training. The pressure is relieved, of course, when the plays are known, the score is available, and the script is memorized.

Just as the football player adjusts his moves according to the design of the play, the musician according to the design of the score, and the actress according to the design of the drama, persons entering the normative role adjust their behavior according to the design of their relationship to the group. That design is given by the norms. As guidelines, they replace their dependence upon moment-to-moment observations of what others do. As guidelines, they free one from the immediate demands of the existing interaction pattern. Instead of following others, one is free to follow the norms.

New latitude is again gained in the shift into the instrumental role. With a clear collective goal to be accomplished, the question of effectiveness takes precedence over the question of conformity. Often the most effective course of action calls for a change both in traditional modes of behavior and in past norms. As a consequence, the norms are less binding. Moreover, deviance is not automatically sanctioned. Instead, it is first assessed from the viewpoint of the group goal, for it may be effective, even though deviant, and therefore may be reinforced rather than punished. With the instrumental perspective, norms become less absolute, and the range of possible behavior widens.

However, with new latitude in the instrumental role comes a new risk; namely, the possibility of failure and of having that failure measured. In this sense our pair of newcomers become more vulnerable as they gain latitude. By the same token, they have an opportunity for being effective and, therefore, of becoming more valuable to the group. The fact that the stakes are higher is another indication that they are operating on a new level of group process.

NOTES

1. Muzafer Sherif and Carolyn W. Sherif, *Reference Groups, Exploration into Conformity and Deviation of Adolescents* (New York: Harper & Row, Pub., 1964), pp. 164–83, 269–73.

2. John W. Thibaut and Harold H. Kelley, "On Norms," in Edwin P. Hollander and Raymond G. Hunt, eds., *Current Perspectives in Social Psychology* (New York: Oxford University Press, 1971), pp. 463–69.

3. Talcott Parsons and Edward A. Shils. eds.. *Toward a General Theory of Action* (Cambridge, Mass.: Harvard University Press, 1951), pp. 80–88. Parsons subsequently dropped the self-collectivity dilemma. Consequently we list the four remaining ones.

4. E. Adamson Hoebel, *The Law of Primitive Man: A Study in Comparative Legal Dynamics* (Cambridge, Mass.: Harvard University Press, 1954), pp. 46–63.

5. For a discussion of the concept of deviance, see Albert K. Cohen, *Deviance and Control* (Englewood Cliffs, N.J.: Prentice-Hall, 1966), pp. 1–23.

6. A. Paul Hare, "Norms and Social Control," in his *Handbook of Small Group Research*, 2nd ed., (New York: Free Press, 1976), pp. 19–59.

7. Leon Festinger and John Thibaut, "Interpersonal Communication in Small Groups," *Journal of Abnormal and Social Psychology*, 46 (1951), 92–99.

8. Leon Festinger, "Informal Social Communication"' in Leon Festinger and others, *Theory and Experiment in Social Communication* (Ann Arbor: Research Center for Group Dynamics, University of Michigan, May 1950), pp. 3–16; also see reprint in Dorwin Cartwright and Alvin Zander, eds., *Group Dynamics*, 2nd ed. (Evanston, Ill.: Row, Peterson, 1960), pp. 286–99.

9. Edward L. Walker and Roger W. Heyns, *An Anatomy for Conformity* (Englewood Cliffs, N.J.: Prentice-Hall, 1962).

10. Ibid., p. 96.

11. R. M. Emerson, "Deviation and Rejection: An Experimental Replication," *American Sociological Review*, 19 (1954), 688–93.

12. Stanley Schachter, "Deviation, Rejection and Communication," *Journal of Abnormal and Social Psychology*, 46 (1951), 190–207; reprinted in Cartwright and Zander, eds., *Group Dynamics*, 2nd ed., pp. 260–85.

13. Albert K. Cohen, "The Study of Social Disorganization and Deviant Behavior," in Robert R. Merton, Leonard Broom, and Leonard S. Cottrell, Jr., eds., *Sociology Today: Problems and Prospects* (New York: Basic Books, 1959), pp. 461–84.

14. Robert A. Dentler and Kai T. Erikson, "The Functions of Deviance in Groups," *Social Problems,* 7 (1959), 98–107.

15. Ibid., p. 101.

16. Ibid., p. 102.

17. For a discussion on the source and consequences of sanctions, see Emile Durkheim, *The Division of Labor in Society*, trans. George Simpson (New York: Free Press, 1933), pp. 70–100.

18. For an illustration of current research on the importance of normative role relations see V. Lee Hamilton and Joseph Sanders, "The Effect of Roles and Deeds on Responsibility Judgments: The Normative Structure of Wrong Doing." *Social Psychological Quarterly*, 44 (Sept. 1981), 237–54.

19. Jurgen Ruesch, *Therapeutic Communication* (New York: W. W. Norton & Co., Inc., 1961), pp. 423–36.

20. Floyd H. Allport, *Social Psychology* (Boston: Houghton Mifflin, 1924), p. 9.

21. Richard Henry Dana, *Two Years Before the Mast* (New York: Bantam, 1963).

22. Ibid., p. 2.

23. For a review of research on effectiveness with suggestions for reorienting the problem-solving model see J. Richard Hackman and Charles G. Morris, "Group Tasks, Group Interaction Process, and Group Performance Effectiveness: A Review and Proposed Integration," in Leonard Berkowitz, ed., *Group Process* (New York: Academic Press, 1978), pp. 1–55.

24. For a review of factors both blocking and promoting group effectiveness see L. Richard Hoffman, "Group Problem Solving" in Leonard Berkowitz, ed., *Group Processes*, pp. 67–113; and for a review of factors affecting group productivity, see A. Paul Hare, "Group Versus Group" in his *Handbook of Small Group Research*, 2nd ed., pp. 330–31.

25. Morton Deutsch, "An Experimental Study of the Effects of Cooperation and Competition Upon Group Process," *Human Relations*, 2 (1949), 129–52, 199–231.

26. L. Berkowitz, "Group Standards, Cohesiveness and Productivity," *Human Relations*, 7 (1954), 509–19.

27. L. Berkowitz, "Group Norms among Bomber Crews: Patterns of Perceived Crew Attitudes, 'Actual' Crew Attitudes, and Crew Liking Related to Aircrew Effectiveness in Far Eastern Combat," *Sociometry*, 29 (1956), 141–53.

28. Ibid.

29. William C. Schutz, *FIRO: A Three-Dimensional Theory of Interpersonal Behavior* (New York: Holt, Rinehart & Winston, 1958).

30. D. Rosenthal and C. N. Cofer, "The Effect on Group Performance of an Indifferent and Neglectful Attitude Shown by One Group Member," *Journal of Experimental Psychology*, 38 (1948), 568–77.

31. N. T. Fouriezos, M. L. Hatt, and Harold Guetzkow, "Measurement of Self-Oriented Needs in Discussion Groups," *Journal of Abnormal and Social Psychology*, 45 (1950), 682–90.

32. F. J. Rothlisberger and W. J. Dickson, *Management and the Worker: Technical vs. Social Organization in an Industrial Plant* (Cambridge, Mass.: Harvard University Press, 1939), pp. 524–48.

33. L. Berkowitz and B. Levy, "Pride and Group Performance and Group-Task Motivation," *Journal of Abnormal and Social Psychology*, 53 (1956), 300–306.

34. H. P. Shelley, "Level of Aspiration Phenomena in Small Groups," *Journal of Social Psychology*, 40 (1954), 149–64.

35. See p. 83. See also Robert F. Bales and others, *SYMLOG*, pp. 176–238.

36. Andrew Aldgren and Herbert J. Walberg, "Basic Dimensions in Characteristics of Classroom Groups," *Alberta Journal of Educational Research*, 24 (Dec. 1978), 244–56.

37. Manson J. Solomon, "Dimensions of Interpersonal Behavior: A Convergent Validation within a Cognitive Interactionist Framework," *Journal of Personality*, 49 (March 1981), 15–26.

CHAPTER 6
EXECUTIVE PROCESSES

This chapter describes the executive role—one entered by those who assume unrestricted responsibility for the group and aim to increase its capabilities.[1] The executive functions, as implied in Chapters 3 and 4, are to develop group consciousness and to influence what the group is to become. These functions not only require more skill than the other roles we have discussed but, as we shall explain, place the executive in an unresolvable conflict. Ultimately, consciousness of the human group demands knowledge of all causes and effects of all events or, relative to our present knowledge, omniscience; and ultimately, determination of group character and history means the power to reconstitute persons and social organizations at will or, relative to most of us, omnipotence. Pragmatically, those in the executive role cannot know all, or do all. Consequently, they must select from among the universe of causes and effects those which are relevant and important; and they must choose among courses of action those which are strategic. For this reason the next chapter presents in broad outline a sociological paradigm which, in combining the structural-functional and cybernetic features discussed in Chapter 1, points to a limited number of issues of strategic importance to the executive. We call them critical issues. The paradigm is meant to serve as a model. That is, if executives applying it are true to their role, they will want to become conscious of the way they are applying it, and of its strengths and weaknesses, and to reformulate it where necessary. Executive and paradigm work together; the paradigm helps executives learn their role and, as they do so, they feed that learning back into an improved paradigm. But to appreciate why they need a paradigm, it will be well for us to understand more fully the demands of that role.

THE EXECUTIVE ROLE

The first of four features of the executive's role is that one's responsibility is not for parts, sectors, sub-systems, or selected levels, but for the total dynamic configuration of whole persons in an organized group within a changing environment. One identifies with this totality (which we call the *meta-group*) much as parents identify with their family in its life situation, or a head of government with the nation in its historical situation. The meta-group is not a single thing but a set of phenomena, all important in group experience: it includes routines of interaction; pervasive feelings such as trust or mistrust, confidence or anxiety, elation or sadness; a configuration of interpersonal and intergroup attachments and animosities; a set of written and unwritten, conscious and unconscious rules and taboos; a system of implicit and explicit beliefs and values; and so on. It has a history, current potentials, environmental demands to be met, and choices to be made. It is both a set of processes within persons, and a web of affiliations and influences extending to other persons, groups, and societies. The executive's concern diffuses throughout this multileveled, differentiated, polycentric, interdependent configuration.

Second, while being identified with this meta-group, the executive acts at any moment to influence what the meta-group is to become. Now, what a meta-group becomes is shaped by sequences of discrete responses to momentary situations. For example, a group that pays tribute to a more powerful one becomes a subordinate group; one that persists in its habitual ways in spite of radical environmental changes becomes a rigid group; one that waits for, and always follows, the orders of the experimenter becomes an automaton; one that cannot discard unrealistic fears becomes paralyzed; and, of course, one that pursues a self-destructive plan perishes. Groups pick their way through a career of responses to momentary situations from which they emerge with their qualities and characteristics. It is to this career that executives direct their interventions.

A parenthetical note: the extent to which momentary responses are determined by, or are explicable in terms of, universal laws is an open question in current sociology. What is less in doubt is (1) that choices are affected by the way members approach the momentary situation; (2) that approaches, or orientations, differ; and (3) that, consequently, laws about choices will vary from one set of orientations to another. For example, when all members are oriented to the moment in terms of a pre-established pattern of action (instinctual or otherwise), the law will be of one order, but when members are chiefly interested in achieving a highly desired objective regardless of what has happened in the past, they will be of another order. They will be of still another order (and perhaps quite difficult to formulate) when each member and the set of them collectively confront the situation as executives, conscious of the moment, of their responsibility in respect to making choices, and of the possible effects of one alternative against another. In short, laws governing momentary responses are likely to differ according to the operation or nonoperation of role-systems in the group. The implication for sociology is that more complex or more viable theoretical models are required when members are in the more advanced roles, such as the executive, than otherwise; and the implication for executives is that in making their own choices they cannot rely upon a simple set of formulas, or upon the ones used in less inclusive roles.

Third, members entering the executive role decommit themselves from the other roles. This process is familiar, for it occurs at each stage as the newcomer advances through the behavioral, primordial, normative, and instrumental roles. However, a review of the difference in commitment of these roles will help clarify the executive role. Whereas in the instrumental role one is committed to the group goal, in the executive role one evaluates alternative goals and, if appropriate, attempts to change the current one. Whereas in the normative role one is committed to the maintenance of the group's rules, in the executive role one is concerned with who sets the rules, how they are set and, if necessary, how their legislation might be modified. Whereas in the primordial role one is committed to the expression and fulfillment of feelings and needs, in the executive role one is concerned with how those feelings, expressed or suppressed, present possibilities for, or place limits upon, what the group as a whole can understand about itself and what it can do. In short, executives assume responsibility for what the group might become and de-commit themselves from what it has been.

Fourth, the executive is both an *insider* and an *outsider*. One's stance vis-à-vis the group is comparable to the stance of the ego vis-à-vis the personality: the ego manages forces both from within and from without, and must maintain this dual orientation if it is not to collapse.

The executive—having libidinal ties, being morally obligated to others and sharing ideas and goals with them—is an insider. Yet, in this role one steps back, "becomes stranger to the familiar," and asks, as an outsider might: "What is this group?" "Who are these people?" "What is their (our) purpose?" "What are they (we) doing (becoming)?" Such questions connote detachment, distance, and estrangement—the more so to those who need the protection of the group and the security of its status quo. They arouse feelings of confusion, defense, and resentment toward the executive ordinarily reserved (as we saw in Chapter 2) for the outside observer. Consequently, with this dual stance the executive can expect to be the object of mixed feelings and, often, to be alone.

In summary, those in the executive role identify with the meta-group. They are committed not to sub-parts but to its entirety, both as it is and is becoming. They intervene in its history and as a consequence influence its qualities and characteristics. They experience, observe, and assess the realities of the momentary situation. They act and assess the consequences of their actions upon the group's capability of coping with immediate demands and future exigencies. Although they take into account the interaction system, the affective (under)structure, the normative system, and group beliefs, values, and goals, they operate independently of these parts. They may confirm or break the routine; they may reinforce or modify the structure of group emotion; they may conform to or deviate from the norms; they may adhere to or contradict the group's beliefs and assumptions; and they may pursue or change the group's goal. As both insider and outsider, then, their commitment is to effect the meta-group as it is in the process of becoming.

As in the case of other roles, entry into the executive role is defined by an emotional, moral, intellectual, and behavioral reorientation rather than by formal assignment, an election, or their equivalent. One may be elected to an office where one *should* operate as an executive but does not in fact do so; and one may, even without office, perform executive functions. And, since most members know something of the nature of their group and influence it by what they do, the line marking entry into and departure from the role is often indistinct.

THE EXECUTIVE SYSTEM

Note an important point: that being in charge and being in the executive role are not one and the same, as subordinates often imagine them to be. The role refers to an orientation to the situation and the performance of certain functions, not to a position or an office such as chair, chief, commander, or president. In line with this, note that although the officer from Washington invites others to join him in the executive role, he does not by this act relinquish his leadership. Others may perform executive functions without taking over his position. The same is true in the teacher-student relationship when the student acquires the teacher's methods of thinking, without becoming the teacher. The distinction between position and process is shown again in the example by the fact that the invitation is (correctly) open to all and by the fact that the acceptance by one member does not preclude (it even encourages) acceptance by others. This is because executive processes can be shared and are not exclusive. There is no reason inherent in the processes themselves why all members of a group cannot (1) assume total responsibility for the group, (2) develop self-consciousness, and (3) participate in the determination of the group's process of becoming.

For this reason, it is useful to conceive of an *executive system*; that is, the set of all executive orientations and processes as they are distributed and organized among and performed by group members. Any member, regardless of position or office, who performs executive functions (such as contribution to the group's awareness of itself) participates in the executive system; and any act (regardless of whether it is habitual or unique for the initiator) that performs an executive function is part of the executive system.

The executive system is the group's center for assessment of itself and its situations, for arrangement and rearrangement of its internal and external relations, for decision making and for learning, and for "learning how to learn" through acting and assessing the consequences of action. As such, its purview extends like an umbrella over the other role-systems we have described. The executive system monitors behavior, emotion, norms, beliefs, goals, and their collective organization. They are contained within its orientation, but not it within theirs. They are subject to rearrangement by the executive system, but not it by them. The executive system is a partly independent, autonomous center where information about the role-systems and about the meta-group as a whole is processed and whence come both ideas about what it should become and acts designed to make it so. It holds this supraordinate relation to the other role-systems because executive processes employ a higher order of feedback process (consciousness) than do goal-seeking, normative control, and so on.

In summary: The executive system is the set of executive orientations and processes, howsoever they are distributed among members.

THE EXECUTIVE FUNCTION
OF CONSCIOUSNESS

It is simple enough to say as we did in Chapter 1, that consciousness—the product of third-order feedback—is a system's awareness of itself. But more specifically, what is there to be conscious *of*, and by what method is it achieved?[2]

Let us take an extreme position by saying that one needs to become aware of all factors and forces (elements) which affect what is and is not possible, or likely and not likely, to occur in the group. In attempting to understand the dynamics of personality, and more precisely why a given person does what he does in a given concrete moment in time, Lewin employed the concept of *field*.[3] The *momentary field* is comprised of any element, and all elements in combination, that exert an active influence (a push, a pull, a block, a detour, and so on) upon what a person does or does not do. The field is a momentary, cross-sectional view of the multiple causes of a bit of human behavior. Lewin argued that comprehension of this field makes all human action understandable and consequently lawful. Behavior, he suggested, is a lawful function of the interplay among elements of the field, or, according to his formula: $B = f(P \cdot E)$ where B is behavior, P is the personality of the actor, and E is the environment. $(P \cdot E)$ is the field.

We may apply Lewin's concept of the field and his formula to groups, providing we make appropriate modifications. The group field—or, as we choose to call it, the *momentary situation*—is comprised of all factors, circumstances, and forces (elements), whatever their nature or location, that have a determinant effect upon what events do or do not occur, or are likely or not likely to occur, in the group. Lewin's formula is modified to read $E_g = f(P \cdot G \cdot C)$—or, translated: a given group event is a function of the interplay among elements in personalities, the group, and the group's context. For example, Peter's taking over John's role, described on pages 60-62, was a joint function of at least (1) the emotional, mental, and internal control processes of the individuals in the class—not only of Peter and John but also of others (P); (2) the students' shared conceptions of what the seminar was to be, expectations about how members would and should act, feelings of surprise, anger, and loss at John's departure, the need on the part of some to replace John, and mixed feelings about John's contribution on the part of others (G); (3) the one-way mirrors, the microphone, the observer behind the mirrors, and probably John's girl, the medical school, and the time of day (C). Were one to know all the factors at play as Peter filled the gap one would, for that moment, approach consciousness of the group; and were that knowledge shared by the participants, they would approach group consciousness.

Table 3 presents a further breakdown of the principal terms in the formula. The basis of the breakdown (which is the one we have used heretofore for the group; namely behavior, feelings, norms, other aspects of culture, and executive processes) is extended to personality and contextual relations in order to indicate corresponding elements in those other systems.[4] Yet the chief purpose of the table is to emphasize three points: (1) that the universe of possible causal elements spreads far beyond the physical and organizational boundaries of the group itself and, at the same time, penetrates into the deeper recesses of personalities; (2) that *any* combination or sub-set of elements within the universe of elements may comprise the momentary situation associated with a given event; and (3) that since events are themselves elements, and therefore possible causes of changes in other elements, the configuration and location of elements in the momentary situation changes from one instant to the other. The complications of this for understanding what is going on are enormous. They are so great, in fact, that social scientists have subdivided the universe of elements into sub-areas, selecting one or another for specialized study while assuming heuristically that other elements are constant. The psychologist, for instance, selects the personality sector, the social psychologist the interplay between personality and group, the sociologist the group sector, and so on. Such a division of labor is a necessary expedient in the making of a science, but it is not available, feasible, nor advisable for the executive who operates within the total complexity of a given moment in time. Those in the executive role are not free to select some sectors and ignore others, but must be prepared to learn about them all. This is to say that not only is the universe of elements they need to become aware of extensive, but *no naturalistic nor a priori grounds exist for excluding sectors of elements*—none, that is, if they are to contribute to group consciousness.

We may imagine consciousness as an aim, but by what method is it achieved? The answer is by direct empirical observation of all that goes on in the group. At least this is the first of four steps.

1. *Observation*. The executive observes overt behavior, listens with "a third ear" as it were, and remembers what he sees and hears. Behavior may be as global as the gap-filling phenomenon or as finite as a glance of the eye or a movement of the forefinger.

2. *Decoding information carried by behavior*. Any event, we have suggested, is caused by a combination of multiple elements. We now assume that each causal element has altered the nature of the event in the sense that without the element the event would be different. This effect is a trace of the element and as such contains information about the elements. The trace contains a message. Events, being multiply caused, carry multiple messages which to the observer are scrambled together.

   Let us refer to the modulators on a telephone line, an analogy used by Wiener.[5] At one end a large number of conversations are collected, encoded, then sent through a trunk line to the other end, where a modulator separates and decodes them before delivery to recipients. Were one to tap into the trunk line, one would simply hear a jumble of noises; yet, these noises are traces of the original conversations. It is only with a modulator which "understands" the encoding procedure that sense can be made out of the noises. To executive-observers, the original conversations correspond to elements in the momentary situation, the jumble of noises to the observable event, while the modulator corresponds to their thought processes in interpreting causal elements. Causal elements encode events; events carry multiple messages and the executive-observer decodes the messages, thereby arriving at information about the momentary situation.

3. *Inferring*. Repeating this process over a series of events and using the classification in Table 3, the executive-observer draws inferences as answers to these questions: What do these messages tell me about the personalities of persons in the group? What do they tell about the operation of the group's role-systems? What do they tell about the relation of the group to its context?

4. *Formulating*. Executive-observers arrange their inferences into a conception of the structure of, and the interplay among, elements which affect group events. They may test their ideas by intervening and judging by reactions whether or not their conceptions are adequate and, in time, formulate their notions as to what the group is and how it operates. As they convey these formulations to others, feeding them in to the group's culture, they contribute to group self-consciousness.

Note that each new event may bring new information and that there is no set number of messages events carry. Consequently, *there are no a priori grounds for attending to one event while ignoring another, or for knowing how many messages a given event will contain.*

Table 3 Classification of Elements in the Momentary Situation

Personality	Group	Context
Behavior Traits How person tends to act and interact under given circumstances.	*Interaction System* The pattern of interpersonal behavior among members	*Physical and Social Contacts* Environmental resources and limits; the pattern of contacts with outside persons, groups, and societies.
Personal Needs and Feelings The structure of physical and psychic needs and affective processes, and the conscious or unconscious processes associated with them.	*Affective Under(Structure)* The distribution of emotional states, and the structure of affective relations among members (conscious and unconscious).	*Emotional Relations* The distribution of libidinal attractions, enmities, and alienations between the group (and its members) and outsiders, including the member's nation and other societies.
Internalized Norms The set of conscious and unconscious ideas about how one should feel, and what one should do.	*Normative System* The set of shared ideas (conscious and unconscious) about how persons, as a group members, should feel, and what they should do under given circumstances; ideas about what the interaction system and group emotion should be.	*Contractual (or "Treaty") Relations* The set of reciprocal obligations and privileges between the group as a unit, and outside bodies.

Beliefs and Values

Explicit and implicit definitions of the world, and of preferences among alternative objects, ideas, and states of affairs.

Group Culture (in addition to norms)

The set of shared (explicit or implicit) definitions of reality; preferences among objects, ideas, and states of affairs; and standard procedures for pursuing the desirable—all as collectively defined.

Cultural Interchange

Definitions and evaluations of one another by group members and outsiders; the content of information, ideas, ways of learning, etc., exchanged between group and outsiders.

The Ego

The person's capabilities for assessing realities and for rearranging his or her habits, feelings, norms, beliefs, and goals according to new circumstances and to new purposes.

The Executive System

The group's capabilities for developing consciousness, for rearranging itself, and for altering its goals according to new circumstances and to new purposes.

The Inter-Group Executive System

The capabilities of the group, together with outsiders, to assess, negotiate, and renegotiate their contacts, emotional relations, obligations, exchange, and, in general, their degree of interdependence.

THE FIRST EXECUTIVE DILEMMA

Our argument is that any element in the universe of elements may be causal and that any event, and any one of the many messages contained in an event, may be informative. On the face of it, all are significant, none are insignificant. There are no naturalistic, or *a priori*, grounds according to which one can, by screening or by exclusion, simplify one's task. In other words, the ultimate demands of gaining group consciousness are for omniscience. However, as suggested above, realistic limitations prevent one from achieving omniscience. Consequently, the executive faces a dilemma.

For one thing, the sheer volume of messages produced in the normal course of group interaction appears greater than participants can process. Although we have no accurate estimate of this volume, its scale is suggested by Pettinger and others (who wrote a sizable book analyzing the first five minutes of a psychiatric interview, and at that were highly selective of the facets they took into account[6]), and by the fact that few observers who have used tape recordings and slow-motion cameras would claim that a still more refined breakdown of analysis would not add new (and perhaps important) information. The more angles taken on interaction, and the more minute its dissection, the more the information found. It would be easy to reduce this matter to the absurd, but the important lesson for the executive is the realization that even the most astute observers of human behavior are, relative to the amount of behavior produced, inefficient information processors, catching and decoding only a small portion of the total.

Even with improved efficiency, the executive faces another limitation to omniscience: active personal and collective resistance to self- and group awareness. As human beings we have unconscious needs and wishes which we are not prepared to acknowledge and against which we construct defenses. Each of us evolves a private view of ourself and the world composed in part of fantasy or illusion which, for our own comfort and esteem, we keep secret, implicit, unformulated, and therefore beyond test. Each person, that is, has a vested, and partly unconscious, interest in preventing causal elements within from becoming known. The same is true for the group as a collective unit. Members are subject to common unconscious needs, assumptions, prohibitions, and so on, which serve defensive functions for the group, and may serve them best by being unknown. For example, groups with a taboo against harming the leader often have a secondary taboo against acknowledging the first one, for to recognize the rule to protect the leader would be to admit the existence of wishes to harm the leader (which wishes are themselves taboo). In the family, incest is not only taboo, but talk about it is unthinkable, for it would acknowledge just those libidinal forces against which the taboo is aimed. And among the Navaho, to know about witches is a sure sign that one is a witch. The general point is that the sense of collective security is supported by unconscious and implicit agreements to keep certain feelings, assumptions, beliefs, and taboos *unrecognized*. Members cooperate, inadvertently or otherwise, to keep these elements out of awareness—to keep them, in the face of inquiry, secret. Add to this the likelihood that executives themselves are both subject to unconscious needs and wishes, and emotionally and culturally bound to the group with which they identify and one realizes the subtlety and strength of resistances to group consciousness.

The first dilemma of executives who aim to increase group capabilities is that, on the one hand, they need to know what the group is and what it can become, while on the other, because of both the volume of information and the built-in resistances to self-awareness, they cannot know all that persons are, all that the group is, nor at any moment, all that is happening. In short, the demands of the role are impossible to fulfill. This distinguishes the role from the others previously discussed: behavioral patte.,1s can be followed, feelings can be expressed and many needs fulfilled, norms can be maintained and reasonable goals can be reached, but *consciousness of the human group, by its very nature, cannot be fully realized.* Awareness of this condition introduces *another* demand of the role: namely, an attitude of humility—which is to say, the combination of a receptivity to new information (even though the past is not understood) with a readiness to revise past assessments (even though the revisions will be incomplete).[7] And, awareness of this condition means a shift from the imperative of omniscience to the imperative of selection. Pragmatically, the executive must select and screen information, must infer and formulate according to some frame of reference which purports to distinguish the relevant and important from the irrelevant and insignificant. The paradigm in the next chapter is one such guide. However, before going to it, let us consider briefly the executive's second dilemma.

THE SECOND EXECUTIVE DILEMMA

Whereas the first dilemma is over *knowing*, the second dilemma is over *doing*. And while the first is common to outside sociologists and executives alike because both are observers, the second involves just executives because they alone operate from within the group and are responsible for acting upon the situation when necessary. As actors *in* the situation, executives assume an orientation similar to experimenters; that is, they ask such questions as: "If act x occurs, what effect will it have upon group characteristic y?" and "If we alter part A of the system, what effect will that have upon part B, or upon the total system?" Actions become significant as causal factors, as well as sources of information. Group process is seen as interplay between elements in the momentary situation, and overt events: a set of elements causes an event and the event changes the original set of elements; this in turn causes a different event—and so on. The second dilemma is that even though one's assessment might indicate what in the group should be changed (what the group could be were one omnipotent), certain basic properties of persons, groups, and the context—as one may have discovered through assessing the situation—are impervious to the will of the one who wishes to change them. For instance, through what action can one person modify at will the basic needs of another—needs such as hunger, thirst, sex, security? Or alter the emotional states of anxiety, fear, antagonism, love, mistrust? Or neutralize internal prohibitions? Or supplant basic assumptions of the nature of reality? Parents, teachers, friends, and physicians are familiar with limitations in this regard. Persons and groups have integrities of their own. Through what action can one alter the nature of a group—a group, for instance, that thinks it is superior to all others, or one that believes it can be rescued only through a messiah, or one that assumes that its cohesion depends upon physical attack against an enemy, or one whose superstitions preoccupy it, or one that is coalesced through common guilt? Prophets and poets and political leaders are all too well acquainted with the difficulties in reforming such collective phenomena.

When through experimental attempts to determine the history of their groups, executives become aware of those elements which are beyond their power either to modify or to create, then they confront another demand of their role: that they be imaginative, as well as humble. They need to devise interventions which, though small in themselves, have disproportionately large consequences upon the system; and for these they need more than a superficial understanding of group dynamics. They need a model which guides them to causes rather than to symptoms, and suggests what is feasible to do as well as what would be ideal to do.

RESPONSES TO THE DILEMMAS

The dualities of the executive role that we have mentioned, such as monitoring the group from outside while operating from within, and identifying with its overall development while being oriented to the immediate situation, test the skill and balance of the group member. Even more severe are the basic dilemmas of being responsible for enlightenment and self-determination, when neither is completely possible. Together these dilemmas pose a conflict to which executives respond in one way or another—a response which has a critical effect upon their groups.

Some would-be executives escape the conflict altogether by anticipating it and by refusing to enter the role, preferring to remain in more specialized roles or in ones lower on the pyramid of responsibility. Others, especially in crises but at other times as well, call on outside help such as aid from the physician, the clergy, the psychiatrist, the lawyer, the management consultant, the diviner, the shaman, and so on as the case might be. Still others respond with pseudosolutions, such as trying to convince others that there is no problem, or forcing others into a closely regulated pattern of action, or blocking anyone else's attempt to change the process.

In contrast, there is a response which offers promise: to begin "to learn how to learn" and to learn how to intervene. A first step in this direction is to ask questions which require judgment: Of the many elements that might be known, which are *relevant*? Of the variety of formulations, which are *important*? Of the many alternative actions, which are *strategic*?[8] Judgment requires a full and intuitive familiarity with the concrete group and situation, but it is aided enormously by an effective way of thinking about groups. As an introductory guide to group dynamics for the executive, the paradigm presented in the next chapter is organized around these questions: (1) What is the purpose of a group—or more generally, what are the orders of group purposes? (2) What feedback processes and what psychological and sociological arrangements are essential for accomplishing given orders of purpose? (3) What contributions can an executive make toward creating those essentials?

NOTES

1. For earlier analyses of executive functions see Chester I. Barnard, *The Functions of the Executive* (Cambridge, Mass.: Harvard University Press, 1948), pp. 139–284; and W. E. Henry, "The Psychodynamics of the Executive Role," in W. L. Warner and

N. H. Martin, eds., *Industrial Man* (New York: Harper & Row, Pub., 1959), pp. 24–33. For a recent conception of executive learning, both individual and collective, see Chris Argyris and D. Schön, *Organizational Learning* (Reading, Mass.: Addison-Wesley, 1978) and Chris Argyris, "The Individual and the System," Chap. 2 in his *Inner Contradictions of Rigorous Research* (New York: Academic Press, 1980), pp. 9–23.

2. For discussion of issues involved in advancing feedback and consciousness see William R. Torbert, *Learning from Experience: Toward Consciousness* (New York: Columbia University Press, 1972) and Chris Argyris, *Increasing Leadership Effectiveness* (New York: Wiley-Interscience, 1976).

3. Kurt Lewin, *A Dynamic Theory of Personality*, trans. D. K. Adams and K. E. Zener (New York: McGraw-Hill, 1935), pp. 66–80; and Kurt Lewin, *Principles of Topological Psychology* (New York: McGraw-Hill, 1936), pp. 30–40.

4. For a discussion of the relation between elements in personality and elements in the group or the social system in general, see Talcott Parsons, "The Superego and the Theory of Social Systems, " in Talcott Parsons, Robert F. Bales, and Edward A. Shils, *Working Papers in the Theory of Action* (New York: Free Press, 1953), pp. 13–29; for an analysis of ego functions, see Anna Freud, *The Ego and the Mechanisms of Defense*, trans. Cecil Baines (New York: International Universities Press, Inc., 1946); and Erik H. Erikson, *Childhood and Society* (New York: W. W. Norton & Co., Inc., 1950), pp. 163–234.

5. Norbert Wiener, *The Human Use of Human Beings* (Boston: Houghton Mifflin, 1950), pp. 4–7.

6. Robert E. Pettinger and others, *The First Five Minutes* (Ithaca, N.Y.: Paul Martineau, 1960).

7. Karl Deutsch, *The Nerves of Government* (New York: Free Press, 1963), pp. 229–33.

8. Needs in this direction underlay the development over the past four decades of training groups (T-Groups), of self-analytic groups, and of "sensitivity training." See Leland P. Bradford, J. R. Gibb, and Kenneth D. Benne, eds., *T-Group Theory and Laboratory Methods* (New York: John Wiley, 1964); and Edgar H. Schein and Warren G. Bennis, *Personal and Organizational Change through Group Methods: The Laboratory Approach* (New York: John Wiley, 1965). For a recent modification in the design of experiential learning settings see Dexter Dunphy, "A Design for the Exploration and Development of Interpersonal Space," in C. P. Alderfer and C. L. Cooper, eds., *Advances in Experiential Social Processes*, Vol. II (New York: John Wiley, 1980), pp. 1–36.

CHAPTER 7
A PARADIGM
FOR GROUPS

"In each period," wrote Alfred North Whitehead, "there is a general form of the forms of thought; and like the air we breathe, such a form is so translucent, and so pervading, and so seemingly necessary, that only by extreme effort can we become aware of it."[1]

We have learned enough about groups to know that the early form of thought from which the study of groups grew is not enough; yet the full contours of a new form are not yet apparent. If and when it comes into view one can hope that it will be broad enough to encompass the billions of groups around the globe, sophisticated enough to somehow integrate the seemingly disparate theoretical models described in Chapter 1, precise enough to serve as a guide for the group executives described in the previous chapter, and finally, that it is put together well enough to generate empirically testable hypotheses that can help advance our science.

If we are correct in suggesting in the Introduction that the shape of early thought on groups was thin and simple but that with the recent explosion of interest and research it became spread out, variegated, segmented, broader and deeper, then it is not improbable that future thought on the group will focus on synthesis and consolidation. The paradigm in this chapter is presented with that as a guess. Without presuming to integrate all viewpoints and findings in the field, we have with broad strokes sketched the region where the personal, the transpersonal, the group, and the societal intersect and suggest some of the linkages that enable their dynamic interplay. In doing so we have had one eye on the advancement of science and the second on the needs of those in the executive role who want to comprehend what is happening in the group and who want to determine the group's history.[2]

Three points at the outset: First, following the cybernetic model the paradigm extends beyond current goal-attainment models to allow for higher-order purposes such as obtaining autonomy and maximizing capabilities for personal and collective growth (as outlined specifically on pages 38-39). Thus, in making room for the participants' values of autonomy and growth (either in their affirmation or their negation) the paradigm is quite explicitly value-directed and certainly not value-free inasmuch as we have selected those values. Second, while our discussion of favorable conditions (such as those under which the "inherent" conflict between the individual and the group tends to dissolve and those where the member's contributions tend to enhance the group and vice versa) may seem open to the charge of idealism, we reassure you that care has been taken to refer to actual group states that we or others have observed—we know they can occur. Quite consciously the paradigm allows not only for what is most probable but also for what is possible. Third, if you are put off by the concept of "purpose," (some associate it with the teleological fallacy of the attribution of a cause subsequent in time to a given effect), then you are invited to reconsider its utility when used in a specific sense; namely, "purposeful reactions which are controlled by the error of reaction—i.e., by the difference between the state of the behaving object [individual or group] and the final state interpreted as the purpose. . . [It is] synonymous with behavior controlled by negative feedback."[3] As stated below, our interpretation of purpose is always a hypothesis, subject to correction.

ORDERS OF PURPOSE

The purposes underlying the formation and operation of groups may be classified into five orders:[4] (1) immediate gratification; (2) sustenance of conditions permitting gratification; (3) pursuit of a collective goal; (4) self-determination; and (5) growth.

First Order of Purpose

Individuals in groups classified according to this order seek immediate gratification of their personal needs, either through interaction with one another or, more directly, from one another. Each approaches and engages the other so as to satisfy one's own needs, which may vary from sex, harm-avoidance, curiosity, warmth, safety, and relief from anxiety, to tension-release and aggression. In any case, needs are primary elements in the encounter. When they are fulfilled the purpose is accomplished, and when they are not, the engagement aborts.

First-order purpose is illustrated in the following instances: (1) male and female meet, copulate, then go their separate ways; (2) persons facing danger band together; (3) mother and newborn child cling to each other; (4) villagers gather around a drummer for singing and dancing; (5) patients in a waiting room tell one another of their problems; (6) friends of a dead person meet and mourn together.

Note that the statement of purpose is a construct. It is used by sociologists to organize their observations of what is occurring. Its relationship to observed events is as follows: the engagement of these parties, their interaction, their conversation, their movement, and so on, are as though the purpose were, in this case, immediate gratification. The notion of purpose may or may not exist in the minds of the parties in the same form as it exists in the mind of the sociologist; it can exist on the conscious or unconscious level; it can be explicit or implicit. In any case, its service in organizing observations is useful to observers—more useful, to be sure, when their constructs are consonant with processes in the minds of group members.

Notice, as well, that our classification refers to *purposes* and not to *groups*, simply because groups often shift from one order of purpose to another, as one does from work to play.

Second Order

The purpose which guides processes of this order is to sustain contact among parties who have previously engaged one another. That is, persons who have experienced gratification (or its promise) with one another seek to continue the relationship or to reconvene it in order to satisfy needs with the same persons. This means that a second purpose—sustaining the conditions which permitted gratification—is added to the first rather than replacing it—a point to which we will return below. For some examples: (1) Copulating creatures pair off as seasonal or permanent mates; (2) gorillas roam as a band to feed and to nest; (3) patients in the waiting room arrange to come early next time to have more time to talk; (4) villagers schedule a weekly dance; (5) young adolescents set up an exclusive club; (6) a seminar forms around a gifted teacher.

Third Order

The purpose guiding groups of this order is to pursue a collective goal. A collective goal, as stated earlier, is an idea about a desirable state of affairs for the group as a unit. Although this goal may arise out of needs, it refers to a much wider range of conditions than simply need-fulfillment. Examples of this order of purpose are commonplace: (1) Father and mother teach the child; (2) one village builds a defensive wall around itself, while (3) another cuts a road to join itself to a neighboring one; (4) hunters form a joint expedition; (5) musicians form an orchestra; (6) an experimental group in the laboratory works on a problem given it by the experimenter; (7) a surgical team performs an operation.

Fourth Order

The purpose of the fourth-order group is self-determination for the group. Members seek to establish conditions which will allow them to set their own goals and pursue them, including enough freedom from external restraints, obligations, and commitments, and sufficient emancipation from past routine, habit, and tradition. They prepare themselves for a wide range of contingencies and for a change of course when they think such a change is desirable. This order of purpose is exemplified by (1) a group of explorers moving in uncharted territory; (2) a scientific research team with promising new leads; (3) a religious sect emigrating to form an ideal community; (3) a group of *avant-garde* artists; (4) a group of investors considering the distribution of their capital; (5) research and development teams. Notice that this order of purpose, referring to the group as a collective unit, corresponds largely to the orientation of the individual who is in the executive role.

Fifth Order

In the case of this order, the purpose is for the group to grow in capabilities and influence, or, as stated in Chapter 1, to become open to wider varieties of information; capable of pursuing a wider range of goals; versatile in producing new ideas, knowledge, and techniques of value both to the group and to others; and increasingly effective in exchanging things of value with others. Certain individuals combine learning, creativity, teaching, and exchange, as in the conspicuous examples of the philosophers, the theologians, the scientists, and so on; and certain institutions do so, as in the examples of the school, the seminary, the artists' colony, and, in particular, the university. Yet the purpose of growth is found in less explicit and more modest form in most types of small groups: a young couple who want to raise a family; an adolescent group which sees itself as a source for new styles of language, dress, music, and dance; a new firm.

These five orders of purpose are meant to be more than a list, for in our arrangement each succeeding one presumes accomplishment of the preceding one. For example, the aim to sustain connections among given individuals presumes that those persons have either been satisfied in an initial encounter, or give promise to being satisfied; goal pursuit presumes success in holding the group together; change of goal presumes experience in reaching an initial one; and so on. The orders are cumulative. This means that the final purpose (growth) presumes the capabilities necessary to accomplish the four lower orders: (1) intermember gratification; (2) sustaining contacts among the parties; (3) reaching a common goal; and (4) altering the goal and rearranging internal and external relations in order to accomplish the new goal. We shall return to the point that the capabilities for accomplishing lower-order purposes are prerequisites for attaining higher-order ones after raising the question of what is required in order for a group to realize any one of the purposes.

PURPOSE, SYSTEM REQUIREMENTS, AND CRITICAL ISSUES

The following discussion of what a group must be and do in order to realize its purpose and to advance to a higher-order purpose is more abstract and selective than most executives (or students) would like. The excuse for its abstractness is simply that the points aim to cover a varied universe of small groups, and for its selectivity that they emphasize those structural and dynamic features familiar from previous sections of the book. Its purpose is to point to matters that are relevant, important, and strategic to the executive whose interest is to increase group capabilities.

The first point of the thesis is that realization of any one of the purposes mentioned above and listed in the first column of Table 4 requires a complex and interdependent set of operations and arrangements. It requires feedback processes which involve connections (open network) among elements in the momentary situation. Such connections depend, in turn, upon the operation of role-systems (which

Table 4   Group Purposes, System Requirements, and Critical Issues*

Order of Purpose	Feedback Required to Accomplish Purpose		Elements in Situation Relevant to Feedback (Selected)	Role-Systems Connecting Elements	Roles Persons Must Enter	Critical Issues Governing Role-Entry
	Person	Group				
1. Immediate gratification	First order	—	Ego's needs, actions; signals of needs and actions	Interaction Affective	Behavioral Primordial	Commitment
2. To sustain conditions for gratification	Second order (Learning)	First order	Environmental resources and limits; personal beliefs; personal and group norms	Normative	Normative	Authority
3. To pursue a collective goal	"	Second order (Learning)	Personal values and technical skills; group beliefs and values; inter-group contacts and loyalities, etc.	Technical	Instrumental	Intimacy Work
4. Group self-determination	Third order (Consciousness)	Third order (Consciousness)	Information on *all* elements, role-systems, etc., listed above and on inter-group obligations	Executive	Executive	Integrity
5. Growth	"	"	Increasing range in personalities, group, and context	Inter-group executive	Generative	Interchange

*The table is cumulative, i.e., as one goes down the table (from lower to higher order of purpose), all entries for preceding purposes are relevant. All entries, for example, are relevant for growth.

open channels among elements), and these, of course, depend upon the actual entry of persons (as sources of energy, perception, thought, and action) into the group roles. Finally, role-entry depends upon the resolution of critical organizational problems. This interdependence is indicated by column headings in Table 4, moving from left to right.

The second point is that, as we shall see, the critical issues (listed in the far right column) are of strategic concern to the executive. When these issues are not resolved, persons are blocked out of roles (and the group); when they are resolved, persons are more willing and able to contribute their energy and thought to the group, as raw material for their development into capabilities. Consequently, success or failure in these arrangements has a disproportionately large effect upon group potential.

The third point is that as one shifts from lower to higher-order purposes (down the rows in the table), system requirements are cumulative. The previous requirements still hold, but new ones are added—such as more advanced feedback processes, connections among more elements, more advanced role-systems, new arrangements governing role-entry—and, therefore, so are additional issues of strategic concern to the executive.

The fourth point is that in the process of realizing one order of purpose, the group (its members, its culture) gains a dividend, as it were, in the form of new learning and abilities, rather than simply returning to a prior state of equilibrium. When, for example, two people find their meeting a gratifying experience, they learn more from the encounter than simply how to gain gratification. They may learn, for instance, what it would take to sustain the relationship, in which case they would be better prepared to step up to that higher-order purpose. In any case, an increment of learning beyond that required for gratification is a consequence of the encounter.

The fifth point is that this increment—this dividend—is potentially greater for higher-order purposes than for lower-order ones. A group is likely to learn more, for example, from trying to survive than from seeking transitory gratification; it is likely to learn more from trying to change its course to a more desirable one than by simply pursuing one already set. There is, in other words, a dynamic relation between purpose, requirements, and capabilities: Though higher-order purposes are more demanding in their realization, they afford a disproportionately greater opportunity for developing capabilities. (This corresponds, of course, to the experience of the pair of newcomers of earlier chapters who, we saw, were able to increase progressively their contributions to the group as they moved into more advanced roles.)

The sixth point is that, as far as is known, the advance of any single concrete group from one order of purpose to the next is not automatic—as though determined by an irrevocable, evolutionary, ontological program—but instead occurs through the vision and effort of group members. It is a bootstrap operation that must be imagined and engineered. Consequently, advance to a higher-order purpose is, we suggest, the second matter of strategic concern to the executive.

These six points underlie the schematic layout in Table 4, to which we return for a more detailed discussion of the first two rows and of the far right column.

SYSTEM REQUIREMENTS
FOR FIRST-ORDER PURPOSE

In obtaining mutual gratification with, or from, one another, the various parties employ first-order feedback (as defined in Chapter 1): a given party directs action (a movement, a gesture, a signal, etc.) toward the other(s), reads its effect upon the other party, redirects action so as to more nearly evoke the desired response, and eventually reads the effect of the interchange as gratifying or not. Being performed more or less simultaneously by the various parties, this order of feedback requires connections, or an open network, between the *egos* (as individual control centers), their *needs and emotions*, and their *actions* (of approach or withdrawal, expressions of frustration or satisfaction, and so on). That is, feedback can operate only if these elements, at the very least, are brought into play.

For *needs* to come into play, one (*ego*) must be responsive to one's own needs (rather than their being repressed) and attentive to the *signals of needs of others* (rather than ignoring them). If one is open to needs and their signals, then, according to our discussion in Chapter 4, one is in the primordial role: *roles*, in general, *link elements in the situation*. The primordial role links a person with his or her own needs and with signals of needs of others. The affective (under)structure—a set of interrelated primordial roles—links needs and their signals among a number of persons. Only with such linkages can the feedback processes function. Thus, entry into the primordial role, and the affective (under)structure, are requisites for those processes.

Actions are brought into play by entry into the behavioral role. The behavioral role links *actions* and *reactions* and the person (*ego*), while the interaction system links the interaction among a number of persons. This second linkage is as essential as the first for the operation of the feedback processes. In short, the role-systems of affect and interaction open channels among persons, needs, actions, reactions, and their signals. For such role-systems to operate, persons must enter primordial and behavioral roles.

But what, one might ask, enables the parties to deal with one another in the first place? Why should they enter role-systems with one another? Or, more specifically, what governs entry into the primordial and behavioral roles? It is this question, we suggest, that is the critical sociological (and executive) issue, for, to repeat, unless persons who are the primary source of both energy and thought join together on some basis, the matters of linkages and feedbacks remain academic. But if and when they do, then they may, through exploration and trial-and-error, eventually work out the kinds of role-systems which open the necessary channels. Entry into the primordial and behavioral roles is governed by the critical social arrangement we call *commitment*.

Commitment is an understanding of give-and-take among the parties. Whether explicit or implicit, it is an arrangement whereby each party agrees, in effect, to give up something for, or give something to, the other on the promise of receiving something in exchange. What is to be given may be little or much, and the balance of the exchange may never be equal, but these details are less important than the basic question of whether or not an arrangement exists, for with it a group is possible, while without it, one is not.

Let us return to the animal world for a simple, primitive example. According to ethologists,[5] when male and female of a given species meet, there is often a rapid exchange of signals serving the function, apparently, of indicating the extent to which each party is willing and able to modify habitual tendencies either to flee or to attack, and instead to come into close enough contact for sexual gratification. If it is true that their initial tendencies are either to attack or to flee, then to the outside observer, their coming together is circumstantial evidence of their having "made" an arrangement according to which the fighting and fleeing responses are to be given up and, instead, sexual access granted to the other. This arrangement, arrived at through the exchange of unambiguous signals, is a prerequisite for successful mating; it is the functional equivalent of what we mean more generally by commitment.

Commitment is essentially promissory: one gives up something with a feeling of promise, or on the promise that something will be forthcoming in return. It is precisely this willingness to give up more than one gets in immediate return (and the signaling of this willingness) that endows the relation with trust and makes it social.

To summarize, and going from left to right in the first row of Table 4, inter-member gratification requires first-order feedback—action, reading effects of action, modifying actions, and so on; feedback entails an open network connecting the energy systems of persons with one another, with their needs and actions, and with signals of needs and actions. Such networks are opened when, and only when, the several members enter primordial and behavioral roles. An interaction system and affective structure are, therefore, requisites. Entry into these systems is governed by the presence or absence of a promissory social arrangement of give-and-take, called commitment.

Such an arrangement, we emphasize, is critical for the group, for without it no meaningful relation exists while with some form of arrangement persons are able to make energy, thought, and other resources available for working out the remaining requirements.

The strategic questions for the executive are: What do members want from the group? What are they prepared to give to it? What does the group want from members, and what can it give them?

SUSTAINING THE GROUP
AND THE ISSUE OF AUTHORITY

Let us follow the second row of Table 4 much as we have the first, in the hope that retracing once more the interdependence between *purpose, feedback, role-systems,* and *issue* will be a sufficient guide so that you may trace the steps in the other rows while we direct attention to the other critical issues.

In sustaining a group—let us assume a continuation or repetition of conditions which have permitted gratification in the past—members (1) observe indications from both themselves and from the external environment as to what is necessary to form a group; (2) through self-control modify or inhibit those demands for immediate gratification which might disperse the parties; and (3) regulate their interpersonal patterns of action and emotions so as to maximize in the end the chances for both group survival and personal gratification. Control processes on behalf of this *dual* purpose entail the formulation of concrete ideas about what must be done for the group to survive, and about what must be done in it to permit gratification. Such ideas, when applied to specific acts and conditions, are, as we stated in Chapter 5, *norms*. Norms are brought into play only when a plurality of members enter the normative role, for the normative role (and the normative system) links *egos, needs, actions*, and *realities* of the internal and external environment, with *ideas* about what should be felt and done. Entry into normative roles calls upon the members to control themselves—to inhibit their desires, postpone gratification, rechannel their energy, restrain their actions, and so on—according to a set of ideas (prescriptions and prohibitions) in their mind and in the minds of others, but at the same time not to so restrict themselves that they are incapable of giving and receiving gratification.

It is at this point, of course, that the classic conflict between the individual and the group arises: The individual must relinquish personal freedom so that the group is able to coordinate itself and survive, while the group (its agents) must allow individuals sufficient freedom and access to gratification to maintain their membership, even though that freedom may endanger group survival. This opposition between individual latitude and collective coordination is, essentially, an issue of *authority*. Its resolution depends upon a moral arrangement among members, providing for an agreed-upon way of setting and modifying rules—a supraordinate set of rules for making rules. When rules are tentative, modifiable, and negotiable, then members are more likely to subject themselves to them without feeling that they jeopardize their chance for gratification, or (in the face of changing circumstances) the group's chance for survival. Fixed rules, on the other hand, lead to a variety of reactions which tend to complicate entry into the normative role: rebellion against the rules and those who symbolize them; over-controlled self-restriction; uncontrolled impulsive behavior; leaving the group; and so on.

The strategic questions for the executive are: What are the group norms? How, and by whom, are they set? Do they take into account the needs of members and the environmental realities? And, finally, what provisions are there for their negotiation and revision?

GOAL-PURSUIT, INTIMACY, AND WORK

The prospect of working together toward a common goal brings people together on new and special terms. If we assume that their earlier relation was for the sake of individual gratification, we can assume that it is now oriented toward the shared idea of a goal—a goal that supersedes the individual. In order to realize the goal it may be necessary to rearrange the interpersonal relationships: those who prefer to stay apart may be brought into close contact; enemies may have to forgo fighting and lovers may have to stay far enough apart to get the job done. In addition, it may call on persons to do things they have been taught not to do and to associate with those they have been taught not to associate with—to break norms and taboos. All this leads to the general point that the attempt of a number of individuals to reach a common goal tends to disrupt the existing structure of emotional and normative relations and to require a redistribution of energy, affect, and action. In this sense, the demands of entering into instrumental roles to accomplish a group goal introduces the classical conflict between self-oriented pairs (or cliques) and the group as a whole.[6] If, on the one hand, members refuse or are unable to give up or modify their primal relations, then they are held back from entering freely into the instrumental role; while on the other, if, for the sake of the goal, they detach themselves from those relations, then they sacrifice a major source of gratification. The conflict creates what we call the *intimacy* issue. It is one of two matters that govern entry into the instrumental role.

Resolution depends, we suggest, upon a social arrangement among the parties which (1) acknowledges the distinction between affective relations and goal-pursuit (e.g., to work with another does not mean that one must like the other; task involvement with another does not mean total personal involvement; and so on); (2) provides that rewards for goal-achievement are to be independent of the nature of interpersonal, affective relations (e.g., enemies who are effective workers are not to be punished because of their negative relation; ineffective lovers are not to be rewarded for their positive relation); and (3) provides, in general, that those who work together have *the option of a variety of affective relations*, so long as they do not interfere with gratification of others, with group survival, or with collective goal-attainment. That is, a work group may be comprised of a set of affective relations varying from close to distant, from warm to cold, from positive to negative—all of which, within the limits suggested above, are negotiable by the parties concerned.

Negotiability of such a variety of interpersonal relations is the first condition that increases the likelihood of entry into the instrumental role. The second involves the arrangement for work. Discovering a common target and aiming for it presents both a possibility of success and a chance of failure. It offers the attraction of joint movement, mastery, productivity, and creativity, and as such, promises its own rewards (as workers in an artisan shop, athletes on a relay team, medics in the operating room, actors in a theatrical troop, students in a seminar, and others often realize). At the same time, specification of a clear target means that it can be missed; or, in the case of specifying clear standards of excellence, that the product can be undesirable or worthless; and, in general, that the group can fail, and suffer from feelings of shame, incompetence, and inferiority. The second issue governing role entry is, therefore, whether the prospects for success and reward are enough to offset the chances and fears of failure. This we call the *work* issue.

Resolution of this issue depends upon a variety of conditions, three of which we emphasize. The first is a design, a plan, or a technical program which both relates one worker's activities with those of others, and links in a more or less unbroken chain their operations to the achievement of the goal. The second is a provision for differential rewards (money, goods, prestige, acclaim, deference from others, and so on) to be given according to differential contributions toward goal-achievement. The third is an arrangement whereby both the technical plan and the reward system may be modified—the plan according to discoveries, inventions, and changing environmental conditions, and the schedule of rewards according to changes both in the importance of operations and in the needs of workers. These provisions, when added to those regarding intimacy, increase the likelihood of entry into the instrumental role.

On *intimacy* the strategic questions for the executive are: how close, how distant, are members? What provision is there for rechanneling energy and feelings associated with interpersonal relations into the collective effort, while at the same time leaving options for members to engage in a variety of interpersonal relations ranging from the more detached to the most intimate? On *work*, the questions are: What provision is there for a flexible plan for reaching the goal and for a modifiable schedule of rewards for goal achievement?[7]

SELF-DETERMINATION AND INTEGRITY

Aside from the technical difficulties which might be enough to discourage the more cautious from entering the executive role (which, as implied by the fourth row of Table 4 is essential for group self-determination), the prospect of self-awareness and goal-changing raises group issues which are likely to discourage even the most able and confident. We call them together the issue of *integrity*.

You will recall the suggestion in Chapter 2 that groups characteristically close ranks against outside observers and that, as a consequence, sociologists are denied inside information unless and until they and the group develop a relationship of mutual trust. And you will recall the suggestion in Chapter 6 that groups, quite beyond their conscious intentions and in the service of cohesion, resist "too much" self-knowledge. In short, the prospect of self-awareness arouses resistance. When observers are outsiders, the group may simply deny them access, but the problem is not so simple when they are fellow members. Groups, like the villagers who stone the prophet, burn the philosopher, and crucify the messiah, turn against their fellows who hold a mirror to them. The question is: How are groups able to admit a detached, objective, alien-like view of themselves (it may be positive as well as negative but, in any case, it reflects present areas of ignorance) without resenting, punishing, and expelling the one who brings it, thereby splitting the group apart?

Resolution depends upon an explicit or implicit arrangement paralleling in major respects the one between the group and the sociologist-observer. Accordingly, *access to*, and *the right to publicize*, the private, personal processes and the more sacred group process is granted only to those who show promise of becoming unconditionally committed to the group (to the executive role). In turn, those who assume a responsibility for self-awareness are granted immunity from punishment because of what they happen to discover and convey. Without such an arrangement, even those who are able to manage the technical difficulties of group self-consciousness are not likely to enter or remain in the executive role.

A second issue arises from the prospect of shifting the group goal. Characteristically, we look back with special interest to the turning points in the histories of nations, families, and individuals, with some sense of pride (and relief) when a decisive choice turns out to have been well-advised. Such interest shows how uncertain (and often how anxious and afraid) we are when major collective goals are in the process of being changed. One reason for the depth of such concern may be the common, though implicit, assumption that a group is synonymous with its goal: the *raison d'être* of a group is its goal (a football team *is* to play; a surgical team *is* to operate; a theater group *is* to perform; and so on). When group and goal are condensed into the same thing, it follows that to entertain an alternative goal is to doubt the legitimacy of the group as it is, to debate various alternatives is to disorient the group, and to select a new goal is to create a new group. Before groups will change their goal, they must in their culture distinguish between themselves and their present goal. The issue is open to question from several sides: (1) To what extent can the group remain intact, its members still committed, its resources still available, its capabilities unimpaired, and its energies in reserve, while it stops its present activity in order to consider alternative goals? (2) If and when it changes its goal, to what extent can it recommit itself without impairment? (3) To what extent can it repeatedly shift directions without its members becoming afraid of losing their way, of wandering, of becoming a lost group?

Holding a group together while it considers what it is and where it might go, and while it alters directions, requires more than a social contract among members. It requires, first, a sociological conception of the group, similar to the notion of the meta-group mentioned on page 105. According to this notion a group is more than a goal, more than a set of rules, more than a structure of affective relations, and more than a pattern of interaction. The meta-group transcends both these sub-aspects and the momentary situation; it includes processes members are unaware of, and potentials which are yet to be realized. Such a conception, when shared by members, supports both a program for self-discovery and the consideration of alternative goals. Beyond this, yet consonant with it, resolution depends upon a shared set of values which Deutsch suggests include humility and faith. "To combine humility with faith, to be capable of rapid and thorough commitment without losing the openness to alternative information, and the capacity for rearrangement and possible recommitment to other goals, or to a different understanding of some of the goals previously sought—that is, perhaps, a requirement for all autonomous systems that are to have a good chance of extended survival."[8]

The strategic questions for the executive are: What is the group's conception of itself? To what extent does this conception acknowledge that the group is more than it can presently know itself to be, is more than its present goal, and is more than what it is currently doing? Is there humility enough to allow increasing self-consciousness, and faith enough to experiment with alternative goals? Can it both know itself and shift its directions without impairing its capabilities?[9]

GROWTH AND INTERCHANGE

A group's capacity to grow, as outlined in Chapter 1, depends upon entry of members into still another role which, after Erikson,[10] we call the *generative* role. Its functions are (1) to explore the past and present physical, cultural, and social environment for information, ideas, designs, techniques, products, and so on, that might be valuable to the group; (2) to import selectively and to create new ideas, knowledge, designs, by recombining the new and the old, the external and the internal; and (3) to become both conscious of this creative experience and able to translate it into a communicable form so that it may be either stored for future use or made the basis for the formation of new groups. This role requires the crossing of traditional boundaries separating insiders from outsiders, one's own group from other groups. It means an expanding network of outside relations: a readiness to contact "foreigners"; to take into the group their ideas, languages, and products; and to send out (or give up) to foreigners one's own ideas, products, and even personnel. It means relinquishing group members and their contributions for the sake of creating new groups with goals that differ from one's own. It means, in short, the progressive permeation of those boundaries which ordinarily define and secure one's group, the reformation of relations with other groups, and the formation of new groups.

One reaction to such a prospect is for the group to give up its identity. The group may become xenophilic—that is, lovers of foreign or strange things—like the mountain-dwelling Arapesh, for instance, who import their good things (like songs, dances, and dress styles) from the neighboring beach people, and their bad things (such as aggression against their fellow Arapesh) from the Plainsmen who are viewed as sorcerers.[11] A second and equally defensive reaction, of course, is to equate group identity with the boundaries themselves, and to solidify them. One's group becomes apprehensive of the consequences of external contact, for example when consciousness of others shows them to be more desirable than oneself; when exchange of persons and products with others diminishes the distinctiveness of one's own culture; and when one's group is shown to be weak, and as a result is surrounded and incorporated by other groups.

The problem of maintaining system integrity while boundaries are being permeated and the group is becoming interdependent with other groups we call the issue of *interchange*. How is it possible for the group to increase its receptivity to new information, to expand its network of intergroup contacts, to increase the volume and variety of its imports and exports, without suffering the loss of its capabilities, its identity, and its autonomy? The issue is critical to the executive, for, if unresolved, not only will the group lose what it might have gained through contact, but it runs the danger of either dissolving into other groups, or becoming increasingly closed off from others and as a result, becoming increasingly ethnocentric.

We suggest two conditions which, among others, help resolve the interchange issue and thereby encourage entry into the generative role. The first is an understanding *among groups* which acknowledges a *differentiated* set of boundaries, some being firm while others are permeable. One may, for instance, be inside a group physically but not an insider; one may be physically away from it but not an outsider; one may use a foreign idea without either being a foreigner or exploiting the foreigner; and one may export group culture and products without impoverishing it or being disloyal to it. Such a condition exists when several groups recognize the distinction between *physical location* and *emotional attachments*. This done, a person, like a guest, may move physically from one group to the other without having that act signify, or require, a shift of primary attachment, loyalty, and responsibility from the first to the second group. And, this done, a group, like a host, may admit the presence of an outsider without having that admission signify or require equating the outsider with other members. Persons, for instance, may marry outside and move away from the clan without giving up membership in the clan and without assuming a status comparable to the spouse in the clan. Distinguishing between the ecological and sociological boundaries enables an interchange of persons among groups which maintain their identity. A similar arrangement may cover cultural exchange, wherein the distinction is between the *source* and the *use* of information, ideas, tools, techniques, and so on, and according to which freedom to *use* is granted on the condition that the *source* not be responsible for the consequences of the use.

The second condition, upon which the first perhaps ultimately depends, is having the groups share a set of values which include what Deutsch in the absence of technical terms, calls "grace and generosity." Grace combines a hospitable orientation to the external world as a possible (though unpredictable) source of benefit to the group, with an acknowledgement that the group is in need of benefit.[12] Generosity combines an appreciation of one's own group as a source of things potentially valuable to others with a readiness to translate the group's experience into words, its operations into technology, and its learning into terms that can be comprehended and used by others. Through sharing these values, groups are able to transcend the temporal, spatial, social, and cultural boundaries blocking interchange and growth while maintaining those boundaries essential for a coherent, though perhaps constantly changing, sense of collective identity.

SUMMARY OF CRITICAL ISSUES

Under five headings we have reviewed the group issues (listed in the far right column of Table 4) of strategic importance to the executive who aims to increase group capabilities. The way they are managed makes a disproportionately large difference to the group because they govern entry of persons into roles. When the issues are not resolved, members are blocked from the roles (and from that sector of the group), but when they are resolved, or show promise of being resolved, members' energy and mental capacities become available to the group. Questions to guide the executive's observation and assessment on the six critical issues are, in summary, as follows:

1. *Commitment.* To what extent are members prepared to give to others and to the group more than they receive in immediate return? In turn, to what extent is the group prepared to do likewise for individual members?

2. *Authority.* What provision is there both for negotiation and revision of the norms and, pending revision, for adhering to current ones?

3. *Intimacy.* What provision is there for rechanneling interpersonal affect toward collective goal achievement while at the same time leaving optional to members a wide variety of interpersonal relations?

4. *Work.* How clear and how viable are the plans for linking and coordinating effort toward achievement of the goal and for distributing the rewards of goal achievement?

5. *Integrity.* To what extent are members' relations and their values such that the group can retain its capabilities while becoming conscious of itself? To what extent are they such that it can hold together while fundamentally altering its goal?

6. *Interchange.* Are the relations with other groups, and the values shared with them, such that the several groups can benefit through the exchange of personnel, goods, techniques, ideas, beliefs, customs, and values without loss of the capacity for self-determination and collective identity?

Regarding accomplishment of a purpose of a given order, we suggest that resolution of the critical issue(s) increases the likelihood of entry into given roles and therefore the likelihood of the operation of role-systems. These role-systems open channels among a wider range of situational elements, thereby enabling the order of feedback processes essential for accomplishing the given order of purpose.

DYNAMICS OF GROWTH

It is one thing to suggest requirements for accomplishing a purpose of a given order, and another to suggest that the requirements of higher-order purposes presume the capabilities for achieving lower-order ones (as goal pursuit presumes sustaining the group). But it is admittedly more controversial and speculative to propose how and why and the conditions under which a group shifts from one order of purpose to another—particularly from lower to higher, because this involves a basic alteration, a mutation as it were, in members' conception of their group. Consequently, the intention of the following remarks is more to recommend consideration of the problem than it is to present a solution.

If your thought on how groups shift from lower- to higher-order purposes were to be led solely by the equilibrium model (discussed on pages 32-34), then the matter would be simple: you would never expect such a shift, for according to the model, success at one level of purpose results in a return to, or toward, the previous state of the group—a state in which there is simply less tension than when trying to accomplish the purpose. For instance, persons at rest experience a need for something, orient toward one another for the purpose of fulfilling their needs, succeed in doing so, and as a result return to, or toward, a state of rest. Though the model does not claim that the system is precisely the same as it was in the beginning, it makes no provision for the possibility of the type of major change, the basic reconstitution, or reorientation, that occurs in a shift in order of purpose.

Less restricted is the structural-functional model of Parsons, Bales, and Shils (discussed on pages 34-36), for it provides for elementary learning. In the course of working toward the accomplishment of a given order of purpose, the group members have an opportunity to learn what is and is not effective. In seeking gratification, for example, they may discover new sources and forms of gratification; in sustaining the group they may learn new modes of normative control; and in pursuing a goal they may discover new and more effective techniques. Yet this learning is within the level of a given order of purpose—an order assumed by the model. Any observed shift from one order to another must be due to factors outside the model and, if the model is of groups, outside the group. In other words, although the model provides for learning within a given orientation, there is no explicit provision for basic reorientation.

The cybernetic-growth model of Deutsch contributes positively by combining an explicit value-position (namely that growth of capabilities, in general, is an ultimate purpose of information-processing systems) with the notion of group consciousness, the products of which are a conception of the group's purpose, an awareness of the group's potentials, and an idea of what the group's purpose might become. In our discussion the value-position and the process of developing consciousness are incorporated within the orientation of the executive. They lead the executive—and the sociologists who share this orientation—to ask how capabilities are related to purpose, and what might be needed for the group to advance to a higher-order purpose, with its greater opportunities for growth.

Aside from specific answers regarding concrete cases which require information about the particular circumstances, we suggest the following general proposition: Although accomplishment of a given order of purpose tends to increase the group's potential for advancing to the next higher order, that advance is not automatic or

Table 5   The Orders of Purpose and the Cumulative Effects of Success*

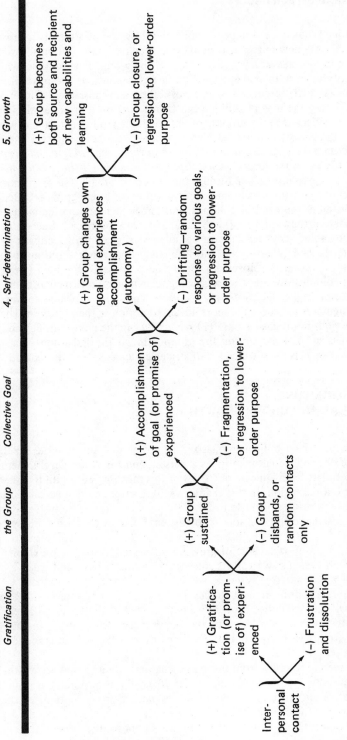

| 1. Immediate Gratification | 2. To Sustain the Group | 3. To Pursue a Collective Goal | 4. Self-determination | 5. Growth |

Inter-personal contact

(+) Gratifica-tion (or prom-ise of) experi-enced

(−) Frustration and dissolution

(+) Group sustained

(−) Group disbands, or random contacts only

(+) Accomplishment of goal (or promise of) experienced

(−) Fragmentation, or regression to lower-order purpose

(+) Group changes own goal and experiences accomplishment (autonomy)

(−) Drifting—random response to various goals, or regression to lower-order purpose

(+) Group becomes both source and recipient of new capabilities and learning

(−) Group closure, or regression to lower-order purpose

*(+) Purpose accomplished; (−) Purpose not accomplished.

predetermined, but instead depends upon the initiative of a member, or members, in conceiving the new purpose, formulating it, conveying it, acting according to it, and having it generally accepted by others in the group. For example, while a mutually gratifying encounter may lead to a desire to continue the relationship, continuance must first be conceived as a possibility, and must then be proposed and accepted. *Seeing* the new possibility and then *acting* on it are relevant, important, and indeed critical to group growth: When done, the group shifts to a new purpose; when not, the group of course remains on the same level of purpose. Consequently, *the redefinition and reconstitution of group purpose according to new capabilities and opportunities is the second major strategical concern for the executive.*

Table 5 presents schematically the order of progression from inital interpersonal contact to the development of capacities for group growth. Orders of purpose are listed at the head of columns, and under each are charted both success in their realization (upward arrow) and failure (downward arrow). Success or failure, we have suggested, depends upon a complex arrangement of feedback processes, open channels, and role-systems, and ultimately upon the resolution of the issues which govern role-entry. Movement from one purpose to the next (from left- to right-hand column), we are now suggesting, depends upon two conditions: (1) success in accomplishing the lower-order purpose, and (2) conceiving, conveying, and inducing members to accept the more advanced notion as their purpose. The critical steps in the entire progression are (1) *reconstituting* the group through adding new role-systems, and (2) *reorienting* the group through the induction of a more advanced purpose. It is these which are of strategic importance to the executive.

GROUP STRUCTURE: INDIVIDUAL AND GROUP GROWTH

Although the paradigm emphasizes the group, the opportunities for the development of the individual member as a person, and for group development, are of course interrelated. To indicate one facet of this relation, let us pull together several strands of our discussion. In this chapter we have suggested that accomplishment of a purpose requires the operation of a certain collection of role-systems, presented this time schematically in Table 6. In the case of growth, all six role-systems are required.

When a group is capable of growth—when a concrete group exhibits the operation of all systems—we call its role-structure *full-fledged*, and when a concrete group displays fewer role-systems, we call it *truncated*. For instance, a "group" with no norms is truncated at the level of interaction and affect, and one with a goal but without executive capabilities is truncated at the technical level. Truncation, in other words, is relative to the requirements for growth. In this respect, truncated groups are incapacitated: They do not have the apparatus for accomplishing a given purpose.

The second strand is from the earlier chapters, where it was argued that as our pair of newcomers advance through roles (from the behavioral and primordial to the normative and on to the executive) they *need* new conceptions of themselves and the group, and new performance capabilities, and they *receive* the benefit of increased opportunities to learn (to grow), and improve the value of their contribu-

Table 6   Order of Purpose and Required Role-Systems

	1. Immediate Gratification	2. To Sustain the Group	3. To Pursue a Collective Goal	4. Self-Determination	5. Growth
Role-Systems Required	Interaction	Interaction	Interaction	Interaction	Interaction
	Affective	Affective	Affective	Affective	Affective
		Normative	Normative	Normative	Normative
			Technical	Technical	Technical
				Executive	Executive
					Inter-group Executive

tions. Although in the beginning their role repertoire may be truncated, the more it approaches the full-fledged, the greater the potential output both to themselves and to the group. Now, the same holds for the group as a whole. For a group to advance from one order of purpose to another it must acquire new capabilities: It must expand its culture, resolve new issues, and add new role-systems. However, as it does so, and as members enter these new roles, the group increases both its potential for growth, and the opportunity for its members to grow.

If these two points are true, then it follows that the potential for personal development and the potential for group growth are maximized under the same set of conditions; namely, with a full-fledged role-structure with an option for members to participate in a full repertoire of roles. This implies that the classical conflict between the individual and the group (freedom *vs.* restraint) is related to the nature of role-systems that may be in operation. We should expect the conflict to be more acute when the group is severely truncated, and to become less intense, or to disappear altogether, when it becomes full-fledged and when individuals' role-repertoires become more complete. From this viewpoint, the paradigm in this chapter presents in broad outline the sociological arrangements which permit resolution of the individual/group conflict through bilateral growth of the individual and the group (it also implies how difficult it is to achieve such a resolution).

THE PARADIGM AND THE EXECUTIVE

The person who enters the executive role, we have said, faces the dilemmas of omniscience and omnipotence. There being no satisfactory way out of these dilemmas, the executive must *select* the more relevant things to become conscious of, and *choose* the more strategic course of action. All persons responsible for groups select and choose on some grounds or other. The grounds offered in the paradigm in this chapter are sociological; they aim to be general enough to give perspective both on the nature of groups and on their long-run potentials, yet specific enough to suggest what is relevant to observe and strategic to do in the momentary situation.

In respect to relevance, the paradigm recommends that instead of trying to interpret the total field of elements [as defined by $E_g = f(P \cdot G \cdot C)$], executives simplify their inquiry (though still tentatively and at some peril) to such questions as: What is the order of the group s purpose? What feedback processes are and are not being employed? What role-systems are and are not operating? What psychological, social, and cultural factors either block or permit entry of persons into roles? If the group *is* operating effectively at its present level of purpose, is it possible and desirable for it to advance to a higher order? Relevance is defined not in terms of all existing causes and effects, but according to a theoretical model of group dynamics and growth. The implication is that one way out of the dilemma of omniscience is to employ (again tentatively) a working model of groups.

In respect to strategy, the recommendation to our pair of newcomers (she now enacting her executive role and he, his) is that actions be directed first toward establishing those arrangements which help resolve the six critical issues (commitment, authority, intimacy, work, integrity, and interchange), and second (and when it is desirable) toward redefining the group's order of purpose. As we have said repeatedly, not only do the critical issues make an emphatic difference to the group, like gateways connecting higher-energy sources with control processes, or like gates cutting them off, but *they involve personality, group, and contextual elements which are relatively responsive to conscious modification.* That is, while executives cannot alter the basic personality of a member, they may influence the member's orientation to the group and increase both the amount the person is willing to give the group and the amount the group is willing to give in return. While they cannot modify deep-seated taboos and unconscious prohibitions, or eliminate fear and suspicion between the powerful and the weak, they may arrange for negotiation among the parties, whereby they work out rules each is willing to abide by. While they cannot change, or create at will, feelings of affection or disaffection among members, they may induce members to rechannel some of those feelings into collective and productive enterprises. While they cannot force others into self-awareness, they may enter the executive role themselves and, to the degree they are effective, demonstrate its usefulness, and by this means induce the group to learn objectively about itself and to reorganize itself consciously. While they cannot alter environmental realities at will, they may teach that the outside world is of potential use to the group rather than simply a threat. While they cannot easily "correct" ethnocentrism, they may open channels of contact and exchange between the group and others, and between its own ideas and past or future thought in other groups. And, finally while they cannot magically lift the group to a higher-order purpose, they may, when the time is ripe, present to it possibilities for development that it had not imagined before.

In sum, then: Executives employing the paradigm define relevance not according to all elements in the momentary situation, but according to the place of the elements within a theoretical model; they govern their strategy of action not according to all demands of the moment, but according to whether or not the demands critically determine the progressive development outlined in the paradigm. And, of course, if the executives are true to their role, they will consciously take note of how they use the paradigm and of how useful it is. As they learn its strengths and weaknesses, they will alter, modify, and improve upon it.

NOTES

1. Quoted in *Behavioral Science*, 12 (1967), 2.

2. For a related approach see Walter Buckley, *Sociology and Modern System Theory* (Englewood Cliffs, N.J.: Prentice-Hall, 1967) and for a brief comparison of the approach taken here with others in sociology see S. N. Eisenstadt, "The Schools of Sociology," in James F. Short, Jr., *The State of Sociology: Problems and Prospects* (Beverly Hills, Calif.: Sage Publications, 1981), pp. 22–39.

3. Arturo Rosenblueth, Norbert Weiner, and Julian Bigelow, "Behavior, Purpose, and Teleology," in Walter Buckley, ed., *Modern Systems Research for the Behavioral Scientist* (Chicago, Ill.: Aldine Publishing, 1968) pp. 221–25.

4. The present list is a modification of the one presented by Karl Deutsch, *The Nerves of Government* (New York: The Free Press of Glencoe, a division of Macmillan Publishing Company, 1963), pp. 90–93. See his discussion of self-determination, integrity, and growth, to which the present paradigm is indebted, pp. 128–40, 245–54. For a summary of empirical observations of groups advancing toward the fifth order, see Theodore M. Mills, "Seven Steps in Developing Group Awareness," *Journal of Personality and Social Systems*, 1 (Sept. 1978), 15–29.

5. See Konrad Z. Lorenz, "The Role of Aggression in Group Formation," in Bertram Schaffner, ed., *Group Processes: Transaction of the Fourth Conference* (New York: Josiah Macy, Jr., Foundation, 1959), pp. 181–252.

6. Philip E. Slater, "On Social Regression," *American Sociological Review*, 28 (June 1963) 339–64.

7. For summaries of empirical observations of developmental trends in goal attainment groups see Bruce W. Tuckman, "Developmental Sequence in Small Groups," *Psychological Bulletin*, 62 (1965), 384–99; and Bruce W. Tuckman and Mary A. Jenson, "Stages in Small-Group Development, Revisited," *Group Organizational Studies*, 2, no. 4 (Dec. 1977), 419–27.

8. Deutsch, *The Nerves of Government*, p. 232.

9. For empirical readings on developmental sequences in groups attempting to employ executive skills, see Michael P. Farrell, "Patterns in the Development of Self-Analytic Groups," *Journal of Applied Behavioral Science*, 12 (1976), 523–42.

10. Erik H. Erikson, *Childhood and Society* (New York: W. W. Norton & Co., Inc., 1950), p. 231.

11. Margaret Mead, *Sex and Temperament in Three Societies*, in the trilogy *From the South Seas* (New York: Morrow, 1939), pp. 3–14.

12. Deutsch, *The Nerves of Government*, pp. 236–40.

CHAPTER 8
EMOTIONAL RELATIONS AND GROUP GROWTH

In this chapter we contrast the structures of emotional relations at the two opposite poles implied in the paradigm in the previous chapter (the first where a truncated structure makes the development of a social group difficult or impossible, and the other where a full-fledged structure both permits and encourages group growth). In order to illustrate selected points between these poles, we sketch brief profiles of affective relations, first between authority and subordinates, and then among peers.

TWO POLES OF GROUP FORMATION

From the beginning of our discussion of the newcomers' experience we have assumed individuals who are capable of both intellectual and emotional growth. Regarding emotional growth, we have assumed that their emotional commitments are "capable of expansion"—a condensed term which, when expanded itself, means that they have the capacity to go beyond the pleasure principle in their relations with others and the group (that they are able both to postpone immediate gratification of their own needs and to respond to the needs of others); that beyond adherence to their respective personal codes, they respect the codes of others; that beyond their individual aims, they appreciate the importance of attaining a collective goal; that beyond the rewards accruing to them through goal accomplishment, they are able to love other persons and to care about them as a group; and finally that beyond attachment to the group as it is, they have wishes for what it might become. From the viewpoint of sociology, expanding commitment means progressive entry into, and emotional investment in, roles on the levels described in Chapters 4, 5, and 6. From the viewpoint of the person, it means a transformation from a *narcissistic* orientation, whose aim is gratification of the self alone, to a *generative* orientation, wherein the aim is to encourage the development of the capabilities of the self, others, and the group. This is a change not unlike that which occurs as the self-centered young child grows to maturity, becomes a parent, and then comes to feel tenderness toward, and concern for, not only one's own, but others' children. Such a change does not mean, of course, that the primordial feelings of love, hate, fear, and anxiety are not experienced, or that the drives of hunger, thirst, sex, and aggression are entirely repressed. Rather, it means that they are rechanneled and reapportioned as libidinal attachments to the self are given up and are diffused progressively to others, to norms, to ideas, to goals, and to the potentials for group development.

Similar to our assumption about the newcomers is the assumption that the group as a whole has the capacity of expanding its emotional commitments from the primordial purpose of gratifying elementary personal needs to other and progressively higher-order purposes. We assume that the members, taken collectively, are capable of going beyond the pleasure principle: that they are able to respond to one another's needs, respect normative ideas, appreciate the group goal, care about each other, and share wishes for what the group might become. In terms of the paradigm in the previous chapter, this means that group emotion becomes invested progressively in new levels and in new role-systems and therefore is diffused throughout the full range of group elements. Such expansion cannot occur for the group as a whole, of course, unless members (or a significant proportion of them) jointly participate in it, for it takes *joint* respect to sustain group norms, *joint* appreciation to accomplish a goal, *mutual* confidence to consider alternative goals and to change goals, and *shared* values to invest in group development.

Again we may conceive of two contrasting poles: again, the *narcissistic*, where group affect is organized around gratification; and the *generative*, where group affect is simultaneously diffused to the group as a whole, and mobilized around a sense of responsibility for its future. In the first case, libidinal attachment is to *selves*; in the second it is to the *idea* of creating a group that is conducive both to individual and to group growth.

The Narcissistic Pole

When one takes into account the differences among persons in their relative size, strength, and influence, Freud's description of the primal horde (referred to in Chapter 4) approximates a "group" near the narcissistic pole. The horde, it will be recalled, consists of the chief, the lesser males, and the females. The chief is omnipotent. Having begotten sons and daughters, he takes all the females to himself, prohibiting sons and all other males from sexual access to them. He claims them and protects them. This exclusive right symbolizes both his character and his relation to others: he is entirely self-oriented; "he need love no one else, he may be of a masterly nature, absolutely narcissistic, but self-confident and independent,"[1] He alone possesses what is valuable; he gives no more than suits him; his omnipotence is unrestrained. In contrast, the lesser males are powerless. Deprived of sexual access, they are entirely excluded from the experience of reproduction. On the periphery of the horde, they remain infantile, sterile, autistic, and unable to rebel for fear of being destroyed by the chief. If, in Bion's terms,[2] we may attribute an underlying, basic assumption to such a "group," it is that it exists in order to fulfill the narcissistic needs and capricious wishes of the chief. In any event, all parties—sons, lesser males, females, and the chief himself—act, interact, and avoid action as though this were true.

The primal horde can be interpreted as a profile of groups which have resolved none of the critical issues listed in the paradigm in the previous chapter. It is devoid of norms, of a goal, of a government, and of a social apparatus for steering. No provision is made for internal and external adjustments as protections against threat or the realities of the passage of time. Instead, members are locked in a rigid structure of primordial roles: The omnipotent chief lords over sons who, through mistrust, avoid one another; the wish to kill the chief and to steal the women is endemic, yet the fear of retaliation inhibits any fundamental change. From the viewpoint of sociology, groups at this pole are not unorganized, not amorphous, not vague masses. Instead, like the primal horde, they tend to be rigidly structured. What distinguishes them is not lack of structure, but lack of capabilities. They are, in terms of the paradigm, truncated. They are "groups" without a normative system, a technical system, an executive system, and a viable arrangement for dealing with a changing external situation. They are organized, yet incapacitated. Their principle of organization is narcissism, which in itself opposes the social arrangements necessary for resolution of the critical issues of their system.[3]

The Generative Pole

Because the capabilities of groups near this pole provide for flexibility and variation, we can expect to find among them a wide variety of arrangements and structures—and, consequently, no simple structural model to be used by way of illustration. In order to assess their generative capacity, therefore, a test is needed, not of their form or structure, but of their viability as a total system. One such test is that of reproducibility: whether they are able to reproduce from their own ranks another full-fledged, self-sustaining group, and to do so without impairing their original capabilities. Are they able through sub-division, emigration, and the transmission of patterns, norms, ideas, techniques, and so on, to generate another group similar to themselves?

Let us imagine a group whose members visualize two equally reasonable and desirable, yet mutually exclusive, goals—for example, explorers at a fork in the route, or a research team that discovers a highly promising lead in the course of a tightly-planned project. One reaction, of course, is to select one alternative and disregard the other. Another is to attempt both, whereupon in the case of the explorers the group voluntarily divides and pursues two routes as separate groups which later on exchange their findings. Two groups are thus created from the original one. In general, when a group is able to divide, and accomplish it without sacrificing cohesion or other original capabilities, then it approaches what we have termed the generative pole.

Questions which test a group's approach to the generative pole are as follows: Is the group able to split into two parts, with each part then being able to develop into a full-fledged system? If so, what is the time lag between the split and the existence of two full-fledged systems? After subdivision, to what extent is each part capable of adapting to its own circumstances, of evolving and maintaining its internal organization, of pursuing an independent goal, and of determining its own history? Do these new groups remain emotionally committed to their common origin (as kinsfolk do), even though they are operationally autonomous and self-determining? Are they able to enter into and honor agreements with each other? Are they able to exchange the products of their separate operations? Do they respect the integrity of each other? Finally, is the original group able to accomplish this division without substantially impairing its own capabilities?

Whether the experimental subdivision of the group is actual or hypothetical, answers to questions such as these provide the sociologist, as well as group members themselves, with information relevant to assessing the group's capacity for growth. Negative answers reveal unresolved issues and areas of conflict; for example, "There is no second person who is able to lead another group," or, "The members are so tightly knit that they cannot get along without each other," or "The groups would become competitive, each trying to undercut the other." Positive answers, on the other hand—and particularly when obtained by an actual experimental division—attest both to the resolution of the critical issues in the paradigm and to the capacity to grow.

Change from the narcissistic to the generative orientations appears to be a highly complex process. For the individual it is only dimly suggested by our previous discussion of the newcomer, and is a problem beyond the scope of this book. You will find a presentation of the major issues, conflicts, and forms of success and failure in Erikson's *Childhood and Society*[4] and, for men, in Levinson and others, *The Seasons of a Man's Life*.[5] For the group, somewhat parallel changes are suggested, though not presented as such nor even as progressive transformations, in Redl's discussion of "Group Emotion and Leadership."[6] Selected aspects of the transformations are treated in the following sections by presenting thumbnail sketches of the types of emotional relations existing between the person in authority and his or her subordinates, and among peers at various points between the two poles. These brief profiles will suggest certain of the dynamic changes involved in shifting from one pole toward the other.

TYPES OF AUTHORITY RELATIONS

Dependent-Nurturant

Because humans' survival in infancy depend upon their being fed, sheltered, and cared for by those who are larger, stronger, and more able, most persons early experience dependence upon authority. Contrary to the popular belief, feelings of dependence are not restricted to infancy. Instead, they reappear in various later relationships as a need and a wish. Bion, a psychiatrist treating patients in groups, reports one of its variations when he notes that on occasion members, seeming to lose conscious awareness of their individuality, interact, speak, think, and otherwise communicate as though they assumed that "the group is met in order to be sustained by a leader on whom it depends for nourishment, material and spiritual, and protection."[7] When (in contradistinction to Bion) those in authority complement members by assuming that they lead *in order that* members be dependent upon them, then the relationship approaches the dependent-nurturant type.

To members the authorities are perceived as kind, beneficent, sensitive to the needs of others, capable of supplying needs—in general, an inexhaustible source of gratification. Whether that which is sought be food or warmth, or whether it be information, guidance, better health, entertainment, answers to problems, ideas, a theory or a philosophy, members assume that it resides in one place alone, and that one's strategy in membership is to acquire it. In return, the leaders find supplication gratifying, for they want to be that source.

The bond forms with the authorities caring for others and the subordinates showing their appreciation to them. This amounts to a normative relation whose contract calls for sustenance and protection on the one hand, and for compliance and appreciation on the other. Between the subordinates no comparable normative arrangement exists; instead, they are depressed because there is not enough of the leaders' love to go around, and consequently are jealous and competitive. The discontent of the subordinates confuses the authorities and can only be interpreted as ingratitude—which of course angers the authorities. However, since all parties know that any overt expression of either ingratitude or anger between authority and subordinate could disrupt the relationship, negative feelings between them tend to be repressed, and their recognition guarded against (the authorities afford more complete care, and the subordinates show clearer signs of gratitude). Still, nothing exists to counteract jealousy among the subordinates.

Insurgent-Coercive

Redl describes an example of this type:

> [The teacher] is in charge of a group of rather problematic adolescents in a school setup which is so well regimented through an established system of suppressive rules that no one dares to rebel, because it would be too futile. These children obey their teacher under the constant application of pressure. They behave sufficiently well to keep out of trouble, but they do so grudgingly. They neither identify with the teacher nor with what he represents. Their relationship toward him—with the possible exception of a "sissy" in the class—is one of intensive hatred, of piled-up aggression which is kept from exploding only by their reality-insight.[8]

In the insurgent-coercive relation, each party perceives the other as an aggressor. To members the leader (who for illustration we assume to be male) is not only powerful, like the chief in the primal horde, but actively and dangerously oriented toward them. They may fantasy his desire to block them, to take away their capabilities, to castrate them. In turn, the authority may imagine the group's desire to dethrone him. Although both attribute aggressive intentions to the other, and both defend themselves by aggressively restraining the other, they are each afraid of their own destructive impulses. The basic assumption, shared by both parties, is that the relation is formed in order to contain aggression.

Subordinates defend themselves by banding together, by moving underground, by initiating loyalty checks in their ranks to spot stooges or would-be traitors, by creating secret signs and codes, and so on. The trusted are selected to organize and secure the band, while active and aggressive members are pressed forward to confront the authority.

Characteristically, the authority "defends" himself against threats of rebellion by sharper surveillance, by loyalty checks of his own, and by tighter controls. As a result, the group is split into two camps, which through interaction evolve a set of rules that permit battle, yet specify its limits. By this means aggression is kept within bounds. A group so divided against itself cannot pursue a collective goal; its energies are devoted instead to an uneasy containment of aggression.

Idealistic

In this type the authority (who for illustration we assume to be female) is devoted to an ideal, whether she be a philosopher devoted to reason, a teacher to knowledge, a world leader to peace, an artist to creation, a lawyer to justice. To others she personifies that ideal.

Subordinates, as followers or disciples, admire and love the leader. She is perceived as good, able, courageous, and generous (albeit demanding). Her grip on reality is firm, and she is unconflicted. Of timeless quality, her words and deeds are recorded as guides and models. Many followers seclude themselves with the leader's works, which they scrutinize, dissect, and laboriously contemplate in an attempt to assimilate their essence into themselves. Those who do not share these intense feelings of admiration for the leader and her work and words either leave the group or are excluded from it; those who do are moved by a deep sense of solidarity.

To the leader, subordinates are apprentices, students, interns—but, too, in a deeper sense, children. She expects devotion to the ideal, and a capacity to give up personal comfort and pleasures for the sake of the ideal. She may nurture and protect, or deprive, test, and challenge, but in any case her acceptance of her "children" is conditional upon their approach to the ideal. To the leader, they are younger versions of herself who can be trained to carry on after she leaves; through them she can transcend limitations and gain immortality.

The basic assumption is that the relation is formed to pursue the ideal. Members are graded and ranked by their approach to it. The route is often marked by tests which members must "pass." Passing is rewarded by insignias, by a title or ceremony, or by other symbols of accomplishment.

Although the *means* by which the ideal may be approached are open to debate, the *ideal*, and the logical or scientific, aesthetic or religious roots of doctrine attending it, are not open to question. Instead, they tend to be accepted as near-sacred. Group formation demands commitment to the single notion personified by the authority. Alternatives which contradict the ideal are not easily imagined because they depreciate both the leader and that part of the self identified with him or her. Alternatives tend to be either denied or subsumed under the ideal; unconsciously, they belong outside the boundaries of the group, as part of the *not-us*. As a consequence of this pattern of identification, commitment to the idealistic type of relationship involuntarily inhibits critical evaluation of ideals in general, and therefore limits the range of the imagination in discovering new and alternative ones. In short, while the idealistic relation encourages collaboration in pursuit of a collective goal, it inhibits the examination and selection of alternative ones in terms of more general values.

Democratic

"Democracy means the power and the freedom of those controlled by law to change the law, according to agreed-upon rules—and even to change these rules; but more than that it means some kind of collective self-control over the structural mechanisms of history itself."[9] When authority and subordinate share this power and freedom, and when they join in "collective self-control over the structural mechanisms of history," we call the relation between them *democratic.*

The emotional orientation of persons in the democratic relationship differs from those in the types we have previously described, where the emotional attachment was either to the self, to the protection of the self, or to an ideal. In contrast, in the democratic it is to the total group—or, more accurately, to the group as it is in the process of becoming. Whereas in other types the explanatory assumptions for their existence refer to some selected sector of the situation (such as the need to be cared for, or the containment of aggression, or the accomplishment of a given ideal), the basic assumption in the democratic relationship is that the relation exists in order to create a group that can be fully identified with. The group itself is the object of emotional attachment. Since what the group becomes is determined by responses to momentary situations, both authority and subordinate, to the extent that they care about how these moments are managed, are drawn into executive roles. They are drawn into "collective self-control over the mechanisms of history itself."

In the democratic type, authority and subordinate relate to each other more nearly as partners than they do in the other types. The superior loves the group rather than an ideal; the subordinate loves the group rather than the authority. Not only do they love the same object, but this object is conceptualized as a whole which incorporates each of them as parts. Through the over-arching group they are conceptually and emotionally connected with each other, and therefore are able to identify with the part each plays in respect to the whole. This enables each party to add to his or her own orientation the orientations, responsibilities, and functions of the other. Each acquires a dual orientation: Each can think both like a superior and a subordinate. Each can take the role of the other.

Familiar properties of democratic groups are consequences of this partnership. First, *any* member may become the official head; second, headship is transitory—a subordinate ascends to authority only to return to subordination; third, the elected authority is subject to the ultimate control of subordinates, for legally the head may either be given emergency powers or be removed; fourth, each party is obligated to represent the interests of the other; and fifth, each is bound by the acts of the other. The important point for our discussion is that under these conditions, persons in positions of authority and subordination are interchangeable. Through the course of actual interchange, each is trained to perform the role of the other. Given a division of the group into two parts, both leaders and subordinates are available.

TYPES OF PEER RELATIONS

In the previous chapter the strategic questions for assessing whether intimacy among members is effectively managed were stated as follows: How close, how distant are members? What provision is there for rechanneling energy and feelings associated with interpersonal relations into the collective effort, while at the same time leaving options for members to engage in a variety of interpersonal relations ranging from the more detached to the most intimate? The following five profiles will illustrate both the stages in the resolution of this issue, and selected points between the narcissistic and generative poles.[10]

Lovers

Here we refer to a special phenomenon: the dyadic narcissistic withdrawal of lovers "all wrapped up in each other," as discussed by Slater.[11] To the exclusion of other persons and of the world of reality, the pair withdraws into itself. Each party wants to be totally loved. Seeing the biological and psychic differences between the self and the other, each needs union with the other in order to complete the self and thereby become more lovable. The attractiveness of the other—the good, the beautiful—are associated with the self and are assimilated by the self through fusion with the other.

Lovers cooperate in presenting themselves to one another for exploration, admiration, and pleasure. Unveiled are the inconsequentialities, the personal, the private, the secret—all without shame. Lovers share a need, first, to discover and then to eliminate whatever differences exist between them. While they dissolve the physical and the psychic boundaries that separate them, they shield themselves against the outside world.

Being incorporated in the pair, lovers know not who or what they are, where one begins, nor where the other ends. There is no independent point from which to think or act. One cannot separate from the other (which is a part of the self) without dividing oneself in two; nor can one love a third person, or become attached to an independent thought, without inflicting some measure of cruelty on one's partner. With one's identity diffused within the pair, one is consigned to the dyad to the exclusion of other roles and social relations. As a consequence, lovers are not only uncertain about who they are, but have no opportunity for learning this. Instead of being oriented toward growth, lovers are, as Slater suggests, oriented toward death together.

Enemies

Enemies seek each other out. When they meet, they fight. Their wish is to square off in the heart of an arena surrounded by spectators who will cheer a champion. Often they are like the sons of a dying chief who fight over the paternal inheritance. More usually, in small groups they appear to be fighting for the right to claim that inheritance—where the inheritance is access to the group's resources of gratification: sex, esteem, promotion, prestige, deference, and worship as a hero or a heroine. Enemies may share the unconscious assumption, in one case, that the right of hero belongs to the strongest, most aggressive, and "coolest" male, while in another, that the right of heroine belongs to the most attractive and most seductive female. In both cases, the actors, having staked their claims, are on the lookout for another whom they both fear and admire and whom they must defeat.

Paradoxically, in fighting for an exclusive right for obtaining something from others, enemies tend to isolate themselves from the source of what they seek. First of all, the contestants demand the right to fight without outside interference, and, second, they become preoccupied with one another's mode of attack, style of defense, and major weakness and strength until in time, they become a pair. Quite involuntarily, perhaps, the contestants become fused into a relationship that tends in many ways to take over control of them. Neither party can withdraw without the shame of cowardice, and any attempt to change the relationship is likely to be interpreted as simply a new tactic in fighting. Meanwhile, the group is likely to demand that they either (1) make up, (2) fight to the finish, or (3) engage in combat period-ically for the vicarious pleasure of the group. The irony of enemies is that in their fight for the exclusive right to sources of gratification, they not only sacrifice their individuality and afford the group vicarious pleasure, but in the process also become pawns of the group. Some enemies resolve this impasse by giving up their claim and turning to one another as potential friends.

Collaborators

Parties in this pair join forces in pursuit of a single collective goal. Personal in-timacy remains an open question—one to be answered in the course of working to-gether. Their relation contrasts with those described above wherein the parties are defending themselves against free and open contact and where the degree of close-ness and distance is fixed by the basic assumption of the relation, in the sense that avoiders must stay apart, lovers must intertwine, and enemies must fight. In these cases, tension is reduced by one type of defense or another. And the degree of close-ness and distance is determined by the type of defense. Among collaborators, ten-sion is reduced by progressive movement toward a joint goal, closeness and distance being left open to their experience together. This is to say that while collaborators are committed to a common goal, they are not committed to a given degree of intimacy.

While working toward their goal, collaborators are free to explore what the self and the other are like, and to test out the satisfactions or tensions that arise when they come closer or move further apart—and in this respect they are free to experiment with various degrees of intimacy without becoming irrevocably com-mitted to any one state. Although some goals demand more closeness than others, the chief point is that by reason of their relationship, collaborators do not *have* to love one another, or hate one another, or fight with one another.

Because demands for intimacy among collaborators are varied and fluid, actual moves toward, away from, and against one another gain greater significance. Since such moves are voluntary—the outcome of experience rather than the result of act-ing out certain compulsions—they are indicative of the actual relation that exists. They provide the parties with valid information about the nature of the pair they are forming. Consequently, the degree of intimacy arrived at helps the parties clarify who and what they are as persons, and what they as a pair can do.

The boundary separating collaborators from other members is more permeable than is the one separating other pairs. Whereas lovers and enemies resist outside in-trusion as a means of protecting their internal defenses, collaborators have no reason intrinsic to their relationship for not expanding to include other persons, if and when it is clear that they are likely to help reach their goal.

There is another reason why the collaborative relation provides the individual with a wider variety of experiences than do other relations. Since immediate obliga-tions end when goals are reached, the relations themselves tend to be transitory—and thus, instead of being locked infinitely as half of an unalterable pair, collabora-tors are committed only temporarily, and may experience a series of relations, each involving both different persons and different goals. This range of experiences pro-vides them with additional information about themselves, enables them to compare partners and working relations, and, in favorable circumstances, helps them to develop their interpersonal skills. It thereby also prepares them for the later step of setting their own goals and choosing their own collaborators.

Friends

Whereas between collaborators the critical question is their ability to work together, the critical factor between friends is the placing of a high value upon respect for each other as persons. While the strength of a collaborative pair is tested by failure and frustration, the strength of friendship is tested by disappointment, in the sense that one of the parties departs from what the other wishes that one to be. And while collaborators are likely to break up either because the goal is reached or because it was unreasonable, or because of incompetence, friends are likely to part because the wishes one party has for the other intrude upon the other person. By "friends," then, we mean a pair who are faithful to one another—who remain loyal to the other even though the other is or becomes other than what one wishes the other to be.

A set goal is not essential for friends. They may shift into and out of the goal-seeking role; they may shift from one goal to the other; they may play at setting up goals they enjoy pursuing together. But, as we have said, goal-setting and seeking is but one of the pleasures of being together; friendship sustains itself in the absence of a goal—its *raison d'être* is the enjoyment of mutual experiences.

Besides being free of the necessity for having a set goal, friends are also free (that is, as free as can reasonably be expected) from restrictions of space, time, and personal or social compulsions. While lovers and enemies seek contact, friends may be friends whether together or apart. After a separation, they pick up where they left off, fill one another in on what happened while they were apart and start a new phase—all on the assumption that though time, space, and events are important, they do not determine the relationship. Although enemies must fight and lovers must love, friends are free both to fight and to love, on the assumption that their relationship encompasses both. And whereas enemies distinguish themselves from one another, and lovers incorporate their differences, friends are free to be alike or different. Finally, lovers, and enemies erect boundaries of exclusion, friends (even more than collaborators) are free to expand: Acquiring a new friend does not exclude an old one; one's friends are introduced to each other; a friend of a friend is a friend.

The upshot of our comparison of peer relations is that friendship—being free as it is from a set goal, free from restrictions of time and space, capable of incorporating both positive and negative feelings, and capable of expansion—is a prototype of the quality of socio-emotional relations which, when existing for the collectivity as a whole, enable the group to subdivide into separate operating parts and still retain emotional commitment to their original unit.

EMOTIONAL RELATIONS AND GENERATIVE CAPACITY

In respect to emotional relations between authority and subordinate, and among peers, the profiles we have sketched suggest that a necessary conditon for group division without impairment (which is our test for capabilities at the generative pole) is a triangular structure wherein authority and subordinate approach what we called the *democratic relation*, and peers approach what we have designated *friendship*.

In the democratic authority relation, each party is not only emotionally and intellectually capable of taking the role of the other, but operates with the understanding that one's actual position is interchangeable with the other. Together the persons identify with the total group in its potentialities and assume responsibility for negotiating new procedures, new rules, and new goals. Unlike the other forms of authority relations mentioned, the democratic tends to draw members into the executive role, and is therefore better prepared to supply skilled persons to lead new, yet affiliated units.

As long as identification among peers depends upon fusion, aggressive contact, or even a set goal, group division is likely to create additional strains both within new groups and between them. These strains can be minimized only when peer relations attain the qualities of friendship and the group as a whole learns, as friends do, that it can retain members' commitment and loyalty even though members are physically separated and oriented to different goals, and belong to a different group.

Although these relations are only two of the number of necessary conditions, we have presented them in order to invite consideration of a more general sociological question: What emotional, social, and technical capabilities must a group possess, and through what processes must it go, in order to grow through the generation of new, autonomous, full-fledged, yet kindred groups? For any given group the question may be used as a guide to a clinical analysis of its capabilities, or may be answered more directly by the simple experiment of dividing the group in two and measuring the consequences of the division. Such a program of analysis and experimentation is one example of the type of research that promises to extend our scientific understanding of groups—beyond the question of how groups are structured, to the question of their capabilities; beyond the description of what groups *are*, to an understanding of what they might *become* when autonomy and growth are values shared by their members.

NOTES

1. Sigmund Freud, *Group Psychology and the Analysis of the Ego* (New York: Liveright, 1949), p. 93.
2. W. R. Bion, *Experiences in Groups, and Other Papers* (New York: Basic Books, 1959), pp. 93–98.
3. In recent history the relation between Jim Jones and his followers represented the authority structure of the primal horde, to a degree that can only be described as remarkable. See reports of survivor's accounts, *New York Times*, November 28 and 29, 1978; *Newsweek* and *Time Magazine* of December 4, 1978.
4. Erik H. Erikson, *Childhood and Society* (New York: W. W. Norton & Co., Inc., 1963) and his *Dimensions of a New Identity* (New York: Jefferson Lectures, 1974).
5. Daniel J. Levinson and others, *The Seasons of a Man's Life* (New York: Knopf, 1978).
6. Fritz Redl, "Group Emotion and Leadership," *Psychiatry*, 5 (1942), 573-96; reprinted in A. Paul Hare, Edgar F. Borgatta, and Robert F. Bales, eds., *Small Groups: Studies in Social Interaction* (New York: Knopf, 1955), pp. 86-87.
7. Bion, *Experiences in Groups*, p. 147.

8. Redl, "Group Emotion and Leadership," p. 80.

9. C. Wright Mills, *The Sociological Imagination* (New York: Grove Press, 1961), p. 116.

10. For a study of a range of relations between husbands and wives see John F. Cuber and Peggy D. Harroff, *The Significant Americans* (New York: Appleton-Century-Crofts, 1965).

11. Philip E. Slater, "On Social Regression," *American Sociological Review*, 28 (June 1963), 339-64.

SELECTED REFERENCES

From the following list of books, and the footnotes in the text, the reader may branch out to a number of academic fields which are relevant to the study of groups.

For a general introduction to the field see Michael S. Olmstead and A. Paul Hare, *The Small Group*, 2nd ed. (New York: Random House, 1978) and Howard L. Nixon II, *The Small Group* (Englewood Cliffs, N.J.: Prentice-Hall, 1979).

For reviews of recent trends in research, see A. Paul Hare, *Handbook of Small Groups Research*, 2nd ed. (New York: Free Press, 1978); the special issue, "What's Happened to Small Group Research," Martin Lakin, ed., *The Journal of Applied Behavioral Science*, 15, no. 3 (1979). Hare's *Handbook* contains a comprehensive bibliography of the field.

Useful collections of professional papers ranging from theoretical formulations to laboratory studies are: Dorwin Cartwright and Alvin Zander, eds., *Group Dynamics*, 2nd ed. (Evanston, Ill.: Row, Peterson, 1960), and 3rd ed. (1968); A. Paul Hare, Edgar F. Borgatta, and Robert F. Bales, eds., *Small Groups: Studies in Social Interaction*, 2nd ed. (New York: Knopf, 1965); Richard J. Ofshe, ed., *Interpersonal Behavior in Small Groups* (Englewood Cliffs, N.J.: Prentice-Hall, 1973); Leonard Berkowitz, ed., *Group Processes: Papers from Advances in Experimental Social Psychology* (New York: Academic Press, 1978); Theodore M. Mills and Stan Rosenberg, eds., *Readings in the Sociology of Small Groups* (Englewood Cliffs, N.J.: Prentice-Hall, 1970); Paul V Crosbie, ed., *Interaction in Small Groups* (New York: Macmillan, 1975); and, Peter B. Smith, ed., *Group Processes: Selected Readings* (Middlesex, Eng.: Penguin, 1970).

For examples of empirical investigations of group processes in the neighborhood, the clinic, and the university, see William F. Whyte, *Street Corner Society: The Social Structure of an Italian Slum*, 3rd ed. (Chicago: University of Chicago Press, 1981); James F. Short, Jr., and Fred L. Strodtbeck, *Group Process and Gang Delinquency* (Chicago: University of Chicago Press, 1965); Dexter C. Dunphy, *The Primary Group: A Handbook for Analysis and Field Research* (New York: Appleton-Century-Crofts, 1972); Morton A. Lieberman, Irvin D. Yalom, and Matthew B. Miles, *Encounter Groups: First Facts* (New York: Basic Books, 1973); Richard D. Mann and others, *The College Classroom: Conflict, Change and Learning* (New York: John Wiley, 1970); and Robert F. Bales, Stephen P. Cohen, with Stephen A. Williamson, *SYMLOG: A System for Multiple Level Observation of Groups* (New York: Free Press, 1979).

For a review of research methods, see Gardner Lindzey and Elliott Aronson, eds., *The Handbook of Social Psychology, Volume II: Research Methods*, 2nd ed. (Reading Mass.: Addison-Wesley, 1968). For discussions of problems in observation and experimentation see Leon Festinger and Daniel Katz, eds., *Research Methods in the Behavioral Sciences* (New York: Holt, Rinehart & Winston, 1953); Joachim Israel and Henri Tajfel, eds., *The Context of Social Psychology: A Critical Assessment* (New York: Academic Press, 1972); and Robert Rosenthal and Ralph L. Rosnow, eds., *Artifact in Behavioral Research* (New York: Academic Press, 1969).

For recent developments in the two promising areas of exchange theory and the theory of expectations states, see Part 3 in Morris Rosenberg and Ralph Turner, eds., *Social Psychology: Sociological Perspectives* (New York: Basic Books, 1981).

Theoretical formulations of the small group as a social system include George C. Homans, *The Human Group* (New York: Harcourt Brace Jovanovich, Inc., 1950); Talcott Parsons, Robert F. Bales, and Edward A. Shils, *Working Papers in the Theory of Action* (New York: Free Press, 1953); and A. Paul Hare, *Creativity in Small Groups* (Beverly Hills, Calif.: Sage Publications, 1982).

Two clear presentations of the social-psychological view of groups are John W. Thibaut and Harold H. Kelley, *The Social Psychology of Groups* (New York: John Wiley, 1959); and Barry E. Collins and Harold Guetzkow, *A Social Psychology of Group Processes for Decision-Making* (New York: John Wiley, 1964).

A selection of provocative papers with emphasis upon neglected areas is contained in Warren G. Bennis, Edgar H. Schein, David E. Berlew, and Fred I. Steele, *Interpersonal Dynamics: Essays and Readings in Human Interaction*, 3rd ed. (Homewood, Ill.: Dorsey, 1973).

For an important departure in the conception and interpretation of the emotional and symbolic processes in groups, see Philip E. Slater, *Microcosm: Structural, Psychological and Religious Evolution in Groups* (New York: John Wiley, 1966); for a scheme for analyzing the interplay of personal and group issues, see Dorothy Stock Whitaker and Morton A. Lieberman, *Psychotherapy Through the Group Process* (New York: Atherton, 1964); and for an attempt to combine the group dynamic viewpoint with the psychoanalytic see Helen Durkin, *The Group in Depth* (New York: International Universities Press, 1964).

On the use of groups in training and teaching, see Leland P. Bradford, J. R. Gibb, and Kenneth D. Benne, eds., *T-Group Theory and Laboratory Methods* (New York: John Wiley, 1964); Warren G. Bennis, Kenneth D. Benne, and Robert Chin, *The Planning of Change* (New York: Holt, Rinehart & Winston, 1961); Edgar H. Schein and Warren G. Bennis, *Personal and Organizational Change Through Group Methods: The Laboratory Approach* (New York: John Wiley, 1965); and Cary L. Cooper and Clayton P. Alderfer, eds., *Advances in Experiential Social Processes*, two volumes (New York: John Wiley, 1978).

On the relevance of small group analysis to political processes see Martin King Whyte, *Small Groups and Political Rituals in China* (Berkeley: University of California Press, 1974); Sidney Verba, *Small Groups and Political Behavior: A Study of Leadership* (Princeton, N.J.: Princeton University Press, 1961); and James David Barber, *Power in Committees: An Experiment in the Governmental Process* (Skokie, Ill.: Rand McNally, 1966).

On the application of mathematical techniques, see Herbert Simon, *Models of Man: Social and Rational* (New York: John Wiley, 1957); Joseph Berger, Bernard Cohen, J. Laurie Snell, and Morris Zelditch, Jr., *Types of Formalization in Small Group Research* (Boston: Houghton Mifflin, 1962); and Joan Criswell, Herbert Solomon, and Patrick Suppes, eds., *Mathematical Methods in Small Group Processes* (Stanford, Calif.: Stanford University Press, 1962).

Major current sources are *Social Psychology Quarterly*, *Journal of Personality and Social Psychology*, *Human Relations*, *Journal of Applied Behavioral Science*, *Journal of Conflict Resolution*, and *The International Journal of Group Psychotherapy*.

INDEX